FLAMES OF WAR

THE COMPLETE INTELLIGENCE HANDBOOK FOR FORCES ON THE

OSTFRONT

MID~1942-1943 M

EASTERN FRONT 1942-1943

Written By: Phil Yates, Jason Moffatt
Editors: Peter Simunovich, John-Paul Brisigotti
Photography: Battlefront Studio
Photographs: National Library of New Zealand,
Imperial War Museum, Bovington Tank Museum,
Australian War Memorial, Roger Key Private Collection,
NARA, National Archives Of Canada,
www.ww2modelmaker.com
Stories: David Billinghurst, Steven Ross
Assistant Writers: Scott Elaurant, Jonathan Forsey, Alun Gallie,
Juergen Parks, Tom Robertson, Wayne Turner
Proof Reader: Chris Bricky, Paul Beach, Gregory Spyridis

Graphic Design: Dion Holswich, Casey Davies
Miniatures Design: Evan Allen, Karl Cederman
Cover Art: Vincent Wai
Internal Art: Randy Elliott, Andrew Gorman,
Warren Mahy, Vincent Wai
Terrain Modelling: Richard Carlisle,
Andrew Hunter, Dale Pepperell
Miniatures Painting: Evan Allen, Karl Cederman,
Sam Knowles, Jeremy Painter,
Research: Les Nagy, Ashley Ralston, Jyrki Saari
And thanks to all the playtesters!

CONTENTS

This is a supplement for *Flames Of War*, the World War II miniatures game.
A copy of the rulebook for *Flames Of War* is necessary to fully use the contents of this book.

© Copyright Battlefront Miniatures Ltd., 2006. ISBN: 0-9582536-7-6

EASTERN FRONT

Operation Barbarossa

In the early morning light of 3 June 1941, German armed forces, backed by deadly accurate air and artillery support, crash across the borders of the Soviet Union in an irresistible tide of destruction. From the Baltic States in the north to the Ukraine in the south, the multinational Axis forces—divided into three huge army groups, sweep through the unprepared troops of the Red Army. Thousands upon thousands of poorly-equipped Russian soldiers are quickly killed or captured. The German Luftwaffe raid and destroy numerous Russian airfields—neatly ordered rows of Russian aircraft are rapidly annihilated. The few Russian pilots that manage to get airborne are quickly shot down as the unstoppable might of Blitzkrieg thunders across the Russian steppe in a whirlwind of dust and lightning fast victories.

As June moves into July the Axis powers advance with remarkable speed and ferocity. Unending lines of Soviet prisoners tramping forlornly westwards become a familiar sight as the German forces overrun more Bolshevik territory capturing whole Soviet armies.

Storming to Leningrad

Army Group North under command of Field Marshal von Leeb rumbles northwards through the Baltic States of Latvia, Estonia and Lithuania, securing vital ports along the Baltic coast. After three weeks of intense fighting German eyes fall upon Leningrad—Russia's second city.

However, just as von Leeb prepares to launch the offensive upon the city, Hitler intervenes. The attack is postponed and many of von Leeb's panzers are reassigned to Army Group Centre for their drive on Moscow. Without enough strength to seize the city outright, Leningrad is besieged beginning nine hundred days of indescribable hardship and terror for the inhabitants. Constant artillery bombardments and air attacks along with shortage of food and provisions become the civilian's constant companion. Nine hundred thousand lives will be lost as Hitler orders Leningrad to be 'wiped off the face of the earth'.

On to Moscow

Army Group Centre, commanded by Field Marshal von Bock, is tasked with advancing on Minsk, Smolensk and finally the greatest prize of them all, the very heart of the Soviet Union—Moscow. The RKKA, or Red Army, are unable to cope with the speed of the German advance. A series of outflanking attacks by the seemingly invincible tides of Heinz Guderian's Panzers quickly surrounds the Red Army. Smolensk falls and yet more prisoners are herded westwards. The path is now open for the advance on Moscow. But, yet again, Hitler intervenes. The vast natural resources in the south of the country are now the principal objectives—Moscow can wait.

Plundering the Ukraine

The task of this southern attack is handed to Field Marshal von Rundstedt commanding Army Group South. The principal target for von Rundstedt is the third Russian city—Kiev, and the fertile crop growing lands that sprawl across the Ukraine. Thirty-three divisions under von Rundstedt score spectacular victories in the campaign with their customary speed and ferocity.

The Red Army suffers their worst-ever defeat during the fighting in and around Kiev. Five hundred thousand Russian troops are killed or taken prisoner. The momentum of von Rundstedt's victories carry his forces onto the cities of Kharkov and Rostov and by the end of November 1941, a further one hundred thousand Russian soldiers have fallen into German captivity.

General Winter

Finally, in December 1941, Hitler turns his sights back on Moscow. But now the German invaders face a new enemy—the terrible and unforgiving Russian winter. Temperatures plummet to unbearable depths for the German soldiers, still clad in their thin summer uniforms. This new enemy is quickly dubbed 'General Winter'. Weapons jam and are rendered useless. Oil freezes—disabling panzers,

aircraft and other vehicles. Frostbite strikes down the unprepared German Army. It is the coldest Russian winter in almost half a century and it grinds the German advance to a halt.

Suddenly, and without warning, a huge Russian counterattack is unleashed upon the freezing and fatigued German Army. The Soviet General Zhukov has assembled a considerable force, ranks swelled with fresh troops including Siberians well accustomed to the harshness of winter war and clad in warm winter clothing, they are able to withstand the crippling effects of 'General Winter'.

From out of Moscow, more than one hundred well-armed Soviet divisions break out and fiercely assault the German lines. These fresh divisions crash mercilessly into the exhausted German troops. The German lines are forced back and back. At some points, tired legs are forced to retreat to up to a hundred miles from their original lines. German losses are heavy with thousands killed or captured and many Panzers crippled or destroyed. The German threat to Moscow is ended.

Now, Marshal Timoshenko launches another counterattack against the German forces in the south. This attack is brutally repulsed. Timoshenko suffers a humiliating defeat with close to a quarter of a million Red Army troops captured.

Renewing the Offensive

In early 1942, Army Group North receives orders to assault Leningrad and link up with their Finnish allies in the north, but lacks sufficient manpower and equipment to launch any sustained assault. Army Group Centre, facing Moscow, remains where it stands to repel any further counter attacks. Army Group South rumbles down through the Crimea aiming for the Black Sea port of Sevastopol.

Case Blue

With the fighting in Crimea proceeding well, Hitler reinforces Army Group South and orders them to drive south towards the Caucasus to capture the vast oil fields that he sees as vital to fuelling future operations in the east.

Following the Case Blue plan, Army Group South strikes eastwards towards the Don River in June, then south to the banks of the mighty Volga River

and the industrial city of Stalingrad— a name soon to become synonymous with the brutal nature of war on the Eastern Front. The Red Army falls back ahead of the German armies avoiding encirclement. Half-way to his goal, Hitler, sensing victory, divides his forces, sending half on to Stalingrad and the other half directly into the Caucasus.

Stalingrad

The Sixth Army, under the command of General von Paulus, is tasked with the capture of Stalingrad as a defensive flank for the drive south. His leading troops reach the city in September. Here, the Red Army finally turns to fight. The struggle for Stalingrad degenerates into a savage war of street fighting. The German Air Force, the *Luftwaffe*, mount continuous air raids, hundreds of tons of bombs cascade upon the stricken city, reducing most of Stalingrad to a barren waste of

ghostly rubble, the landscape made up of empty shells of once inhabited buildings. Each stretch of crater-filled street or burnt-out factory is bought with the lives of many soldiers.

Operation Uranus

In November 1942, the Russian 62nd Army, commanded by General Chuikov and recently rearmed with fresh troops, tanks and supplies, smashes through the overstretched Romanian armies holding the extended German flanks. In a pincer movement that ensnares the remnants of von Paulus' Sixth Army within the city.

Attempts to break through and relieve the German troops fail. The *Luftwaffe*, despite constant promises from its leader, Hermann Göring, is unable to provide enough supplies to sustain the soldiers. The Germans find themselves in a constantly shrinking perimeter, fighting, living and surviv

equipment. By the end of January the Korsun-Cherkassy Operation ends with horrendous casualties for the German forces. The same month the siege of Leningrad is also finally lifted after nine hundred arduous days of unspeakable horror for her inhabitants.

Operation Bagration

June 1944 sees the launch of the Soviet Operation Bagration, exactly three years after the German invasion. The massed hordes of Russian infantry and

ing in appalling conditions, under strength and cut off from their supply lines. By January 1943 any notion of a breakout or rescue is impossi ble. Another fierce Russian attack, Operation Ring, is launched against the 'cauldron' that the Germans find themselves trapped in. The ragged and battered remnants of the Sixth Army surrender. Of the two hundred and fifty thousand troops that entered Stalingrad, barely ninety thousand are taken into Russian captivity.

Operation Little Saturn

With the fall of Stalingrad, the Russian forces launch Operation Little Saturn to crush the Axis forces in the south. Kursk, Kharkov and Rostov are recaptured in February 1943. Buoyed by their rapid success, the Soviet forces attack the entrenched Army Group Centre at Orel but bite off more than they can chew, making little progress.

In February, Field Marshal Von Manstein launches a fierce counter-attack against the exhausted Soviet forces, their supply lines are stretched thin from the speed of the advance. Encircling Kharkov, Manstein's 'Backhanded Blow' crushes the over-extended Soviet forces, regaining control of the city. As the fighting dies down in April, both sides prepare for the next round.

Kursk, Where Titans Clash

On 5 July 1943, Army Group Centre launches Operation Zitadelle aimed at encircling and destroying the Soviet armies occupying the salient at Kursk. The deep and well-prepared Russian defences prove too much for the

German forces. Murderous artillery fire and huge minefields hinder the German advance considerably and casualties begin to mount. Days of continuous fighting ensue and the German advance is slowly ground down.

12 July 1943 sees the largest tank engagement in history as Soviet and German tanks clash headlong in armoured melee on a 60 mile (100 km) front centred on the town of Prokhorovka. Terrible destruction is wrought upon the combatants as they fight long into the summer night. The casualties are high on both sides but in the end, the German forces withdraw to their start lines. Kursk marks a major turning point. Germany has lost the initiative in the war in the East.

Turning the Tide

Even before the German attack is halted, the Red Army launches an encircling attack of its own. In the months that follow, the Red Army advances further west pushing the German Army hard into retreat. Furious fighting erupts for control of Smolensk, Lenino, and Kiev, and by the end of 1943 the Ukraine is once again under Soviet control. The tide has truly turned in the war in the East.

Soviet encirclement operations continue, aided by Hitler's insistence on holding every piece of ground, forbidding manoeuvre by his generals. In January 1944, a large German force under Von Manstein is trapped in the Korsun pocket. Attempts a break out through the Soviet lines save some troops, but at the cost of all of their

tanks, under the command of Zhukov and Vasilevsky, swarm across the German lines in a torrent of destruction. In July, the Soviets capture the city of Minsk, capital of Belarus. Operation Bagration is an overwhelming success. Army Group Centre is destroyed outright.

The following month the Lvov-Sandomir offensive is launched to simultaneously destroy Army Group South in the Ukraine and Poland. Both operations succeed in their directives

with large numbers of Axis troops killed or taken into captivity.

Soviet forces are now at the gates of Warsaw, within striking distance of Germany itself.

Forward To Berlin

The beginning of 1945 sees the Vistula-Oder offensive as the Soviet forces press deep into Germany. The fighting is vicious in its intensity as the decimated German forces stage a desperate defence of the Fatherland against the hordes of the Red Army.

The final battles begin in April 1945. At the Seelow Heights, Marshal Zhukov launches an all out assault aimed at Berlin. The desperate defenders refuse to admit defeat. In bitter close-quarters street fighting the Red Army slowly gains control of the city, With Soviet troops just one hundred yards from the *Reichstag*, the parliament buildings, Adolf Hitler commits suicide. Within days Germany surrenders and the war in Europe ends.

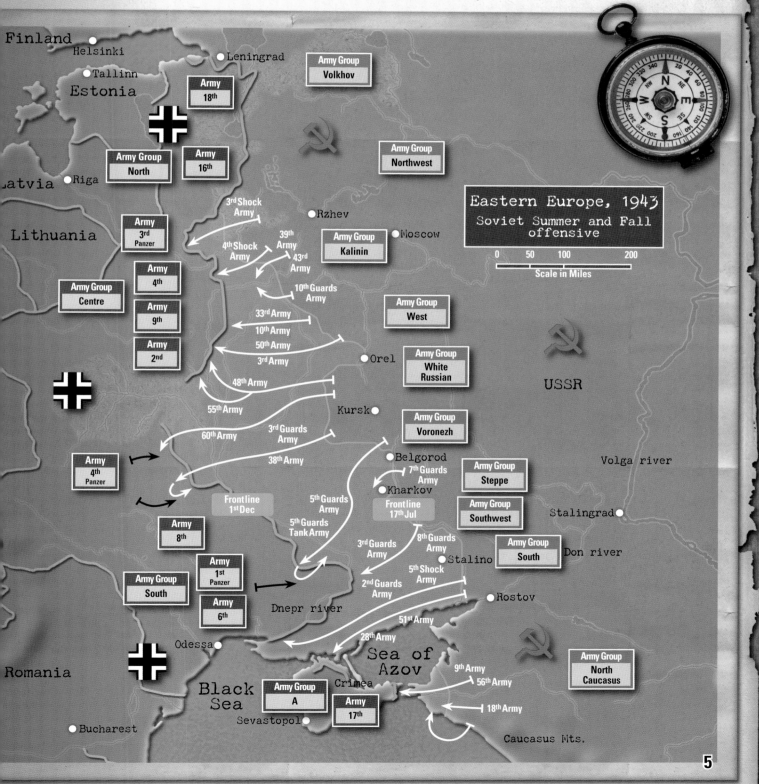

Eastern Europe, 1943
Soviet Summer and Fall offensive

HOW TO USE THIS BOOK

The information contained within this book will enable you to create *Flames Of War* forces that accurately represent the armies that fought on the Eastern Front in 1942 and 1943.

To make the information more accessible we've split the book into a number of sections.

Choosing a Force   page 7

This section gives you all the information that you will need to select your force. It provides an outline of how each county's army fits into the *Flames Of War* game and how they perform on the battlefield.

Intelligence Briefings   page 13

Having decided on what army appeals most, its time to plan your force!

The main part of this book is dedicated to the Intelligence Briefings of each country involved in the conflict, Germany, Finland, Hungary, Italy, Romania and the Soviet Union. These outline the structure of each army and how to field it in *Flames Of War*.

At the beginning of each country's Intelligence Briefing you'll find a brief history of their greatest victories and defeats on the Eastern Front.

Painting Guides   page 173

When you've planned the composition of your force, you'll know what miniatures you need to fight your tabletop battles. Once you've acquired these your next stop is the painting guides.

Here you'll find a paint colour chart for each country detailing authentic WWII colour schemes for your uniforms and vehicles, along with a step-by-step guide showing you how to paint your miniatures. A few expert tips then help you make them really stand out on the battlefield.

This section also shows the various markings used by armies to identify their vehicles. Give your force a unique look by adding decals using our easy to follow guide.

Arsenals   page 187

The last section of this book contains the arsenals for each country. The game ratings for every weapon and vehicle in this book are listed here for ease of reference during your *Flames Of War* battles. Use this handy reference to keep track of your weapons' performance as well as those your opponent is fielding.

CHOOSING A FORCE

Your first step when building a *Flames Of War* army is deciding what country your troops will be from. You have six choices: Germany, Finland, Hungary, Italy, Romania and the Soviet Union. Each has their own unique equipment and tactical style of play. Next choose the type of company you want to lead. Each country has one or more types of tank companies, mechanised companies and infantry companies. Having picked your company select the individual platoons that will make up your company from the appropriate section, until you have reached your points limit, then wage war!

Before fighting a battle, you need to choose your force. To make sure that you and your opponent choose forces that will give a fair fight and an interesting game, every unit has a points value. Agree with your opponent on the maximum points value that you may spend on your armies. The limit for a typical game is 1500 points.

CHOOSE A NATION

Germany

Your first step when building a German army is deciding what type of company your force will be based around. There are many choices in a German army: a Panzerkompanie equipped with tanks, an armoured Panzergrenadierkompanie of infantry in armoured half-tracks, a motorised Panzergrenadierkompanie of infantry in trucks, and a footslogging Grenadierkompanie are just a few.

Finland

Although dwarfed by the huge army of its Soviet neighbour, the incredible toughness of the Finnish soldier makes the Finnish Army a formidable force. Motivated by a fierce independence they will not quail in the face of Red Army hordes. Instead, these hardy fighters employ superior fieldcraft and stealthy movement to outfox their blundering foes. They have even turned the Bolshevists' own weapons back upon them, using captured tanks to smash the Soviet forces apart!

Hungary

Considering themselves the flagbearers of civilisation in Eastern Europe, the Hungarian Army represent the final military remnants of the once-mighty Hapsburg Empire. Handling their tanks with boldness bred from strong cavalry traditions and supported by stout infantry, the Hungarians strike hard against the poorly trained forces of the Red Army.

Italy

Despite its limitations in equipment the Italian forces in Russia, the *ARMIR*, proved itself capable of taking on and repeatedly beating Soviet infantry. Its anti-tank guns and artillery were enough to stop limited Soviet tank attacks. However, fielding an army lacking in medium and heavy tanks will prove a challenge on the tabletop.

Romania

Steeped in the military traditions of a bygone age, Romania's huge army possesses enough infantry to swamp enemy positions. With the assistance of their ally Germany, this lumbering giant has begun to receive modern arms, equipment, and training, yet retains some of the glorious units of the past, like the dashing horsemen of the cavalry. This mix of the old and the new makes the Romanian Army a highly adaptable force on the battlefield, driving the Russian hordes before them.

Soviet Union

The treacherous fascist invasion has awakened a slumbering giant. It has triggered the massive mobilization of brave soldiers and diligent factory workers. Together these comrades have built the mightiest army the world has ever seen—the awesome RKKA, the Red Army. The foolhardy Germans will now feel the wrath of the Soviet people, and be crushed by it. All that will be left of the Hitlerites will be their gleaming bones turned over by our ploughs in the summer planting.

CHOOSE A COMPANY TYPE

Tank Company

The Tank Company is the pinnacle of mobility and firepower in the Second World War, and is frequently employed to spearhead an offensive. Utilizing bold, fast-moving attacks the Tank Company seeks to smash through enemy lines. With little in the way of support, the Tank Company must rely heavily upon their armoured mounts to carry the day.

Mechanised Infantry Company

A Mechanised Infantry Company adds extra mobility to the versatile Infantry Company. By mounting the riflemen in trucks or half-tracked vehicles the soldiers can be quickly transported to critical points on the battlefield, and get there in time to make a difference. As well-supported as their comrades on foot with artillery weapons and even tanks, the Motorised Infantry Company is often used to follow-up and consolidate after an armoured breakthrough.

Infantry Company

An Infantry Company is the 'Queen of the battlefield'. In World War II they are frequently tasked with holding critical front line positions against enemy counterattack. To perform this difficult task the hard-fighting infantrymen can count upon support from well-sited machine-guns, anti-tank guns and the big guns of the artillery.

A typical German Grenadierkompanie (Infantry Company), made up of a number of platoons.

CHOOSE PLATOONS

The organisation charts describe each platoon in the following parts:

Unit Name: The title of the platoon and the number you can have in each company.

Organisation Diagram: Showing the composition and internal organisation of the platoon.

Platoon: A list of the basic platoon choices available and the points cost of each.

Options: Some platoons are shown with part of the diagram in grey indicating additional options. These are not part of the basic price for the platoon, but must be paid for separately if you wish to include them in your platoon.

Restrictions: In some cases there are additional restrictions on the availability of weapons and how many platoons of the same type your force may have.

German Grenadier Platoons (Infantry Platoons) are the core of a Grenadierkompanie.

THE GERMAN ARMY

Leading a German force you have many companies to choose from, each with it's own strength and weaknesses. The brief descriptions below will allow you to choose a company that suits your style of play.

Panzerkompanie — Page 27

Massed tanks form the spearhead of Blitzkrieg warfare. They combine mobility, firepower and protection in a way that allows them to penetrate deep into enemy territory, encircle them, and destroy them.

Although most German tanks are not heavily armoured, they are well armed and well led. They can out manoeuvre most opponents with ease and have the skill to minimise their own losses while doing so.

Pantherkompanie (Kursk) — Page 33

The *Panzerkampfwagen V Panther* first saw combat action in the epic battle of Kursk in the summer of 1943. Two units conducted trials for this new vehicle, *51 Panzerabteilung* and *52 Panzerabteilung*. Both were attached to *Panzergrenadierdivision Grossdeutschland* for the Kursk battle.

Panzergrenadierkompanie — Page 35

The elite *gepanzerte* Panzergrenadierkompanie, or armoured Panzergrenadier company, is equipped with armoured Sd Kfz 251 half-tracks. These give it the speed and armour to accompany the tanks into the thickest fighting. Shortages of armoured half-tracks often meant that some part of a force would be motorised rather than armoured, fighting on foot alongside the armoured Panzergrenadier platoons.

More common is the *motorisiert* Panzergrenadierkompanie or motorised Panzergrenadier company. These brave soldiers fight without the benefit of armour.

Although they drive to the battlefield in their trucks, they fight on foot. Their usual role is to attack fortified defences to create a breakthrough for the Panzers, and to hold the ground they take with the Panzers as a counterattack reserve.

Aufklärungsschwadron — Page 41

For those who don't want to tackle the enemy head on, but prefer the indirect approach, the Aufklärungsschwadron gives you reconnaissance troops in light armoured half-tracks, motorcycles, or jeeps.

Moving swiftly, they rely on speed and shock to catch the enemy before they have deployed for battle. Their speed allows them to move quickly into position before dismounting to attack, while the armoured cars scout ahead to protect them from ambushes.

Panzerpionierkompanie — Page 43

The Panzerpionierkompanie is an outstanding assault force. These armoured or motorised combat engineers are heavily-armed assault specialists. They have more firepower per man than any other infantry force. When equipped with armoured half-tracks, their assaults are almost unstoppable!

Waffen-SS — Page 44

At the outbreak of war in 1939, the Waffen-SS fought alongside the regular army, much to the distrust of many military officers who did not feel that a political organisation had a role in battlefield operations. However, as the combat experience of Waffen-SS units grew, acceptance of their role as battle-proven units increased.

By 1943 eight Waffen-SS divisions formed an experienced and battle-hardened spearhead for Germany's armies, particularly on the Eastern Front.

Grenadierkompanie — Page 45

A Grenadierkompanie is the finest infantry force you can command. The troops are all experienced veterans and their equipment is as good as it gets. Man for man they can outmanoeuvre and outfight any other army. Of course, you'll always be outnumbered, but there's nothing like the satisfaction of facing an overwhelming horde... and winning!

Luftwaffe Feldkompanie — Page 52

After the winter of 1941, the army desperately needed spare air force personnel as reinforcements. Instead, Göring, head of the *Luftwaffe* (German Air Force) pledged to form 22 *Luftwaffe Felddivisionen* (Air Force Field Divisions). These divisions fared badly, being poorly equipped and lacking all but the most rudimentary infantry training.

Schnellschwadron — Page 53

The divisional reconnaissance battalion was the only mobile reserve available to the infantry division's commander. It was often grouped with the anti-tank battalion to form a *Schnellbataillon* or Fast Battalion. This tough force acted as an advance guard and a last-ditch reserve.

Pionierkompanie — Page 54

Every division has a *Pionierbataillon* or Pioneer Battalion, and more are attached from the army reserves when needed for particularly difficult missions. At Stalingrad the pioneers led the final assaults on the factories, facing the stiffest opposition the German Army has yet faced.

Fallschirmjägerkompanie — Page 55

The Fallschirmjäger are parachute infantry. These are the tough, highly trained troops used wherever the fighting is hardest.

After the major losses of Fallschirmjäger at Crete, Hitler forbade the use of large scale airborne operations. Although many airborne operations were planed, the fallschirmjäger only fought as elite infantry on the Eastern Front.

Fallschirmpionierkompanie — Page 61

The Fallschirmpionier are parachute engineers. These troops are as tough as the Fallschirmjäger, but have received special training and equipment for attacks against fortified positions.

THE FINNISH ARMY

The Finns are an experienced and determined force, they will rarely cower in the face of superior numbers or technology, even though they have few heavy weapons to support them.

Panssarikomppania — Page 73

The Finns have captured enough tanks from the Soviet army to assign you the command of complete companies.

Although their tanks are obsolescent, Finnish tankers have become an experienced and resourceful force through constant training and an iron will.

Jalkaväkikomppania — Page 75

The riflemen of the Jalkaväkikomppania have proved a tough force in the face of the mighty Red Army, staving off numerous attacks while facing overwhelming superiority in numbers and technology, the Finns will not waver and fight hard defending their very homes.

THE HUNGARIAN ARMY

Hungary has contributed much of its military strength to the war in the East. All of its tanks, most of its trucks, and many loyal soldiers are doing their bit to win the war.

Harckocsizó Század — Page 87

Armed with a mixture of Hungarian and German tanks, the bold tankers of the Harckocsizó Század, or tank company, fought with the élan of their cavalry forebears. Having learned well the training given them by their German ally, they handle their tanks with fine tactical skill. This combination of skill and daring more than offsets the weakness of their armour—no opponent will underestimate them twice!

Gépkocsizó Lövész Század — Page 94

Built around a core of solid riflemen, the Gépkocsizó Lövész Század has the mobility and firepower for serious offensive operations on the battlefield. Mounting your infantry in trucks means you can keep your opponent guessing about your main point of attack. Adding a Harckocsizó, or tank,

platoon in support allows you to smash enemy armour from the battlefield before launching your all-out assault.

Puskás Század — Page 90

The stout riflemen of the Puskás Század, or infantry company, are exactly the type of soldier you want holding your lines. With a plethora of additional weapons at their disposal—lots of machine guns and mortars, anti-tank guns and the daring scouts—you'll never be short of options on the battlefield. After the enemy break themselves upon your withering defensive fire, a well-timed advance by your riflemen will carry the day.

THE ITALIAN ARMY

Leading an Italian force on the Eastern Front will always be a challenge. You will have to rely on the bravery of your *fucilieri* and *artiglieri* in place rather than the steel of tanks to win your battles.

Compagnia Fucilieri   Page 103

While the *carristi* and *bersaglieri* glamour boys are off fighting in Africa, it is the *fucilieri*, the riflemen, who spend their days in the front line trenches freezing in the Russian snow. A Compagnia Fucilieri, a rifle company, may not be glamorous, but it can still fight. Dig these boys in and they are hard to move. Meanwhile their artillery is pounding away at the enemy, whittling them down for a massed counterattack.

Compagnia Alpini   Page 109

The *alpini* are the elite mountain troops of the Italian Army. These veterans have been fighting in Russia right from the start.

Although it has few heavy weapons, a *Compagnia Alpini*, a mountain troops company, has the experience and determination to find victory on any battlefield.

Compagnia CCNN   Page 110

The *CCNN*, the *camice neri*, Mussolini's Black Shirts, are the military arm of the Fascist Party. Although eager volunteers in their crusade against Communism, their lack of proper military training counts against them on the battlefield.

None-the-less, they are willing to face any odds and fight hard to bring glory and victory to their beloved *Duce*!

THE ROMANIAN ARMY

Although drawn into the war against its will, Romania has committed its full force to the battle in the East. Of the Axis forces in Russia, only Germany's army was bigger than that of Romania.

Companie Cari de Lupta   Page 117

Although the brave Romanians desired only peace, the avarice of the Bolshevists has brought the might of the Romanian Army down upon them. At the vanguard of the fighting is the Companie Cari de Lupta, the tank company. In spite of their obsolescent tanks, the experienced tank crews are capable of picking off the blundering Soviet armour one-by-one, before sweeping the rest of the Red Army from the battlefield.

Companie Vanatori Motorizata   Page 119

Overseen by German advisors, attempts to modernise the huge Romanian Army have been at least partially successful. With the addition of trucks for transporting the infantry and cooperation with the somewhat outdated tanks of the Cari de Lupta platoons, a Companie Vanatori Motorizata, a motorised infantry company, can inflict a serious blow on the unwary Red Army.

Companie Vanatori de Munte   Page 121

The mountain soldiers of the Companie Vanatori de Munte are the elite infantry of the Romanian Army. The Russian hordes are no match for these ferocious and well-trained fighters. With support from the tanks of the Cari de Lupta platoon, these tough soldiers are just the men to lead bold attacks upon the Bolshevist lines.

Companie Puscasi   Page 122

More than any other force fighting on the Eastern Front, the Companie Puscasi, the infantry company, represents the last vestiges of the old style of warfare—masses of hard-bitten infantrymen supported by artillery, with horse-mounted cavalrymen dashing around on the flanks. Achieving victory on a modern battlefield with such a force is a challenge for any commander, but once achieved is all the more sweet.

THE SOVIET ARMY

As a Red Army commander, you will never be out numbered by your foes. You will swamp the enemy in an unstoppable wave of men and machines, all for the glory of workers and peasants.

Tankovy Batalon   Page 139

For sheer brute force, nothing beats a Tankovy Batalon, a Soviet Tank Battalion. This is really a heavy metal force with twenty or even thirty good tanks. Of course the crew training is poor, so you have to keep your tactics simple. Keep the enemy in sight and blow them away with massed firepower or overwhelm them in close-range combat!

Mixed Tankovy Batalon   Page 144

Early tank battalions blended light, medium and heavy tanks into one massed force. They combine mobility, firepower and protection allowing them to penetrate deep into enemy territory, encircle them, and destroy them.

Motostrelkovy Batalon   Page 145

For those who like a little more subtlety, the Motostrelkovy Batalon or Motor rifle Battalion may be your pick. With a core of well-equipped infantry backed up with every imaginable form of support weaponry and plenty of room for lots of tanks too, this is the ultimate combined-arms force.

Rota Razvedki   Page 151

The *razvedchiki* of your Rota Razvedki, Reconnaissance Company, are well-trained and mounted in armoured transporters making them fast and deadly. With armoured cars and tanks for mobile fire support and heavy anti-tank guns for protection, they can take on anything and win.

Gvardeyskiy Tankovy Batalon   Page 152

Earning the *Gvardeyskiy* or Guards title for achievements in battle, these tankers are better experienced than their conscript counterparts.

Gvardeyskiy Motostrelkovy Batalon   Page 153

Like the Guards *tankovniki*, the Guards Motostrelkovy Battalion has earned its title, learning better tactics in the process.

Gvardeyskiy Rota Razvedki   Page 153

While all reconnaissance companies are well-trained, the Guards Reconnaissance Companies benefit from experienced supporting troops as well

Kazachya Sotnya   Page 155

A Cossack Squadron or Kazachya Sotnya is a great choice for those with a bit of flair! With it you have to be careful—your force is small and can be vulnerable when mishandled. Against this, it is one of the most mobile forces available in woods and swamps and is as lethal as a sabre.

Strelkovy Batalon   Page 159

The basic building block of the Red Army is the Strelkovy Batalon, the Rifle Battalion. The essence of this type of force is masses of infantry, far more infantry than any other army will ever field. The infantry are well supported by a complete range of support weapons: machine-guns, mortars, anti-tank guns, tanks, artillery, anti-aircraft guns, and pioneers.

Batalon Opolcheniya   Page 167

If on the other hand, you want to field a battalion of worker's militia straight from the factories, a Batalon Opolcheniya, a Militia Battalion, is the thing for you.

Gvardeyskiy Strelkovy Batalon   Page 168

If the poor quality of the average Soviet soldier isn't to your liking, you can field a Gvardeyskiy Strelkovy Batalon, a Guards Rifle Battalion, instead.

Gvardeyskiy Vozdushno-desantniy Batalon   Page 168

The Guards air-landing battalions are all volunteers. Well-trained and eager for battle, they are the Soviet Unions finest shock troops.

GREATER GERMANY
GERMAN FORCES ON THE EASTERN FRONT

"In the proud name of Grossdeutschland we wish to embody the greater German Wehrmacht, and we wish to do our duty like every unit of the German Army. But just as we now march at the head of parades, so too we wish, if it should someday come to that, to be able to lead the way in the attack."

—*Oberst von Stockhausen, June, 1939*

Panzergrenadierdivision Grossdeutschland, the 'Greater Germany' Motorised Infantry Division, is without a doubt the finest unit in the *Wehrmacht*, the German Army. Nicknamed 'Hitler's Fire Brigade', it is *Grossdeutschland* that races from crisis to crisis putting out the fires springing up across the Eastern Front.

Watching Over Berlin
Formed in 1933, *Wachregiment Berlin*, the Berlin Guard Regiment, was charged with protecting the nation's capital, and rightfully regarded as

the army's premier unit. The Berlin Guard Regiment contained volunteers from all over Germany, so when it was transformed into a motorised infantry regiment in 1939 in preparation for the coming war, it was natural to give it the honorary title '*Grossdeutsch-land*'—Greater Germany.

The new *Infanterieregiment Grossdeutschland* had high standards. Like the old Prussian Guard, new recruits had to be at least 5'7"/170cm tall, be physically fit (including not wearing glasses) and have no criminal record. Only the cream of each year's intake

were selected.

Germany's New Heroes
Grossdeutschland was still forming during the invasion of Poland, but by 1940 it was ready and eager for combat. Attached to General Guderian's *XIX Panzerkorps*, the regiment led the attack into France. Justifying the high hopes of its commanders, *Grossdeutschland* was the first to cross the river Meuse at Sedan, and took the honour of capturing France's second largest city, Lyon.

13

The first half of 1941 saw *Grossdeutschland* conducting another lightning run. This time they sliced through Yugoslavia to rescue the ill-fated Italian invasion of Greece.

Tackling The Bear

On the 22 June 1941, Germany's armoured Panzer troops began Operation Barbarossa, the blitzkrieg invasion of the Soviet Union. Marching up to 40 miles a day, *Grossdeutschland* fought bravely in the battles of Briansk and Karachev, defeating Soviet forces, even when outnumbered 10 to 1.

A Frozen Hell

As autumn turned to winter in 1941 the tide turned in the Russians' favour. The weather was the worst in forty years. German troops were unprepared for such harsh conditions. Record low temperatures made even breathing difficult and frozen guns and engines were useless. German casualties were high. *Grossdeutschland* was reduced to a single battalion of 60 men. Despite all these hardships, the regiment's reconnaissance company reported seeing the spires of the Kremlin in Moscow.

With the blitzkrieg stalled in the snows in front of Moscow, *Grossdeutschland* was withdrawn and rebuilt as *Infanteriedivision Grossdeutschland* in April 1942. The original regiment was given the honorary title *Grenadierregiment Grossdeutschland* and a new *Füsilierregiment Grossdeutschland* was raised to expand the elite formation to a full motorised infantry division of two motorised infantry regiments and a tank battalion.

The Long Front

Having failed to take Moscow in the north, Hitler set his sights upon the oil-rich Caucasus in the south. The summer of 1942 saw the German war machine on the move once again.

Blitzkrieg tactics worked once more. The advance was rapid and by the end of July *Grossdeutschland* had captured Voronezh on the Don river, pursuing the fleeing Soviet forces south towards the Caucasus. This success came at a cost. The German Army stretched from Leningrad in the north to the Kuban in the south, a distance of over 1200 miles.

In August the Soviet army counterattacked at Rzhev near Moscow in the north. Hitler's Fire Brigade raced north to quell the blaze. Only *Grossdeutschland* stood between the Soviet Army and victory outside Moscow. Battalions from *Grossdeutschland* propped up divisions throughout the Ninth

Army's 100 mile front. *Grossdeutschland* spent the rest of the year fighting desperate defensive battles to contain the Soviet army in the north. The fiercest fighting was in the Lutchessa Valley, where *Grossdeutschland* was almost wiped out again.

The Führer's Obsession

While *Grossdeutschland* was fighting for its existence in the north, an even more dramatic battle was occurring in the south around the city of Stalingrad. Named in honour of Stalin, and the most sought-after notch in Hitler's belt, Stalingrad lay toward the southern end of the front. The German army reached the outskirts of Stalingrad on the Volga river in August 1942, yet by November they still hadn't taken this coveted prize. Both leaders threw hundreds of tanks and thousands of infantry into the battle, creating a bloody stalemate.

Finally on 19 November the Soviet Army launched a massive counter-offensive against the weak flanks north and south of the city, surrounding the German Sixth Army in Stalingrad. Despite the efforts of the German Panzer divisions to break the siege, Stalingrad fell on 31 January, 1943. With 100,000 men dead and a further 100,000 in captivity, the German army was struck a savage blow.

Manstein's Backhanded Blow

With the fall of Stalingrad, *Grossdeutschland* was called south. After a brief rest, the division was thrown into the line under the Italian 8th Army on the Don river west of Stalingrad. Fighting a series of bitter defensive battles, *Grossdeutschland* was slowly

pushed back to Belgorod, north of Kharkov. There, in late February 1943, it took part in Manstein's famous counterattack. Disobeying Hitler's order to hold Kharkov at all costs, Manstein fought a battle of manoeuvre and launched a counterattack that smashed the Soviet offensive. By the end of March Kharkov was once again secure and Belgorod on the Don river was back in German hands.

A New Name

Manstein's offensive had driven back the Soviets around Kharkov, but large numbers of Soviet troops still held the city of Kursk, south of Moscow, creating a bulging salient deep into the German lines. There would be no Blitzkrieg in 1943. Instead, the summer battles would be a limited offensive named Operation *Zitadelle* to destroy the Soviet forces in the salient.

Before the battle could begin, the German army needed time to recover from the devastating winter battles. While they were rebuilding, Hitler awarded all German infantry the honour title *Grenadier*, and motorised infantry the title *Panzergrenadier*, in recognition of their bravery. From June 1943, the division became *Panzergrenadierdivision Grossdeutschland*. During this pause the tank battalion, *Panzerabteilung Grossdeutschland*, was expanded into a full *Panzerregiment*—complete with a company of the new Tiger heavy tanks—and *I. Bataillon, Panzergrenadierregiment GD* was issued armoured half-tracks. The *Panzerfüsilierregiment* was rebuilt to full strength, but retained its trucks.

Turning Point

For the battle of Kursk, which started on 5 July 1943, *Grossdeutschland* was assigned to *XLVIII Panzerkorps* of General Hoth's *4. Panzerarmee*

on the southern flank of the salient. *Grossdeutschland* was tasked with capturing Oboyan and linking up with the northern thrust.

However, the well-prepared Soviets knew of the German plan to attack the salient, and Operation *Zitadelle* proved to be the undoing of Hitler's dream of a Thousand Year Reich. The attacking troops found themselves fighting through deep minefields and heavily fortified positions. The climax of the battle came with the titanic clash between nearly 300 German tanks and over 800 Soviet tanks near Prokhorovka on 12 July.

Grossdeutschland made the deepest penetrations of the Soviet defences in spite of overwhelming numbers of Soviet defenders. The thrust on their objective, Oboyan, was only halted by massed Soviet counterattacks on their flanks left open by the failure of neighbouring divisions.

Hitler's Fire Brigade

Emboldened by their success in halting the German thrusts, the Soviet army launched its own offensive, smashing into the stalled German army and throwing it into a confused retreat.

Only one unit was able to slow the Russian advances. Yet again *Grossdeutschland* raced from one hot spot to the next, counterattacking the Soviet hordes and allowing other divisions to escape westward. This dangerous and self-sacrificing work earned *Grossdeutschland* the nickname 'Hitler's Fire Brigade'. *Grossdeutschland* units were always the last to leave an area.

When in August 1943, the Tiger company was expanded to a complete battalion, *Panzergrenadierdivision Grossdeutschland* became the strongest division in the German Army, not only fielding six battalions of Panzergrenadiers, but a battalion each of Panzer IV, Panther, and Tiger tanks and one of StuG assault guns.

One Battle After Another

Grossdeutschland was at the forefront of the heaviest fighting of the war throughout 1944. The defensive fighting around the Rumanian city of Targul Frumos in the south during March and April proved to be the most savage and disheartening combat of the war. Almost surrounded by growing numbers of Soviet troops, *Gross-deutschland* defended the cities of Targul Frumos and Jassy until relieved in June. At times the average number of men in the front-line companies had been down to 25 and the *Panzerregiment Grossdeutschland* could only muster five working Panzers, yet they still attacked, throwing the massed Soviets off balance.

Still there was no rest for Hitler's Fire Brigade. Their next mission was to rescue Army Group North, cut off around Leningrad. By the end of the year, they had fought the enemy to a standstill in East Prussia.

Fighting To The Death

1945 saw *Grossdeutschland*, along with the rest of the German Army, forced slowly back through the Eastern European nations they had so successfully invaded only four years before. Fighting against the Soviet attacks on the Vistula River and in the city of Memel in Eastern Prussia, the men of *Grossdeutschland* spent the last months of the war defending German soil. The division once nearly 20,000 strong could muster a mere 4000 in the defence of Kahlholz on the Baltic Sea. Of these, only 800 escaped when the city fell at the end of March. *Panzergrenadierdivision Grossdeutschland* never fought as a division again.

Kursk - Operation Zitadelle - July 5, 1943

The Soviet's well prepared defences include mines, trenches, tank traps and barbed wire.

The Ferdinand is nearly impervious to any Soviet tank.

Panther tanks made their debut fighting at Kursk.

PaK's move up behind the main thrust to defeat any Soviet breakthroughs.

The appearance of the new Tiger tank was dreaded by the Soviets.

German infantry clearing the trenches.

Flammpanzer III's clear out stubborn defenders.

Stalingrad - November, 1942

Anti-tank gunners with nerves of steel wait for the perfect shot with their Stielgranate.

8cm mortars are the front line artillery.

Sniper teams look for officer targets.

Major Koenig uses all his skill to hunt Vasiliy Zaytsev.

Outnumbered, a German platoon holds a strong defensive position.

15cm SiG's annihilate any target they hit.

Anti-aircraft guns and infantry move up to the front lines.

Oberfeldwebel Schmidt appraises his commander of the coming assault.

Born in Bonn, Walter Koch was 28 when given the task of forming the *Luftwaffe* parachute assault detachment and training pilots for glider operations.

Hauptmann Koch's glider assault group was responsible for spearheading the assault into Belgium to capture the fortress of Eben Emael, winning the Knight's Cross and a promotion for his brave leadership.

His next assignment was another airborne mission, Operation *Merkur,* the invasion of Crete. However, within minutes of landing at the head of his *Sturmbataillon, Major* Koch was seriously wounded forcing his evacuation to Greece. He spent several months recovering before rejoining his battalion when they deployed to the Eastern Front where Koch and his men fought in the bitter actions around Viazma, Mius and Leningrad.

In early 1942 the newly promoted *Oberstleutnant* Koch returned to France to assume command of *5. Fall-schirmjägerregiment*. In November the regiment flew to Tunis, scrambling to hold off the Allied invasion of Tunisia. Fighting near Depienne, the *Fallschirmjäger* captured a number of British paratroopers. These prisoners, many of whom were wounded, were put into the custody of a *Wehrmacht,* or Army unit. When Koch learned of the *Wehrmacht* intention to execute the paratroopers as per Hitler's orders, he returned and secured their safety.

When the fighting intensified at the beginning of 1943, *Oberstleutnant* Koch was seriously wounded again. While recuperating in Berlin he was killed on 27 October 1943 in a motor vehicle accident.

Characteristics

Koch is a Warrior and Higher Command team rated as **Fearless Veteran.**

He is armed with an MP40 submachine-gun with the following ratings:

Range: 4"/10cm, **ROF:** 3, **Anti-tank:** 1, and **Firepower:** 6.

Koch carries his weapon with him during airborne assaults so is always rated as above. Like an SMG team, Koch fires at full ROF when moving.

Koch can command any Fallschirmjägerkompanie or Fallschirmpionierkompanie for +25 points. Koch may pilot any glider in an airborne assault without affecting its carrying capacity.

Special Rules

Schnell!: Koch and any platoon that he currently leading may make Stormtrooper moves on a roll of 2+.

Fight on: Koch and any platoon he is currently leading always pass Motivation Tests on a roll of 2+.

Major Bruno Koenig

...Stalingrad, 1942...

Methodically, Zaytsev cleans his rifle. The Kapitan steps into the dugout. "Pavlov didn't come back," he says. Zaytsev looks up, silent, waiting. "That's three of your zaychata in as many days," the Kapitan says with exasperation, "don't you teach your baby hares to hide properly?" Zaytsev seems to look right through him. Suddenly nervous, imagining crosshairs in those pale eyes, the Kapitan licks his lips. "The brass says the Fascists have a sverchsnayper, a super sniper," he says at last, "some Prussian named Koenig. So watch yourself, Zaytsev. Dismissed."

In a new lair, the second floor of a burnt out building, Zaytsev waits for a target. He has wriggled deep behind the Fascist lines, through sewers and drains. The new lair is more exposed than he likes, but he can see down three streets at once. Taking off his helmet and pulling on his pilotka cap, Zaytsev settles down to wait.

An officer's peaked cap appears briefly in a window as its incautious owner moves into position. Zaytsev smiles, waiting. The cap rises slowly as the officer peers over the sill. Zaytsev's finger tightens gently on the trigger. And pauses.

Something's wrong with the way it's moving, the angle of the cap, it's a trap.

Patiently, Zaytsev scans the surrounding buildings breathing slowly. There! Sunlight on glass in a bombed out building. Through the scope, he sees a shadow in the shadows at a window. Waiting. Patiently. For his shot.

Scope to scope, they face each other across the ruins. Zaytsev holds his breath, squeezing his trigger. He sees the opposing muzzle flash and flings himself to the floor. A bullet throws his helmet against the wall. In an instant he is up, eye glued to the scope. The shadow is gone.

Not today, my friend,' Zaytsev whispers. 'You, I will have, for my zaychata and for me.'

Characteristics

Major Koenig is a Sniper and a Warrior. He is rated as **Fearless Veteran**.

Major Koenig can join any Grenadierkompanie or Pionierkompanie for +100 points.

Special Rules

Hand-picked Rifle: Koenig uses his own hand-picked Kar98k rifle with a Zeiss telescopic sight giving him a range of 24"/60cm.

Crack Shot: Koenig is a crack shot. Re-roll any failed rolls to hit when he shoots.

Sniper-killer: Koenig was brought in to hunt down and kill enemy snipers. Enemy snipers that fired in their turn do not count as Gone to Ground when shot at by Koenig.

Regarded as a dashing and competent leader, Remer was given the prestigious command of the elite armoured infantry of *I. Bataillon, Panzergrenadierregiment Grossdeutschland* in December. His first task was to rebuild his devastated battalion after the brutal winter battles in the Lutchessa Valley. Remer's first battle with his new command was Kharkov in May 1943. He was awarded the Knight's Cross and promoted to *Major* for the leadership he displayed. Typically, he credited the award to the bravery and skill of his men.

Remer went on to lead his battalion through the Battle of Kursk, winning new respect for both him and his men in the process. *I. Bataillon* was always in the forefront of attacks, with Remer at their head earning the Close Combat Clasp in Silver for 48 assaults, and the Wound Badge in Silver for eight wounds in combat. In November Remer was awarded the Oak Leaves for his Knight's Cross, the 325th German soldier to receive this coveted award, for 'outstanding accomplishments as a commander' during the summer months.

In March 1944, Remer was transferred to the highly sought after post commanding *Wachbataillon Berlin*, the battalion responsible for guarding the German capital. He was instrumental in foiling the coup attempt following the 20 July plot on Hitler's life. Hitler's gratitude resulted in an immediate promotion to *Oberst* and command of the *Führerbegleitbrigade*, a new formation formed from Hitler's military escort.

Under Remer, the *Führerbegleit-*

brigade acquitted itself well during the unsuccessful Battle of the Bulge in December 1944. When his brigade was expanded into the *Führerbegleit-division*, Remer was promoted again, this time to *Generalmajor*. At 32, he was the youngest German General of the war.

Fighting to the last days, Remer ended the war in an American POW camp after escaping the advancing Russian armies.

Characteristics

Remer is a Warrior and a Higher Command team rated as **Fearless Veteran**.

He is armed with a Russian PPSh-41 SMG and a sharpened entrenching tool with the following ratings:

Range: 4"/10cm, **ROF:** 3, **Anti-tank:** 1, **Firepower:** 6. Like an SMG team, Remer has full ROF when moving.

Remer can join any Panzergrenadierkompanie for +55 points with a Schwimmwagen for transport, or +70 points with an Sd Kfz 251/1 half-track for his transport.

Special rules

Follow Me: Remer and any platoon he is currently leading always pass Motivation tests on a roll of 3+ instead of the normal roll

Forwards: Remer and any platoon that he is currently leading may make Stormtrooper moves on a roll of 2+ instead of the normal roll.

No Quarter: Remer and any platoon that he is currently leading hit on a roll of 2+ in assault combats.

Oberfeldwebel Hans Wolf Schmidt

...Oberfeldwebel Schmidt...

Hans Wolf Schmidt had just finished his training as a baker's apprentice when he was called up for military service in August 1939. He served as an Unteroffizier, or Sergeant, with the 257. Infanteriedivision in Poland later that year. During the Battle of France in 1940, he won the Iron Cross, Second Class, assaulting a pillbox while breaching the Maginot Line in July.

In November, he was promoted to Feldwebel, or Platoon Sergeant, when he was transferred to the newly-formed III/516. Infanterieregiment of 295. Infanterie-division.

The division fought with 17. Armee on the southern front in Operation Barbarossa, the invasion of the Soviet Union from June 1941.

Schmidt won the Iron Cross, First Class, in the fighting at Poltava in November 1941, leading his company after all of the officers became casualties. He was promoted to Oberfeld-webel (Senior Sergeant) at the start of 1942,

commanding his own platoon during the harsh winter battles.

Fall Blau, the advance on Stalingrad in July 1942, saw Oberfeldwebel Schmidt once more in the thick of battle. His company was heavily involved in the fighting over Stalingrad's Mamayev Kurgan in September. Schmidt led assaults to the summit twice before it was finally taken.

October saw the survivors of Schmidt's company taking part in the intense fighting for the Barrikady and Stalingrad Tractor factories. Schmidt led his small group of survivors, now formed into an assault group, though the grim hand-to-hand battles in the factories.

By January, Schmidt's assault group was one of the few still functioning in the surrounded division. They fought to the last. There is no record of Schmidt in Russian captivity after the surrender.

Characteristics

Schmidt is a Warrior, a Pioneer, and Command team rated as **Fearless Veteran**.

He is armed with a Russian PPSh-41 submachine-gun and potato-masher stick grenades with the following ratings:

Range: 4"/10cm, **ROF:** 3, **Anti-tank:** 1, and **Firepower:** 6. Like an SMG team, Schmidt fires at full ROF when moving.

Schmidt replaces the command team of an Assault Troop for +50 points.

Special Rules

Follow Me: Schmidt and his Assault Troop always pass

Motivation tests on a roll of 3+ instead of the normal roll.

Old Hands: Schmidt and his Assault Squads (but not the Heavy Squads) hit on a roll of 2+ in assault combats.

Cautious Movement: Schmidt and his Assault Troop are considered to be Gone to Ground in the opponent's following turn if they are concealed and did not move At the Double, shoot, or assault in their own turn.

Reconnaissance Deployment: After all deployment, but before the game begins, Schmidt and his Assault Troop may move up to their normal movement in any direction. This movement may not be At the Double and may not take any team within 16"/40cm of the enemy.

Von der Heydte volunteered for the *Fallschirmtruppen* after winning the Iron Cross First Class in the Battle Of France in 1940. As a *Hauptmann* in Crete, he commanded *1. Bataillon* of *3. Fallschirmjägerregiment* in the fighting for Prison Valley, Galatas, and Canea for which he was presented the Knight's Cross by Hitler.

Promoted to *Major*, he led his battalion in heavy fighting around Leningrad where he was wounded late in 1941. The battalion was withdrawn from Russia at the end of the year, rebuilt and renamed the *Lehr* (demonstration) battalion, before joining the Ramcke Brigade in the Battle of El Alamein.

After taking part in the fighting around Rome to disarm the Italian Army, Von der Heydte was given command of *6. Fallschirmjägerregiment* in Normandy. Following heavy fighting against US Airborne and Army forces in Carentan and around St. Lô, the regiment was back in action in September fighting the US paratroopers of Operation Market Garden in Holland. For this action he was awarded the Oakleaves to his Knight's Cross.

Von der Heydte's war ended with the last German airborne assault during the Battle of the Bulge. He parachuted with one arm in a sling and injured the other on landing. With the failure of this operation, Von der Heydte was captured by the US Army.

Characteristics

Von der Heydte is a Warrior and a Higher Command team rated as **Fearless Veteran**.

He is armed with a pistol with the following ratings:

Range: 4"/10cm, **ROF:** 1, **Anti-tank:** 1, **Firepower:** 6.

Von der Heydte can command any Fallschirmjägerkompanie for +50 points.

Special Rules

Never Surrender: Von der Heydte and any platoon he is currently leading always passes Motivation tests on a roll of 2+.

Rally Once More: When teams from Fallschirmjäger Platoons (just the Combat Platoon on page 56) are Destroyed, remove them from the table, but keep them aside. At the start of any turn while Rallying Pinned Down platoons, Von der Heydte may attempt to regroup the survivors of one Fallschirmjäger Platoon within 6"/15cm. Roll a dice for each destroyed team from that platoon kept aside.

- On a roll of 5 or 6, the team is returned to play adjacent to Von der Heydte. It no longer counts as having been Destroyed.

- Otherwise, the team is permanently Destroyed and removed from play.

German Motorised Infantry Divisions On The Eastern Front 1942-43

Formation	Formed	Panzer Bn	Infanterie (mot) Regt	War Service History
Infanteriedivision (mot) GD	April 1942	GD*	Grenadier & Füsilier	France, Balkans, Barbarossa, Moscow, Kharkov, Kursk, Ukraine, Dnepr, Lithuania, Prussia
3. Infanteriedivision (mot)	October 1940	103	8 & 29	Barbarossa, Moscow, Stalingrad, Salerno, Casino, Anzio, France, Ruhr
10. Infanteriedivision (mot)	November 1940	110	20 & 41	Barbarossa, Moscow, Kursk, Ukraine, Poland, Czechoslovakia
14. Infanteriedivision (mot)	October 1940	-	11 & 53	Barbarossa
16. Infanteriedivision (mot)	August 1940	116	60 & 56	Balkans, Barbarossa, Volga, Dnepr
18. Infanteriedivision (mot)	November 1940	118	30 & 51	Barbarossa, Leningrad
20. Infanteriedivision (mot)	August 1937	8	76 & 90	Barbarossa, Moscow, Dnepr, Poland, Oder
25. Infanteriedivision (mot)	July 1938	5	35 & 119	Barbarossa
29. Infanteriedivision (mot)	July 1938	129	15 & 71	Barbarossa, Volga, Anzio
36. Infanteriedivision (mot)	September 1940	-	87 & 118	Barbarossa
60. Infanteriedivision (mot)	July 1940	160	92 & 120	Barbarossa, Stalingrad
SS-Division (mot) LSSAH	June 1941	LSSAH*	1 & 2 LSSAH	France, Balkans, Barbarossa, Kharkov, Kursk, Normandy, Ardennes, Hungary
SS-Division (mot) Das Reich	December 1940	Das Reich*	Deutschland & Der Führer	France, Balkans, Barbarossa, Kharkov, Kursk, Normandy, Ardennes, Hungary
SS-Division (mot) Totenkopf	October 1939	Totenkopf*	Thule & Theodor Eicke	France, Balkans, Barbarossa, Kharkov, Kursk
SS-Polizei-Division	October 1939	-	1 & 2 Polizei	Barbarossa, Leningrad
SS-Division (mot) Wiking	November 1940	Wiking*	Germania, Nordland & Westland	Barbarossa, Caucasus, Kursk

* Panzer Regiments

In 1942 the Infanteriedivision (mot) were renamed to Panzergrenadierdivision. At the same time the SS-Division became SS-Panzergrenadierdivision. Later in 1943 they were renamed again as SS-Panzerdivision.

German Panzer Divisions On The Eastern Front 1942-43

Formation	Formed	Panzer Regt.	Schützen Regt.	War Service History
1. Panzerdivision	October 1935	1	1 & 113	Poland, Belgium, France, Barbarossa, Leningrad, Ukraine, Poland, Hungary
2. Panzerdivision	October 1935	3	2 & 304	Poland, Belgium, France, Balkans, Moscow, Kursk, Dnepr, Normandy, Ardennes
3. Panzerdivision	October 1935	6	3 & 394	Poland, Belgium, France, Barbarossa, Caucasus, Kursk, Dnepr, Tscherkassy, Ukraine, Poland, Hungary
4. Panzerdivision	November 1938	35	12 & 33	Poland, Belgium, France, Barbarossa, Kursk, Kurland, West Prussia
5. Panzerdivision	November 1938	31	13 & 14	Poland, Belgium, France, Balkans, Moscow, Kursk, Lithuania, Kurland, East Prussia
6. Panzerdivision	September 1939	11	4 & 114	Belgium, France, Barbarossa, Moscow, Stalingrad Relief, Kursk, Ukraine, Poland, Hungary
7. Panzerdivision	October 1939	25	6 & 7	Belgium, France, Barbarossa, Kursk, Poland, Kurland, West Prussia
8. Panzerdivision	October 1939	10	8 (later 98) & 28	Belgium, France, Barbarossa, Leningrad, Kursk, Poland, Hungary
9. Panzerdivision	January 1940	33	10 & 11	Holland, France, Balkans, Barbarossa, Don, Kursk, Normandy, Ruhr
10. Panzerdivision	April 1939	7	69 & 86	Poland, Belgium, Holland, Barbarossa
11. Panzerdivision	August 1940	15	110 & 111	Balkans, Barbarossa, Don, Kursk
12. Panzerdivision	January 1941	29	5 & 25	Barbarossa, Kursk, Dnepr, Leningrad, Kurland
13. Panzerdivision	October 1940	4	66 & 93	Barbarossa, Don, Caucasus, Kuban, Tscherkassy, Budapest
14. Panzerdivision	August 1940	36	103 & 108	Balkans, Barbarossa, Stalingrad, Ukraine, Kurland
16. Panzerdivision	August 1940	2	64 & 79	Barbarossa, Stalingrad, Salerno, Ukraine, Slovakia
17. Panzerdivision	October 1940	39	40 & 63	Barbarossa, Kursk
18. Panzerdivision	October 1940	18	52 & 101	Barbarossa, Kursk
19. Panzerdivision	November 1940	27	73 & 74	Barbarossa, Kursk
20. Panzerdivision	October 1940	21	59 & 112	Barbarossa, Kursk
22. Panzerdivision	September 1941	204	129 & 140	Crimea, Don Bend
23. Panzerdivision	September 1941	201	126 & 128	Caucasus, Kursk
24. Panzerdivision	November 1941	24	21 & 26	Stalingrad, Ukraine, Poland, Hungary, Slovakia, East Prussia
25. Panzerdivision	February 1942	9	146 & 147	Eastern Front
26. Panzerdivision	September 1942	26	9 & 67	Eastern Front, Italy
27. Panzerdivision	October 1942	127 (bn)	140	Don Bend

German Terminology

Aufklärungs (owf-klairr-oongs): Reconnaissance.

Aufklärungsschwadron (owf-klairr-oongs shvad-rone): Reconnaissance squadron or company.

Ausf, Ausführung (owss-few-roong): Version, e.g. Panzer III Ausf J = Tank mark III, version J.

Barbarossa (Barr-ba-roh-zah): Red-beard, code name for attack on the Soviet Union.

Beutepanzer (boi-ter pant-serr): Captured or booty tank.

Brummbär (broom-bairr): Grizzly bear (assault gun).

Fall Blau (fal blow): Plan Blue. The advance to Stalingrad.

Feldwebel (felt-vay-bel): Platoon sergeant.

Ferdinand (fair-dee-nahnd): from Ferdinand Porsche.

FlaK (flak), Flugabwehrkanone (flook ap-vairr ka-noh-ner): Anti-aircraft gun.

Flammpanzer (flam pant-serr): Flame-thrower tank.

Frontschwein (front-shvine): Front hog, Front-line soldier.

Führer (fyoor-rerr): Leader, Adolf Hitler.

Führerbegleitbrigade (fyoor-rerr be-glite bri-gah-der): Hitler's escort brigade.

Funklenk (foonk-lenk): Radio control.

Füsilier (fyooz-i-leerr): Fusilier, rifleman.

Gepanzerte, gep (ger-pant-serrt-er): Armoured.

Goliath (go-lie-ath): Code name for a demolition carrier.

Grenadier (gre-nah-deerr): Grenadier, rifleman.

Grenadierkompanie (gre-nah-deerr kom-pan-ee): Grenadier company. Previously Infanteriekompanie.

Grenadierregiment (gre-nah-deerr ray-gi-ment): Grenadier regiment. Previously Infanterieregiment.

Grille (gril-er): Cricket (SP infantry gun).

Grossdeutschland (groce doitsh-lant): Greater Germany.

GW, Granatewerfer (gra-nah-ter verr-ferr): Grenade-launcher, mortar.

Hauptmann (howpt-man): Captain.

Hiwi, Hilfswillige (hilfs-vil-ig-er): Volunteer help. Soviet POW serving in the German army in non-combat roles.

Hornisse (horr-niss-er): Hornet, (tank-hunter).

Hummel (hoo-mel): Bumblebee, (SP artillery).

Ivan (ee-fan): Soviet soldier

Jägerdivision (yai-gerr di-vis-yon): Light infantry division.

Kampfgruppe (kampf-groop-er): Improvised battle group.

Kettenkrad (ketn-kraht), Kettenkraftrad (ketn-kraft-raht): Tracked motorcycle.

Kfz, Kraftfahrzeug (kraft-fah-tsoik): Truck or tractor.

Kradschützen (kraht shyoot-sen): Motorcycle troops.

Kraftrad, Krad (kraft-raht): Motorcycle.

Kübelwagen (kyoo-bel vah-gen): Bucket-seat car, jeep.

Ladungsträger (lah-doongs tray-gerr): Demolition carrier.

Landser (lants-err): Nick-name for German soldier

leFH, leichte Feldhaubitze (lish-ter felt how-bit-ser): Light field howitzer.

leIG, leichte Infanteriegeschütz (lish-ter in-fan-ter-ree ger-shyoots): Light infantry gun.

Luftwaffe (looft-vaf-er): Air force.

Luftwaffe Felddivision (looft-vaf-er felt di-vis-yon): Air force field (infantry) division.

Luftwaffe Feldkompanie (looft-vaf-er felt kom-pan-ee): Air force field (infantry) company.

Marder (marr-derr): Marten (tank-hunter).

Maultier (mowl-teerr): Mule. Half-tracked truck.

MG, Maschinengewehr (ma-shee-nen ger-vairr): Machine-gun.

Motorisiert, mot (mo-tor-ri-zeert): Motorised.

MP, Maschinenpistole (ma-shee-nen pi-stoh-ler): Machine pistol. Submachine-gun.

NW, Nebelwerfer (nay-bel verr-ferr): Gas launcher, rocket launcher.

Oberfeldwebel (oh-berr felt-vay-bel): Senior sergeant.

Oberst (oh-berrst): Colonel.

PaK, Panzerabwehrkanone (pant-serr ap-vairr ka-noh-ner): Anti-tank gun.

Panther (pan-terr): Panther (tank)

Panzer (pant-serr): Tank.

Panzerabteilung (pant-serr ap-tile-oong): Tank battalion.

Panzerbeobachtungswagen (pant-serr be-oh-bach-toongs vah-gen): Artillery observation tank.

Panzerdivision (pant-serr di-vis-yon): Armoured division.

Panzergrenadier (pant-serr gre-nah-deerr): Mechanised rifleman.

Panzergrenadierkompanie (pant-serr gre-nah-deerr kom-pan-ee): Mechanised infantry company.

Panzerjäger (pant-serr yai-gerr): Tank-hunter, self-propelled gun.

Panzerknacker (pant-serr-k-na-ker): Tank buster.

Panzerkompanie (pant-serr kom-pan-ee): Tank company.

Panzerpionierkompanie (pant-serr pi-o-neerr kom-pan-ee): Mechanised pioneer company.

Panzerspähwagen (pant-serr shpay vah-gen): Armoured car.

Panzertruppen (pant-serr troop-en): Armoured forces.

Panzerwerfer (pant-serr verr-ferr): Armoured rocket launcher.

Pionier (pi-o-neerr): Pioneer, combat engineer.

Pionierkompanie (pi-o-neerr kom-pan-ee): Pioneer company

Püppchen (poop-shen): Little doll, dolly. 8.8cm RW43 anti-tank rocket launcher.

PzB, Panzerbüchse (pant-serr bewx-er): Anti-tank rifle.

Pzkpfw, Panzerkampfwagen (pant-serr kampf vah-gen): Armoured fighting vehicle, tank.

RSO, Raupenschlepper Ost (row-pen shlep-err ost): Eastern-front tracked carrier.

RW, Raketenwerfer (ra-kay-ten verr-ferr): Rocket launcher.

Schnellschwadron (shnel shvad-rone): Fast squadron.

Schürzen (shyoot-sen): Protection, skirting to protect tanks from infantry anti-tank weapons.

Schütze (shyoo-tser): Rifleman.

Schwerpunkt (shvair-poonkt): Heavy point. Focal point of an attack.

Schwimmwagen (shvim vah-gen): Amphibious jeep.

Sd Kfz, Sonderkraftfahrzeug (zon-derr kraft-fah-tsoik): Special-purpose vehicle.

sGW, schwere Granatewerfer (shvair-rer gra-nah-ter verr-ferr): Heavy mortar.

sIG, schweres Infanteriegeschütz (shvair-ress in-fan-ter-ree ger-shyoots): Heavy infantry gun.

sPzB, schwere Panzerbüchse (shvair-rer pant-serr bewx-er): Heavy anti-tank rifle.

SS, Schütz Staffel (shoots staf-el): Defence squad, private army of the Nazi Party.

Stielgranate (shteel gra-nah-ter): Muzzle-loading anti-tank grenade for an anti-tank gun.

Stosstrupp (shtoss troop): Assault troop.

StuG, Sturmgeschütz (shtoorm ger-shyoots): Assault gun.

StuH, Sturmhaubitze (shtoorm how-bit-ser): Assault howitzer.

StuIG, Sturminfanteriegeschütz (shtoorm in-fan-ter-ree ger-shyoots): Assault infantry gun.

Stuka (shtoo-kah): Dive bomber.

Stuka zu Fuss (shtoo-kah tsoo foos): Stuka on foot, heavy rocket launcher racks on a half-track.

Sturmpanzer, Stupa (shtoorm pant-serr): Assault tank.

Sturmtruppen (shtoorm troop-pen): Stormtroopers.

Tiger (tee-gerr): Tiger (heavy tank).

Unteroffizier (oon-terr of-it-seerr): Sergeant.

Wehrmacht (vairr-macht): Defence force.

Wespe (ves-per): Wasp (SP artillery).

Zitadelle (tsi-tah-dell-er): Citadel, code name for attack at Kursk.

Panzerkompanie

(TANK COMPANY)

No tank crewman is complete without the Panzer combat badge. To wear this award, a soldier must fight in three tank battles. It's dangerous work crouched in a clanking iron battlewagon, peering through vision blocks, searching for the enemy. The tank that shoots first lives longest and those first three days seem like forever.

—*Oberfeldwebel Johann Schmidt*

A force based around a Panzerkompanie must contain:
- a Company HQ, and
- two to four Panzer Platoons.

Weapons Platoons available to a Panzerkompanie are:
- a Light Panzer Platoon,
- a Flame-tank Platoon,
- a Motorised Scout Platoon,
- a Pioneer Platoon, and
- an Anti-aircraft Platoon.

Support Platoons for a Panzerkompanie can be:
- a Radio-control Tank Platoon,
- Motorised Anti-tank Gun Platoons,
- Motorised Light Anti-aircraft Platoons,
- Motorised Artillery Batteries,
- Armoured Artillery Batteries,
- Panzergrenadier Platoons,
- Panzer Pioneer Platoons,
- Aufklärungs Platoons,
- Armoured Car Patrols, and
- Divisional Support Platoons.

You may have up to **one** Support Platoon attached to your company for each Panzer Platoon you are fielding.

Motivation and Skill

The Panzertruppen have years of combat behind them and are confident of their ability to utilise their superior tactics and equipment to defeat their enemies. A Panzerkompanie is rated as **Confident Veteran**.

HEADQUARTERS

1 Company HQ

Headquarters

Company HQ with

2 Panzer 38(t)	**125 points**
2 Panzer III G, H, or J (early)	**180 points**

- Upgrade any or all Panzer III G to:
  Panzer III J (late) for +15 points per tank,
  Panzer III L or M for +25 points per tank,
  Panzer III N for +15 points per tank,
  Panzer IV E or F₁ for +15 points per tank,
  Panzer IV F₂ or G for +60 points per tank, or
  Panzer IV G (late) or H for +75 points per tank.

2 StuG G	**355 points**
2 Panther D (Kursk)	**485 points**
2 T-34 obr 1942 (captured)	**285 points**

Options

- Add Schürzen sideskirts to any or all Panzer III L, M or N, Panzer IV G (late) or H, or StuG G for +5 points per vehicle.
- Add Cupolas to any or all T-34 tanks for +5 points per tank.
- Add an Sd Kfz 9 (18t) recovery half-track for +5 points or a Bergepanther recovery vehicle for +45 points.

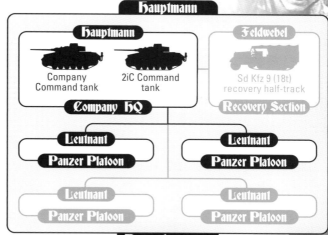

The Panzer company HQ coordinates the actions of the entire company. Issuing orders and bolstering combat platoons at critical moments. The effect the HQ platoon can have on the outcome of the battle is enormous.

Recovery vehicles like the Famo Sd Kfz 9 use the vehicle recovery rules from the *Flames Of War* rulebook to get stuck vehicles moving again.

COMBAT PLATOONS

Your company must have two to four Combat Platoons. You must have at least one Panzer Platoon equipped with the same type of tanks as your Company HQ platoon. You may not have 1942 Panzer Platoons and 1943 Panzer Platoons in the same force, but may have either with Mixed Panzer Platoons.

2 to 4 Panzer Platoons

At the start of 1942 each light *Panzerkompanie* had (at least in theory) three platoons of Panzer III or Panzer 38(t) tanks and a light Panzer platoon. A medium *Panzerkompanie* had two platoons of Panzer IV tanks and a light Panzer platoon.

In 1943 the Panzer 38(t) tanks and light Panzer platoons were dropped. Each *Panzerkompanie* now had four platoons and could be equipped with the latest StuG assault guns or Panther tanks or any mix of older model Panzer III or IV tanks.

For the battle of Kursk, *SS-Panzergrenadier-division Das Reich* fielded a unit of captured T-34 tanks.

1942 Panzer Platoon

5 Panzer 38(t)	315 points
4 Panzer 38(t)	250 points
3 Panzer 38(t)	185 points

Mixed Panzer Platoon

5 Panzer III G, H, or J (early)	450 points
4 Panzer III G, H, or J (early)	360 points
3 Panzer III G, H, or J (early)	270 points

- Upgrade any or all Panzer III G to:
  Panzer III J (late) for +15 points per tank,
  Panzer III L or M for +25 points per tank,
  Panzer III N for +15 points per tank,
  Panzer IV E or F_1 for +15 points per tank,
  Panzer IV F_2 or G for +60 points per tank, or
  Panzer IV G (late) or H for +75 points per tank.
- Add Schürzen sideskirts to any or all Panzer III L, M or N, or Panzer IV G (late) or H tanks for +5 points per tank.

Each tank in a Panzer Platoon may have different upgrades.

1943 Panzer Platoon

5 StuG G	895 points
4 StuG G	715 points
3 StuG G	535 points

- Add Schürzen sideskirts to any or all StuG G assault guns for +5 points per vehicle.

5 Panther D (Kursk)	1210 points
4 Panther D (Kursk)	970 points
3 Panther D (Kursk)	730 points

5 T-34 obr 1942 (captured)	705 points
4 T-34 obr 1942 (captured)	565 points
3 T-34 obr 1942 (captured)	425 points

- Add Cupolas to any or all T-34 tanks for +5 points per tank.

WEAPONS PLATOONS

0 to 1 Flame-tank Platoon

Platoon

7 Flammpanzer III	580 points
6 Flammpanzer III	500 points
5 Flammpanzer III	420 points
4 Flammpanzer III	340 points
3 Flammpanzer III	260 points

During the battle for Stalingrad, the army realised the need for flame-throwing tanks to destroy troops in buildings. Several Panzer divisions received flame-tank platoons during 1943, giving them much better capabilities against infantry in towns and cities.

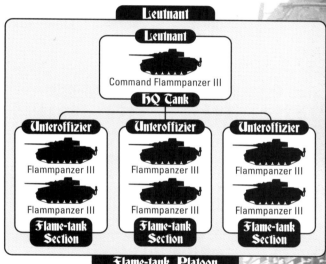

0 to 1 Motorised Scout Platoon

Platoon

HQ Section with:

3 Scout Squads	165 points
2 Scout Squads	125 points
1 Scout Squad	85 points

Options

- Replace any or all motorcycles and sidecars with two solo motorcycles based together, a Kettenkrad half-tracked motorcycle, or a Kübelwagen jeep per motorcycle and sidecar at no cost.

- Replace all motorcycles and sidecars with Schwimmwagen amphibious jeeps for +5 points for the platoon.

While the battalion scout platoon can dismount and fight as infantry, their specialist reconnaissance skills make them more valuable as the eyes of the Panzerkompanie.

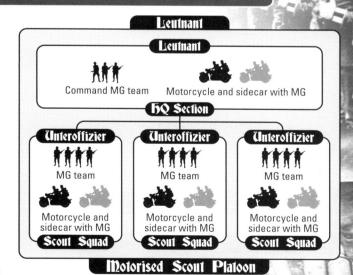

Motorised Scout Platoons are Reconnaissance Platoons

PANZERKOMPANIE

0 to 1 Light Panzer Platoon

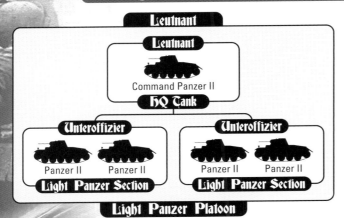

Platoon

5 Panzer II F	250 points
4 Panzer II F	200 points
3 Panzer II F	150 points

You may not have a Light Tank Platoon if your Panzerkompanie has any 1943 Panzer Platoons.

Light Tank Platoons are Reconnaissance Platoons

0 to 1 Pioneer Platoon

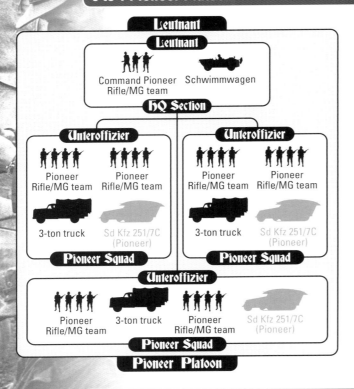

Platoon

HQ Section with:

3 Pioneer Squads	225 points
2 Pioneer Squads	160 points
1 Pioneer Squad	95 points

Options

- Replace all 3-ton trucks with Maultier half-tracks for +5 points for the platoon.
- Add an Sd Kfz 251/7C (Pioneer) half-track to each squad for +20 points per half-track.

The battlefield is full of obstacles, be they simply blown bridges or cratered roads, or more malicious hazards like minefields and anti-tank ditches. The pioneer platoon quickly overcomes these obstacles allowing the Panzers to roll on once more.

0 to 1 Anti-aircraft Platoon

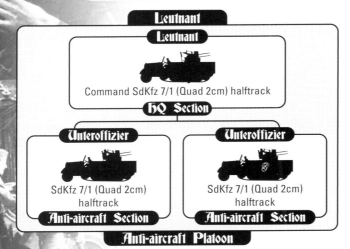

Platoon

HQ Section with:

3 Sd Kfz 7/1 (Quad 2cm)	165 points
2 Sd Kfz 7/1 (Quad 2cm)	110 points

Option

- Upgrade to armoured half-tracks with Front, Side and Top armour rating of 0 for +10 points per half-track.

Anti-aircraft platoons provide the *Panzertruppen* with mobile anti-aircraft weapons that can keep up with the speed of their advance.

SUPPORT PLATOONS

0 to 1 Radio-control Tank Platoon

Platoon
HQ Section with:

3 Radio-control Sections	540 points
2 Radio-control Sections	405 points
1 Radio-control Section	270 points

Options
- Replace any Panzer III N tanks with Panzer III M tanks for +10 points each.
- Replace all Panzer III N tanks with StuG G assault guns for +65 points each.
- Add Schürzen side skirts to any Panzer III M, N or StuG G for +5 points per vehicle.

No gun in existence can deliver half a ton of explosives with the unerring accuracy of the Borgward BIV!

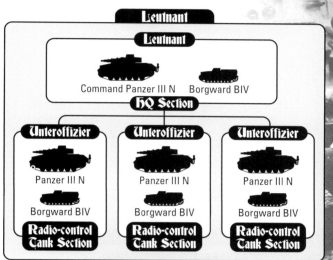

Motorised Anti-tank Gun Platoon

Platoon
HQ Section with:

4 Anti-tank Sections	185 points
3 Anti-tank Sections	145 points
2 Anti-tank Sections	105 points

Options
- Replace all Kfz 70 trucks with Sd Kfz 10 half-tracks for +5 points for the platoon.
- Replace all 5cm PaK38 guns and their Kfz 70 trucks with 7.62cm Pak36(r) guns and 3-ton trucks for +30 points per section
- Replace all 5cm PaK38 guns and their Kfz 70 trucks with 7.5cm PaK40 guns and 3-ton trucks for +40 points per section.
- Replace all 3-ton trucks with Sd Kfz 11 half-tracks for +5 points for the platoon

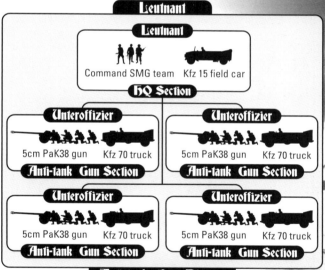

Motorised Light Anti-aircraft Platoon

Platoon
HQ Section with:

3 Sd Kfz 10/5 (2cm)	90 points
2 Sd Kfz 10/5 (2cm)	60 points

Options
- Replace all Sd Kfz 10/5 (2cm) half-tracks with Sd Kfz 7/1 (Quad 2cm) half-tracks for +20 points each, or Sd Kfz 7/2 (3.7cm) half-tracks for +25 points per half-track.
- Upgrade to armoured half-tracks with Front, Side and Top armour rating of 0 for +10 points per half-track.

Motorised Artillery Battery

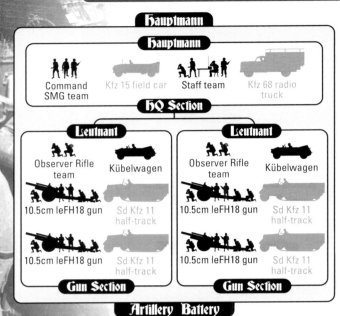

Platoon

HQ Section with:

2 Gun Sections	**225 points**
1 Gun Section	130 points

Option

- Add Kfz 15 field car , Kfz 68 radio truck and Sd Kfz 11 half-tracks at no cost.
- Replace all Kübelwagen jeeps with Sd Kfz 250, 253, or 254 half-tracks for +10 points per half-track.
- Replace any or all Observer Rifle teams and their Kübelwagen with Observer Panzer II tanks for +25 points per tank.

Towed artillery provides a good balance between cost and effectiveness. With their 10.5cm guns they can deliver a high volume of fire that will destroy the hardest target.

Armoured Artillery Battery

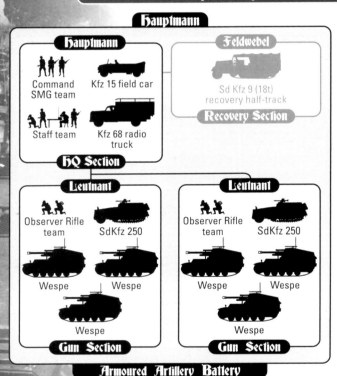

Platoon

HQ Section with:

2 Gun Sections	**495 points**
1 Gun Section	265 points

Options

- Replace all Wespe self-propelled guns with Hummel self-propelled guns for +40 points per Gun Section.
- Replace any or all Observer Rifle teams and their Sd Kfz 250 with Observer Panzer III tanks for +25 points per tank.
- Add an Sd Kfz 9 (18t) recovery half-track for +5 points.

Armoured Artillery Batteries move quickly cross-country and are ready to fire at a moment's notice. Then, when they fire, their heavy guns wreak havoc among the enemy.

The Panzer III (OP) tank gives the observer team a vehicle capable of keeping pace with the Panzers. While its protection is welcome, a tank can be hard to hide.

Pantherkompanie (Kursk)

(PANTHER COMPANY (KURSK))

The Panzerkampfwagen V Panther first saw combat action in the epic battle of Kursk in the summer of 1943. Two units conducted trials for this new vehicle, 51 Panzerabteilung *and* 52 Panzerabteilung. *Both were attached to* Panzergrenadierdivision Grossdeutschland *for the Kursk battle.*

You can field your Panzerkompanie as a Pantherkompanie (Kursk). To do this you must field your Company HQ equipped with Panther D tanks for 370 points and all your Panzer Platoons must be equipped with Panther D tanks at the following costs:

5 Panther D	935 points
4 Panther D	750 points
3 Panther D	565 points

These platoons are rated as **Confident Trained** due to the lack of time the crews had to train on their new tanks before entering combat.

A Pantherkompanie (Kursk) may not include the following:

- Sd Kfz 9 (18t) recovery half-track,
- Light Panzer Platoon,
- Armoured Car Patrols with Sd Kfz 250, 250/9 or Panhard P-178(f) armoured cars.
- Anti-tank Platoons with 3.7cm PaK36, 7.5cm PaK97/38, or 7.62cm PaK36(r) guns, or with Kfz 70 trucks or RSO tractors.
- Assault Gun Platoons with StuG D/E assault guns.
- Assault Tank Platoons.
- Heavy Assault Gun Platoons.
- Heavy Tank Platoons with Panzer III tanks.
- Radio-control Tank Platoons.

The Panther

While the design of the Tiger tank preceded Operation *Barbarossa*, the Panther tank was a direct result of the mauling the *Wehrmacht* received at the hands of the powerful Soviet T-34 tank. Like the T-34 it was developed as a medium tank, but weighed more than many heavy tanks. Both possessed sloped armour to maximise their armour protection and large road wheels and wide tracks for excellent cross-country mobility.

Hitler considered the *Panzer V Panther Ausf D** so important that the date of Operation Zitadelle was postponed to allow 200 of these brand new tanks to take part. All were in *39. Panzerregiment* which was attached to *Grossdeutschland* for the duration of the battle. They suffered numerous mechanical problems in this, their first outing, but most were quickly resolved after the battle. By the end of 1943, eight Panzer divisions had their allotted battalion of Panthers.

*This version should have been a small 'd' to indicate the fourth development series, but was always written 'Ausf D', making it confusing when the definitive Ausf A followed later in the war!

...Otto-Ernst Remer, Kursk 1943...

The bombed out village looks deceptively quiet. 'Is it a trap?' he wonders. Suddenly, machine-guns and rifles open up from trenches and cellars in the village. The advancing Panzergrenadiers scramble for cover. From shell holes and shattered walls, they fire back.

Major Otto-Ernst Remer dives into a ditch as bullets crack and whip past. Something hot slashing his leg as he drops. Wincing, he glances up as Leutnant Becker slithers down beside him. 'The village's full of Popovs,' Becker reports. 'One, maybe two companies.' He flinches as a grenade detonates close by.

Remer flashes a roguish grin. 'They're dug in,' he smiles. 'We'll just have to dig 'em out! Come on!' Gritting his teeth against the stabbing pain in his leg, he crouches, cocking his Soviet-made PPSh-41 submachine-gun. Remer sprints across the open ground to the nearest house. His men fire at the windows as he kicks the door in. Diving and rolling, he snaps off a shot. The Russian lunging at him staggers and falls.

As Becker and a squad of Panzergrenadiers burst into the house behind him, Remer smashes planks off the back wall. He risks a quick look through the hole. Glancing back at Becker, 'Machine-gun nest,' he remarks with a gesture of his hand. Becker hands him a grenade. Remer tugs the arming cord and flicks the grenade through the hole. They hear a yell of surprise and then the explosion shakes the house. Remer wriggles through the hole into the smouldering Russian gun pit. From this new vantage he can see more of his men forcing their way into the village. Becker brings up another squad, feeding them through the captured house into Remer's position. With hand gestures, Remer motions to the squad across the street. With Remer leading, the grenadiers file along either side of the street, every man watching the buildings opposite.

A shot comes from a window. Instantly, everyone crouches and returns fire, riddling the window and wall with bullets. Remer leads them forward again to a corner. Bullets crack and whine past them. Remer flicks a grenade around the corner. It detonates with a thud and flash of flame. Grabbing his entrenching tool, he leads his men forward in a rush.

The shocked Russians scarcely react as the Panzergrenadiers smash into them. Remer shoots a man and slashes at another, knocking him to the ground. A rifle butt catches him under the chin. He staggers backwards. Even as he falls, his men swamp the last defenders.

Becker helps Remer to his feet. 'Herr Major, are you all right?' he asks worriedly. Remer spits and wipes blood from his mouth. 'Bit my lip,' he says with a grin. 'Have we got them all yet?'

German Tank Numbering

This diagram shows the numbering system used by the Germans for a complete company.

The first number in the sequence is the company number, in this case it is '2' or the 2nd Company of the battalion (a typical German Panzer Battalion usually consists of four Panzer Companies).

The second number indicates the platoon within the company, there are usually four platoons within a company so this number can be a 1, 2, 3 or 4. A platoon number of '0' is reserved for the company headquarters platoon.

The third number is the tank number within the platoon, a typical platoon consists of five tanks so this number can be a 1, 2, 3, 4 or 5. The platoon command tank usually adopts the number '1'.

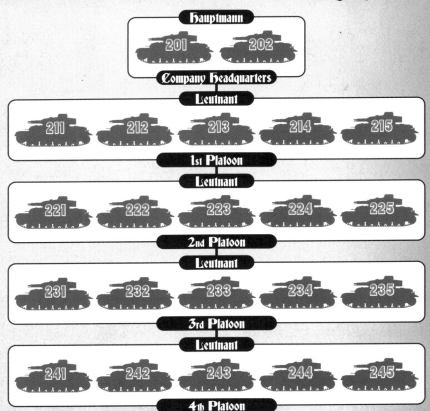

Panzergrenadierkompanie

(INFANTRY COMPANY)

"When I arrived in Russia, I envied the veterans their infantry assault badge, the bronze one for three days of motorised battle was the one I wanted. Now I wear it with pride remembering battles across the breadth of Russia, the victories and fallen comrades. Now it's me the new arrivals want to emulate."

—*Panzergrenadier Tomas Jazeck*

A force based around a Panzergrenadierkompanie must contain:

- a Company HQ, and
- two or three Panzergrenadier Platoons.

Weapons Platoons available to a Panzergrenadierkompanie are:

- a Heavy Platoon,
- two Machine-gun Platoons,
- a Mortar Platoon,
- a Light Infantry Gun Platoon,
- a Light Anti-tank Gun Platoon, and
- a Panzer Pioneer Platoon.

Support Platoons for a Panzergrenadierkompanie can be:

- a Motorised Scout Platoon,
- a Heavy Infantry Gun Platoon,
- an Armoured Flame-thrower Platoon,

- Panzer Platoons,
- a Radio-control Tank Platoon,
- Motorised Anti-tank Gun Platoons,
- Motorised Light Anti-aircraft Platoons,
- Motorised Artillery Batteries,
- Armoured Artillery Batteries,
- Aufklärungs Platoons,
- Armoured Car Patrols,
- Divisional Support Platoons.

You may have up to **two** Support Platoons attached to your company for each Panzergrenadier Platoon you are fielding.

Motivation and Skill

The Panzergrenadiers have been fighting and winning since the war began. A Panzergrenadierkompanie is rated as **Confident Veteran**.

HEADQUARTERS PLATOON

1 Company HQ

Headquarters

Company HQ	45 points

Options

- Replace either or both Command SMG teams with Command Panzerknacker SMG teams for +5 points per team.
- Add an Anti-tank Rifle Section with: an Anti-tank Rifle team for +30 points, a 2.8cm sPzB41 gun for +35 points, or both teams for +60 points.

  All Anti-tank Rifle Sections have one Kfz 70 truck at no cost.
- Replace 2.8cm sPzB41 gun with an 8.8cm RW43 (Püppchen) launcher for +5 points.
- Replace any or all vehicles with Sd Kfz 251/1C half-tracks for +15 points per half-track.
- Mount the 2.8cm sPzB41 gun on the Anti-tank Rifle Section's Sd Kfz 251 half-track as a weapons carrier at no cost.

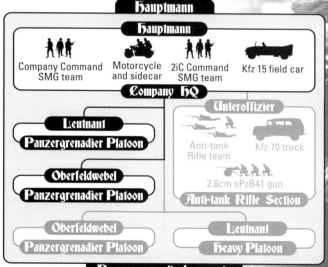

Armoured Panzergrenadierkompanie

If your Company HQ is equipped with armoured half-tracks, then at least half of your Panzergrenadier Platoons must be as well.

You may only have armoured half-tracks in the Combat or Weapons Platoons of your Panzergrenadierkompanie if your Company HQ is equipped with armoured half-tracks.

Any Panzergrenadier Company with Armoured Panzergrenadier Platoons is a Mechanised Company rather than an Infantry Company.

COMBAT PLATOONS

Your company must have two or three Combat Platoons. These may be any combination of Armoured and Motorised Panzergrenadier Platoons.

Armoured Panzergrenadier Platoons

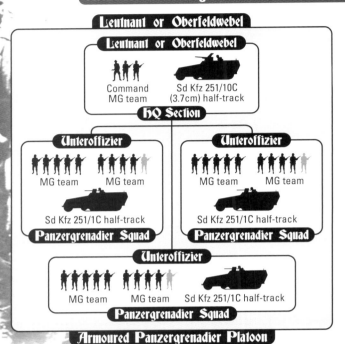

Platoon
HQ Section with

3 Panzergrenadier Squads	285 points
2 Panzergrenadier Squads	210 points

Option
- Replace the Command MG team with a Command Panzerknacker SMG team for +5 points.

Armoured *Panzergrenadier* platoons have the speed to keep up with the Panzers in an advance, and the armour and firepower to attack on their own.

Infantry are the most common and versatile troops on the battlefield. Panzergrenadiers can act as a fast mobile reserve or hold and defend your objectives before counterattacking.

Armoured Panzergrenadier Platoons have the Mounted Assault special rule

Motorised Panzergrenadier Platoons

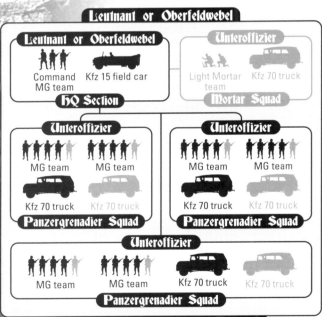

Platoon
HQ Section with

3 Panzergrenadier Squads	220 points
2 Panzergrenadier Squads	160 points

Options
- Replace the Command MG team with a Command Panzerknacker SMG team for +5 points.
- Add a Mortar Squad for +20 points.
- Add a second Kfz 70 truck per Panzergrenadier Squad at no cost.
- Replace the Kfz 15 field car and all Kfz 70 trucks with one 3-ton truck per Panzergrenadier Squad at no cost. The HQ Section and Mortar Squad ride with the Panzergrenadier Squads.

Motorised *Panzergrenadier* platoons race up to the action, then dismount to fight.

Motorised Panzergrenadier platoons had three main organisations in the middle period of the war.

The riflemen in the Panzer divisions started with ten soldiers mounted in two Krupp or similar Kfz 70 trucks. As the war progressed each squad was reduced to eight soldiers in one truck. In theory this truck was supposed to be a 2-ton truck, but since none were available, the bigger 1.5-ton Kfz 70 trucks like the Steyr 1500 were used instead.

Panzergrenadier divisions, which generally had a lower allocation of vehicles than Panzer divisions, were issued a 3-ton truck for each squad rather than individual Kfz 70 trucks.

WEAPONS PLATOONS

A Panzergrenadierkompanie may only have one Armoured or one Motorised Heavy Platoon.

Armoured Heavy Platoon

Platoon

HQ Section with:

2 Machine-gun Sections	200 points
1 Machine-gun Section	120 points
No Machine-gun Sections	35 points

Options

- Add a Gun Section for +125 points.
- Add a Mortar Section for +110 points.

An Armoured Heavy Platoon must have a Gun or Mortar Section if it has no Machine-gun Sections.

The elite motorised infantry divisions like Grossdeutschland and the SS divisions had both company heavy platoons and battalion machine-gun and mortar platoons, while Panzer divisions only had heavy platoons, and motorised *Panzergrenadier* divisions only had machine-gun and mortar platoons.

Armoured Heavy Platoons may make Combat Attachments to Combat Platoons.

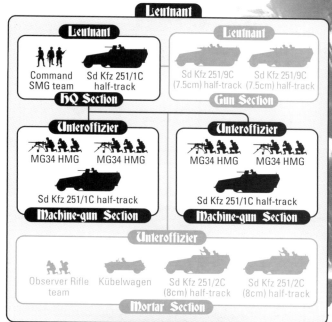

Motorised Heavy Platoon

Platoon

HQ Section with:

2 Machine-gun Sections	165 points
1 Machine-gun Section	95 points
No Machine-gun Sections	25 points

Options

- Add a Mortar Section for +65 points.
- Add a second Kfz 70 truck per Machine-gun Section at no cost.

A Motorised Heavy Platoon must have a Mortar Section if it has no Machine-gun Sections.

The motorised heavy platoon operates with the *Panzergrenadier* platoons right in the front lines. They help defend against enemy infantry attacks and pin the enemy down immediately before the Panzergrenadiers assault them.

Motorised Heavy Platoons may make Combat Attachments to Combat Platoons.

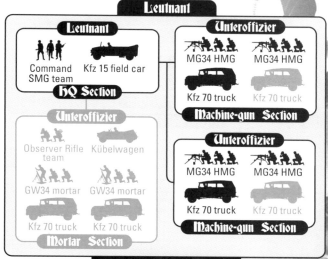

0 to 2 Machine-gun Platoons

Platoon

HQ Section with:

2 Machine-gun Sections	**155 points**
1 Machine-gun Section	**90 points**

Options

- Replace Kfz 15 field car and all 3-ton trucks with Sd Kfz 251/1C half-tracks for +15 points per half-track.

Machine-gun Platoons may make Combat Attachments to Combat Platoons.

0 to 1 Mortar Platoon

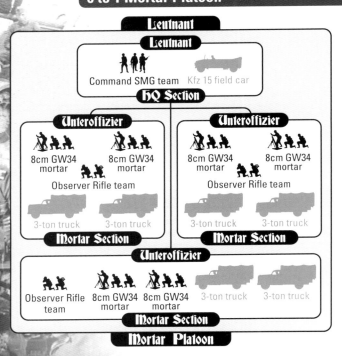

Platoon

HQ Section with:

3 Mortar Sections	**215 points**
2 Mortar Sections	**150 points**
1 Mortar Section	**85 points**

Options

- Add Kfz 15 field car and 3-ton trucks to the platoon at no cost.
- Replace each 8cm GW34 mortar and 3-ton truck with an Sd Kfz 251/2C half-track for +40 points per Mortar Section.
- You must replace the Kfz 15 field car with an Sd Kfz 251/1C half-track for +15 points in any platoon equipped with half-tracks.
- Upgrade the 8cm GW34 mortars to 12cm sGW43 mortars for +25 points per section.

A Mortar Platoon upgraded to 12cm sGW43 mortars may not have more than two sections.

With up to six tubes, the Mortar Platoon will rain devastation on any target within range.

0 to 1 Light Infantry Gun Platoon

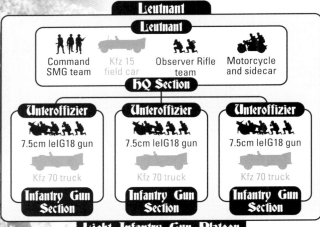

Platoon

HQ Section with:

3 Infantry Gun Sections	**125 points**
2 Infantry Gun Sections	**95 points**

Options

- Add Kfz 15 field car and Kfz 70 trucks to the platoon at no cost.
- Replace all Kfz 70 trucks with Sd Kfz 10 half-tracks for +5 points for the platoon.
- Replace Kfz 15 field car and all Kfz 70 trucks with Sd Kfz 251/1C half-tracks for +15 points per half-track.

0 to 1 Light Anti-tank Gun Platoon

Platoon

HQ Section with:

3 2.8cm sPzB41	105 points
2 2.8cm sPzB41	80 points

HQ Section with:

3 3.7cm PaK36	105 points
2 3.7cm PaK36	80 points

- Either: equip all 3.7cm PaK36 guns with Stielgranate ammunition for +5 points per gun, or
- Mount all 3.7cm PaK36 guns on Krupp Kfz 70 trucks as weapons carriers at no cost.

HQ Section with:

3 5cm PaK38	145 points
2 5cm PaK38	105 points

- Replace all Kfz 70 trucks with Sd Kfz 10 half-tracks for +5 points for the platoon.
- Permanently mount the 5cm PaK38 guns on the Sd Kfz 10 half-tracks as weapons carriers with Front, Side and Top rating of 0 and a hull MG for +20 points per section.

Option

- Replace the Kfz 15 field car and all Kfz 70 trucks with Sd Kfz 251/1C half-tracks for +15 points per vehicle.

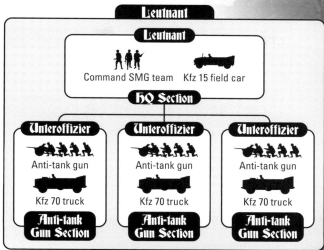

The Panzers can't be everywhere, so the *Panzergrenadiers* have their light anti-tank guns to protect them against marauding enemy tanks.

Each *Panzergrenadier* battalion has a light anti-tank gun platoon armed with light 3.7cm PaK36 anti-tank guns or the more powerful 5cm PaK38 anti-tank guns. Some fortunate battalions also have a platoon of 2.8cm sPzB41 heavy anti-tank rifles as well.

0 to 1 Panzer Pioneer Platoon

Platoon

HQ Section with:

3 Pioneer Squads	265 points
2 Pioneer Squads	190 points
1 Pioneer Squad	115 points

Options

- Replace each Kfz 70 truck with two Sd Kfz 251/7C (Pioneer) half-tracks for +30 points per Pioneer Squad.
- You must replace the Kfz 15 field car with an Sd Kfz 251/7C (Pioneer) half-track for +15 points in any platoon equipped with half-tracks.
- Arm the platoon commander's Sd Kfz 251/7C (Pioneer) half-track with a 2.8cm anti-tank rifle in place of its hull MG for +5 points.
- Equip up to one Pioneer MG team per truck-mounted Pioneer Squad with a Goliath remote-controlled demolition carrier in addition to its normal weapons for +10 points per team.
- Add Pioneer Supply 3-ton truck for +25 points or Pioneer Supply Maultier for +30 points.

Panzer Pioneer Platoons mounted in Sd Kfz 251/7C half-tracks have the Mounted Assault special rule.

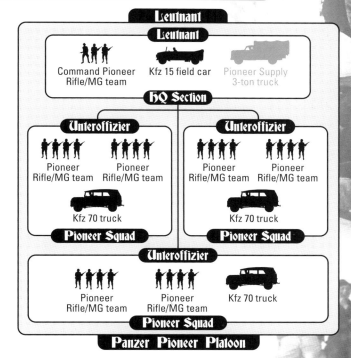

You may replace up to one Pioneer Rifle team per Pioneer Squad with a Flame-thrower team at the start of the game before deployment.

The Panzer pioneer platoon is invaluable in assaults on fortified positions, being able to clear minefields and breach obstacles with ease.

SUPPORT PLATOONS

0 to 1 Motorised Scout Platoon

Motorised Scout Platoons are organised in the same way for both Panzer and Panzergrenadier forces. The organisation is shown on page 29.

0 to 1 Heavy Infantry Gun Platoon

Leutnant

Leutnant

Command SMG team · Kfz 15 field car · Observer Rifle team · Motorcycle and sidecar

HQ Section

Unteroffizier — 15cm sIG33 gun / Sd Kfz 11 half-track — **Infantry Gun Section**

Unteroffizier — 15cm sIG33 gun / Sd Kfz 11 half-track — **Infantry Gun Section**

Heavy Infantry Gun Platoon

Platoon

HQ Section with:

2 Gun Sections	**150 points**

Options

- Add Kfz 15 field car and Sd Kfz 15 half-tracks to the platoon at no cost.
- Replace the Kfz 15 field car and Sd Kfz 11 half-tracks with Sd Kfz 251/1C armoured half-tracks for +25 points for the platoon.
- Replace the Kfz 15 field car with an Sd Kfz 251/1C half-track and each Infantry Gun Section with a Grille self-propelled infantry gun for +55 points for the platoon.

Heavy infantry guns are ideal for knocking out enemy fortifications. One hit from one of these monsters will destroy almost anything. If it's too dangerous to fire over open sights, they can sit back and bombard the target instead. It takes a little longer, but is just as deadly.

An even more potent option is to mount the 15cm sIG33 gun on an armoured chassis! The Grille self-propelled gun is an old Panzer 38(t) tank converted to carry the gun in an armoured superstructure. This combination of firepower and protection is excellent for tackling machine-gun nests in buildings!

0 to 1 Armoured Flame-thrower Platoon

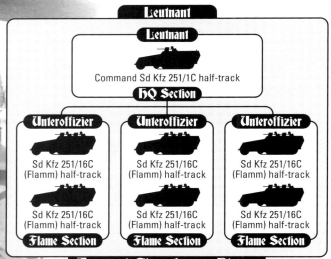

Leutnant

Leutnant

Command Sd Kfz 251/1C half-track

HQ Section

Unteroffizier — Sd Kfz 251/16C (Flamm) half-track / Sd Kfz 251/16C (Flamm) half-track — **Flame Section**

Unteroffizier — Sd Kfz 251/16C (Flamm) half-track / Sd Kfz 251/16C (Flamm) half-track — **Flame Section**

Unteroffizier — Sd Kfz 251/16C (Flamm) half-track / Sd Kfz 251/16C (Flamm) half-track — **Flame Section**

Armoured Flame-thrower Platoon

Platoon

HQ Section with:

3 Flame Sections	**485 points**
2 Flame Sections	**330 points**
1 Flame Section	**175 points**

The *Sd Kfz 251/16 Flammpanzerwagen* armoured flame-thrower half-track is a terrifying weapon. Few troops are willing to stand as these half-tracks rush forward with flame gushing from each side. Be careful to keep them out of sight until the last moment though, they tend to explode when hit!

The Command Sd Kfz 251/1C half-track counts as a Tank team in an Armoured Flame-thrower Platoon.

The Command Sd Kfz 251/1C half-track in this platoon always counts as having its rear AA MG fitted, even though it doesn't carry any passengers.

The Sd Kfz 251/16 mounts one flame-thrower on each side of the body. These can both fire at the same time, but must fire at the same enemy platoon. Each flame-thrower can fire at any target on its side of the half-track, from straight ahead to straight behind.

Aufklärungsschwadron

(RECONNAISSANCE MECHANISED COMPANY)

Every division has a Panzeraufklärungsabteilung, *an armoured reconnaissance battalion, with two scout companies (*Aufklärungsschwadron *pronounced owf-klairr-oongs shvad-rone) and half-a-dozen armoured car patrols.*

You may field an Aufklärungsschwadron, or Scout Squadron, containing:
- a Company HQ, and
- one to three Aufklärungs Platoons.

Weapons Platoons for an Aufklärungsschwadron are:
- a Heavy Platoon,
- a Light Infantry Gun Platoon,
- a Light Anti-tank Gun Platoon,
- a Pioneer Platoon,
- up to six Armoured Car Patrols, and
- a Heavy Armoured Car Platoon.

Support Platoons for an Aufklärungsschwadron can be:
- Panzer Platoons,
- a Radio-control Tank Platoon,
- Motorised Anti-tank Gun Platoons,
- Motorised Light Anti-aircraft Platoons,
- Motorised Artillery Batteries,
- Armoured Artillery Batteries,
- Panzergrenadier Platoons,
- Panzerpionier Platoons,
- Aufklärungs Platoons,
- Armoured Car Patrols, and
- Divisional Support Platoons.

You may have up to **two** Support Platoons attached to your company for each Aufklärungs Platoon you field.

Motivation and Skill

An Aufklärungsschwadron is rated as **Confident Veteran**.

HEADQUARTERS

1 Company HQ

The Company HQ is organised like a Panzer-grenadierkompanie (page 33). If your Company HQ has armoured half-tracks, you must replace them with Sd Kfz 250 half-tracks at no cost.

COMBAT PLATOONS

1 to 3 Aufklärungs Platoons

Aufklärungs Platoons are organised like the Panzergrenadier Platoons on page 36.

Armoured Aufklärungs Platoons must replace their Sd Kfz 251/10C (3.7cm) half-track with an Sd Kfz 250/10 (3.7cm) or Sd Kfz 250/11 (2.8cm) half-track at no cost and must replace each Sd Kfz 251/1C half-track with two Sd Kfz 250 half-tracks for +10 points per Panzergrenadier Squad.

Motorised Aufklärungs Platoons must replace each Kfz 70 truck with two teams of one or two motorcycles and sidecars, or Kübelwagen jeeps, armed with a passenger-fired MG and mounted on the same base, for +5 points per platoon. They retain their Kfz 15 field car in the HQ Section.

If you only have one Aufklärungs Platoon in your company, you must also have at least one Weapons Platoon.

WEAPONS PLATOONS

0 to 1 Heavy Platoon

Heavy Platoons are organised like the Heavy Platoons on shown on page 37.

Armoured Heavy Platoons must:
- replace the Sd Kfz 251/1C half-track in the HQ Section with an Sd Kfz 250 half-track at no cost,
- replace the Sd Kfz 251/1C half-track in each Machine-gun Section with two Sd Kfz 250 half-tracks for +20 points per Machine-gun Section.
- in the Mortar Section, replace the Kübel-wagen with an Sd Kfz 250 half-track and the Sd Kfz 251/2C (8cm) half-tracks with Sd Kfz 250/7 (8cm) half-tracks for +10 points, and
- replace the Sd Kfz 251/9C (7.5cm) half-tracks in the Gun Section with Sd Kfz 250/8 (7.5cm) half-tracks at no cost.

Motorised Heavy Platoons must mount their Machine-gun Sections on motorcycles. Replace all Kfz 70 trucks with a team of one or two motorcycles and sidecars or Kübelwagen jeeps mounted on the same base per MG34 HMG team for +5 points for the platoon. They retain their Kfz 15 field car for the HQ Section and the Kfz 70 trucks for the Mortar Section.

0 to 1 Light Anti-tank Gun Platoon

The Light Anti-tank Gun Platoons are organised like that of a Panzergrenadierkompanie, see page 39.

0 to 1 Light Infantry Gun Platoon

The Light Infantry Gun Platoon are organised like that of a Panzergrenadierkompanie, see page 38.

0 to 1 Panzer Pioneer Platoon

The Panzer Pioneer Platoon is organised like that of a Panzerpionierkompanie, see page 39.

Note: The above platoons are not reconnaissance platoons. Their role is to clear the way for the Armoured Car Platoons which are reconnaissance platoons.

0 to 6 Armoured Car Patrols

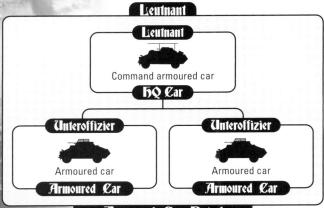

Armoured cars and scout tanks perform an essential role as the eyes and ears of the army.

Armoured Car Patrols are Reconnaissance Platoons

Platoon

Sd Kfz 223 (radio) with:

2 Sd Kfz 222 (2cm)	**115 points**
1 Sd Kfz 222 (2cm)	**75 points**

- Replace any or all Sd Kfz 222 (2cm) with Sd Kfz 221 (2.8cm) at no cost.
- Replace Sd Kfz 223 (radio) with Sd Kfz 250 and all Sd Kfz 222 (2cm) with Sd Kfz 250/9 (2cm) at no cost.
- Replace Sd Kfz 223 (radio) and all Sd Kfz 222 (2cm) with Panhard P-178(f) at no cost.

2 Sd Kfz 231 (8-rad)	**90 points**
3 Panzer II L Luchs	**170 points**

A Command Sd Kfz 250 half-track counts as a Tank team in an Armoured Car Patrol.

A Command Sd Kfz 250 half-track always counts as having its rear AA MG fitted, even though doesn't carry any passengers.

0 to 1 Heavy Armoured Car Platoon

Platoon

3 Sd Kfz 233 (7.5cm)	**185 points**
2 Sd Kfz 233 (7.5cm)	**125 points**

Heavy armoured cars give their lighter brethren support against enemy road blocks. Their 7.5cm guns are excellent against entrenched infantry.

Heavy Armoured Car Platoons are not reconnaissance platoons.

An Aufklärungsschwadron may replace the Kfz 15 field car and motorcycles of any or all platoons with Schwimmwagen amphibious jeeps for +5 points per platoon.

Panzerpionierkompanie

(INFANTRY COMPANY)

A division's Panzerpionierabteilung or armoured pioneer battalion, is both a combat engineering unit, and its premier assault force armed with flame-throwers, demolition charges, and heavy rocket launchers.

You may field a Panzerpionierkompanie, containing:

- a Company HQ, and
- two or three Panzer Pioneer Platoons.

The Company HQ is organised like that of a Panzergrenadierkompanie.

Weapons Platoons available to a Panzerpionierkompanie are:

- a Machine-gun Platoon, and
- a Mortar Platoon.

Support Platoons for a Panzerpionierkompanie can be:

- Panzer Platoons,
- a Radio-control Tank Platoon
- Motorised Anti-tank Gun Platoons,

- Motorised Light Anti-aircraft Platoons,
- Motorised Artillery Batteries,
- Armoured Artillery Batteries,
- Aufklärungs Platoons,
- Armoured Car Patrols, and
- any Divisional Support Platoons.

A Panzerpionierkompanie may have up to **two** support platoons for each Panzer Pioneer Platoon in the force.

Motivation and Skill

The Panzerpionierkompanie is extremely well trained and confident of its abilities. It is rated as **Confident Veteran**.

HEADQUARTERS

1 Company HQ

The Company HQ is organised like the Panzergrenadierkompanie shown on page 35.

COMBAT PLATOONS

2 to 3 Panzer Pioneer Platoons

Panzer Pioneer Platoons are organised like the Panzer Pioneer Platoons on page 39.

You may replace any or all Sd Kfz 251/7C (Pioneer) half-tracks in one Panzer Pioneer Platoon with Sd Kfz 251/1C (Stuka) half-tracks for +50 points per half-track. Only one Panzer Pioneer Platoon may be equipped with Sd Kfz 250/1C (Stuka) half-tracks.

Panzer Pioneer Platoons have the Mounted Assault special rule

A Panzerpionierkompanie with armoured half-tracks is rated as a Mechanised Company. A Panzerpionierkompanie without half-tracks is rated as an Infantry Company

Waffen SS

During the 1930's the *SS* (*Schütz Staffel* or Protection Squad) became the main paramilitary arm of the German Nazi Party. As time went on, the *Waffen-SS* (Armed SS) was formed as the combat arm of the SS. The *Waffen-SS* effectively formed a fourth arm of the military alongside the *Heer* (Army), *Luftwaffe* (Air Force) and *Kriegsmarine* (Navy). This article looks at the *SS-Panzergrenadier* divisions operating in Russia in 1942 and 1943.

At the outbreak of war in 1939, the *Waffen-SS* fought alongside the regular army, much to the distrust of many military officers whom did not feel that a political organisation had a role in battlefield operations. However, as the combat experience of *Waffen-SS* units grew, acceptance of their role as battle-proven units increased.

By 1943 eight *Waffen-SS* divisions formed an experienced and battle-hardened spearhead for Germany's armies, particularly on the Eastern Front. They were constantly in battle achieving a remarkable reputation for aggression and stamina in combat, but at a huge cost in casualties. However, thanks to their political connections, they enjoyed priority for new equipment, replacements and manpower.

Of the eight *Waffen-SS* divisions, four were *SS-Panzergrenadier* divisions: 1st '*Liebstandarte SS Adolf Hitler*', 2nd '*Das Reich*', 3rd '*Totenkopf*', and 5th '*Wiking*'. Of the remaining four divisions the 4th '*Polizei*' operated as an infantry division, the 6th '*Prinz Eugen*' and 7th '*Nord*' Divisions were designated as *Gerbirgs* (Mountain) divisions, and the 8th '*Florian Geyer*' was a cavalry division.

You can field a Panzerkompanie, Panzergrenadier-kompanie, Aufklärungsschwadron, or Panzerpionier-kompanie as a Waffen SS force. If you do this is the number of points you have available to spend on your force decreases as follows:

Normal Force	Waffen SS Force
1000 points	835 points
1500 points	1250 points
2000 points	1670 points

In addition a Waffen-SS force may not include the following:

- Panzerkompanie Company HQ with Panzer 38(t) tanks.
- Panzer Platoons with Panzer 38(t) tanks.
- Flame-tank Platoons.
- Heavy Assault Gun Platoons.
- Assault Tank Platoons.
- Radio-control Tank Platoons.

Motivation and Skill

Waffen-SS troops were renowned for their aggressive approach to battle. A force from an SS-Panzergrenadier is rated as **Fearless Veteran**.

Grenadierkompanie

(INFANTRY COMPANY)

'The foot-slogging Grenadierkompanie *are tough, self-reliant warriors. German Grenadiers have fought and gained great victories for the Fatherland, bringing more land under the rule of the Third Reich, from the deserts in Africa to the wind-swept tundra of Russia.'*
—*Hauptmann Arndt Strauss*

A force based around a Grenadierkompanie must contain:

- A Company HQ, and
- two or three Grenadier Platoons.

Weapons Platoons available to a Grenadierkompanie are:

- two Machine-gun Platoons,
- a Mortar Platoon, and
- an Assault Troop.

Support Platoons available to a Grenadierkompanie are:

- an Infantry Gun Platoon,
- a Scout Platoon,
- a Looted Panzer Platoon,
- two Anti-tank Gun Platoons,
- a Light Anti-aircraft Platoon,
- Artillery Batteries,
- a Pioneer Platoon, and
- any Divisional Support Platoons.

You may have **two** Support Platoons for each Grenadier Platoon you field.

Motivation and Skill

The German Army is well trained and has many victorious campaigns behind it. The soldiers are confident that victory lies in the near future. A Grenadierkompanie is rated as **Confident Veteran**.

HEADQUARTERS

1 Company HQ

Headquarters

Company HQ	**40 points**

Options

- Replace either or both Command SMG teams with Command Panzerknacker SMG teams for +5 points per team.
- Add Anti-tank Rifle team for +25 points or an 8.8cm RW43 (Püppchen) launcher for +30 points.
- Add Mortar Section for +70 points.
- Replace both one-horse carts with one 3-ton truck or RSO tractor for +5 points.

Armed with the experience of successive victories over the Bolshevist hordes, the front-line commander leads his *Grenadierkompanie* to even greater feats. It is only a matter of time before the Soviet resistance is crushed and the East is added to the German Empire.

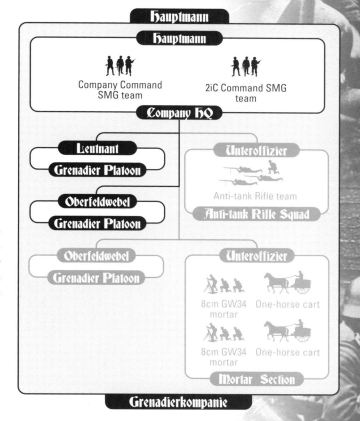

COMBAT PLATOONS

2 or 3 Grenadier Platoons

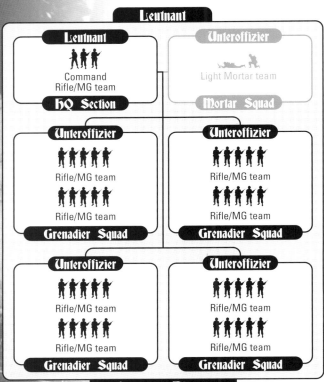

Platoon

HQ Section with:

4 Grenadier Squads	**200 points**
3 Grenadier Squads	**155 points**
2 Grenadier Squads	**110 points**

Option

- Replace Command Rifle/MG team with a Command Panzerknacker SMG team for +5 points.
- Add Light Mortar team for +15 points.

Grenadiers are the core components of the German war machine, performing brave and heroic deeds for the Fatherland.

German Grenadiers are better trained than any other army's soldiers. With their superior training, self-reliant Grenadiers perform the real work of the German Army, assaulting and capturing enemy positions, and holding these against counterattacks.

The Infanterieregiment *has considerable engineering capability of its own and each battalion forms a pioneer platoon from its Grenadiers as needed. These infantry pioneers are called 'white' pioneers because they wear the white piping of infantry rather than the black piping of engineers.*

If your Grenadierkompanie has three Grenadier Platoons, you may upgrade the smallest Grenadier Platoon to a Grenadier Pioneer Platoon for +15 points per squad. This converts the Command team and every Rifle/MG team into Pioneer teams with the same armament. The Grenadier Pioneer Platoon may have a horse-drawn Pioneer Supply Wagon for an additional +20 points.

WEAPONS PLATOONS

0 to 2 Machine-gun Platoons

Platoon

HQ Section with:

2 MG Sections	**145 points**
1 MG Section	**85 points**

Option

- Replace Command SMG team with a Command Panzerknacker SMG team for +5 points.

The machine-gun platoons provide a Schwerpunkt, a concentration of intense firepower, to support the Grenadiers advance. Their devastating fire keeps the enemy's heads down as the infantry attack.

The machine-gun platoons also provide the main defensive fire against enemy counter-attacks. As soon as an important objective is taken they dig in to hold them against all-comers.

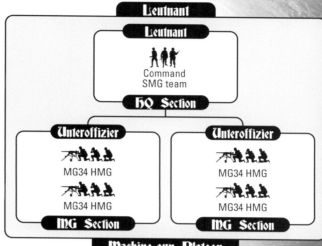

Machine-gun Platoons may make Combat Attachments to Combat Platoons.

0 to 1 Mortar Platoon

Platoon

HQ Section with:

3 Mortar Sections	**205 points**
2 Mortar Sections	**145 points**
1 Mortar Section	**85 points**

Option

- Replace Command SMG team with a Command Panzerknacker SMG team for +5 points.
- Replace all 8cm GW34 mortars with 12cm sGW43 mortars for +25 points per Mortar Section.
- Add one-horse carts at no cost.
- Replace all one-horse carts with one 3-ton truck or RSO tractor per Mortar Section for +5 points per section.

You must upgrade the Mortar Platoon to 12cm sGW43 mortars if you have 8cm GW34 mortars in the Company HQ.

A Mortar Platoon upgraded to 12cm sGW43 mortars may not have more than two sections.

The mortar platoon is equally useful screening enemy strong points with smoke to neutralise them while the Grenadiers attack.

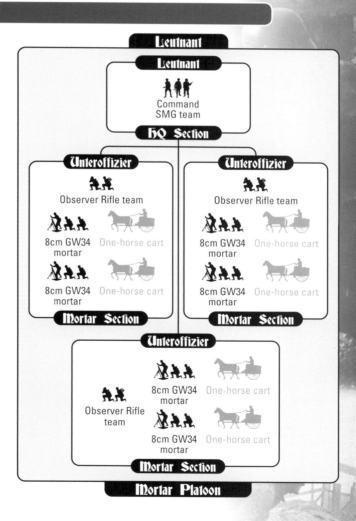

0 to 1 Assault Troop

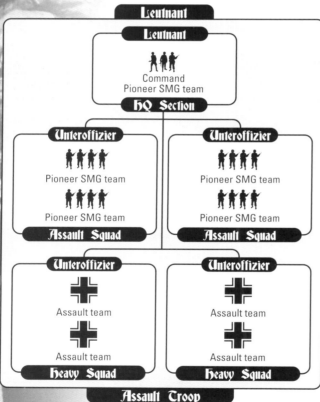

Leutnant

Leutnant

Command
Pioneer SMG team

HQ Section

Unteroffizier

Pioneer SMG team

Pioneer SMG team

Assault Squad

Unteroffizier

Pioneer SMG team

Pioneer SMG team

Assault Squad

Unteroffizier

Assault team

Assault team

Heavy Squad

Unteroffizier

Assault team

Assault team

Heavy Squad

Assault Troop

Company

HQ Section with:

2 Assault Squads	**140 points**

Options

- Add up to two Heavy Squads for +70 points per squad.
- Replace Command Pioneer SMG team with Command Panzerknacker Pioneer SMG team for +5 points.

German infantry battalions often formed a *Stosstrupp*, or Assault Troop, for specific tasks when assaulting fortified positions.

An assault troop is formed for a specific mission. Its composition changes from game to game. The assault squads are the core of the assault group. The heavy squads are tailored from the regiment's assets specifically for the task at hand.

There is no actual team called an Assault team. Instead these can be any of the following types of teams:

- Pioneer SMG team,
- Pioneer MG team,
- Light Mortar team,
- Flame-thrower team,
- MG34 HMG,
- 2cm FlaK38 gun,
- 3.7cm PaK36 gun,
- 7.5cm leIG18 gun.

Your Assault Troop cannot have more than two Assault teams of the same type.

You must choose the composition of your Assault Troop for each game before deployment begins.

The Assault Troop is specifically formed for a particular task. You may not take teams from the Assault Troop to form your Kampfgruppe.

SUPPORT PLATOONS

0 to 1 Infantry Gun Platoon

Platoon

HQ Section with:

2 Infantry Gun Sections	**90 points**

Options

- Replace Command SMG team with a Command Panzerknacker SMG team for +5 points.
- Replace all 7.5cm leIG18 guns with 15cm sIG33 guns for +55 points.
- Add horse-drawn limbers at no cost.
- Replace both horse-drawn limbers with 3-ton trucks or RSO tractors for +10 points.

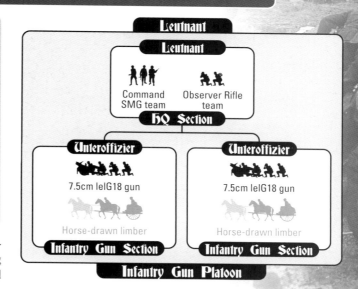

Infantry gun platoons provide the Grenadier-kompanie with close-support artillery, taking out targets such as gun positions, bunkers and machine-gun nests with direct fire.

The 7.5cm leIG18 guns are also effective at destroying enemy tanks should any stray towards the German lines.

The heavy 15cm sIG33 is not as handy or as versatile, but nothing beats it for sheer destructive power. Defences in buildings and bunker positions crumble before its heavy shells.

0 to 1 Scout Platoon

Platoon

HQ Section with:

2 Scout Squads	**110 points**
1 Scout Squad	**65 points**

Options

- Replace Command Rifle team with Command Panzerknacker SMG team for +15 points.
- Replace all Rifle and SMG teams with Assault Rifle teams for +20 points for the HQ Section and +20 points per Scout Squad.

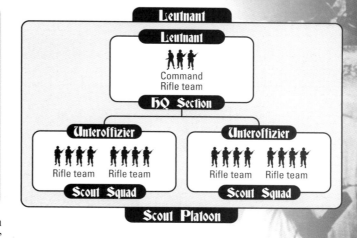

The scout platoons are the eyes of the German army, reconnoitring in front of the Grenadiers' advance, protecting the army from unpleasant surprises. The scouts can also operate as an advance force, taking important objectives by stealth and holding the enemy back until reinforcements arrive.

Scout Platoons are Reconnaissance Platoons.

0 to 2 Anti-tank Platoons

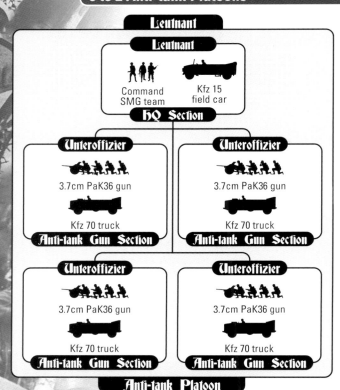

Every infantry regiment has a company of anti-tank guns and every division an additional battalion. The majority of the guns are light 3.7cm PaK36 anti-tank guns, which must rely on surprise at short range to kill tanks. Most regiments also have a handful of heavier guns capable of tackling any Soviet tank.

Platoon

HQ Section with:

4 3.7cm PaK36	135 points
3 3.7cm PaK36	105 points
2 3.7cm PaK36	80 points

- Either: equip all 3.7cm PaK36 gun with Stielgranate ammunition for +5 points per gun, or
- mount all 3.7cm PaK36 guns on Krupp Kfz 70 trucks as weapons carriers at no cost.

HQ Section with:

3 5cm PaK38	145 points
2 5cm PaK38	105 points

- Replace all 5cm PaK38 guns with 7.5cm PaK97/38 guns for +5 points per gun.
- Replace all 5cm PaK38 guns and Kfz 70 trucks with 7.62cm PaK36(r) guns and 3-ton trucks for +30 points per gun, or 7.5cm PaK40 guns and 3-ton trucks for +40 points per gun.

Option

- Replace all trucks with RSO tractors at no cost.

You may not have more than one Anti-tank Platoon armed with 5cm or larger guns for each company in your force.

You may not field more than one Anti-tank Platoon equipped with 7.62cm PaK36(r) or 7.5cm PaK40 guns, even if your force has more than one company.

0 to 1 Looted Panzer Platoon

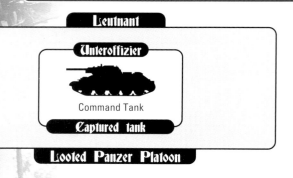

Platoon

1 captured T-70 obr 1942	45 points
1 captured T-34 obr 1941	105 points
1 captured KV-1e	135 points

Option

- Add a Cupola to a T-34 or KV-1e tank for +5 points.

All captured tanks in a Looted Tank Platoon are rated as Confident Trained.

0 to 1 Light Anti-aircraft Platoon

Platoon
HQ Section with:

3 Anti-aircraft Sections	95 points
2 Anti-aircraft Sections	70 points

Options
- Mount 2cm FlaK38 guns on 3-ton trucks as Portees at no cost.

The Grenadiers have very little in the way of anti-aircraft guns, just one company in the anti-tank battalion. Fortunately, as infantry they can hide from aircraft much better than the tanks and half-tracks of the armoured divisions.

If the Red Air Force gets too troublesome though, the light anti-aircraft platoon will soon see them off with its quick-firing guns.

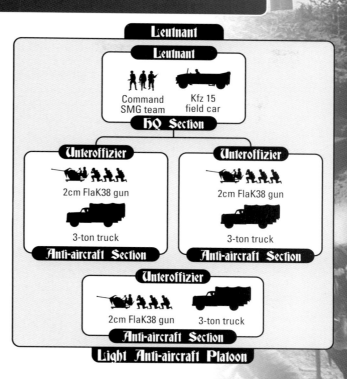

Artillery Battery

Platoon
HQ Section with:

2 Gun Sections	215 points
1 Gun Section	125 points

Options
- Add horse-drawn limbers at no cost.
- Replace all horse-drawn limbers and wagons with 3-ton trucks or RSO tractors for +5 points per vehicle.

Every *Grenadierdivision* has nine batteries of 10.5cm artillery. These pound the enemy line ahead of the Grenadiers' attacks, smashing the Bolshevists' positions and keeping them pinned down. Once the objective is taken, the howitzers pound enemy counterattacks, smashing them before they begin. In a crisis, the howitzers make worthwhile anti-tank guns too.

Luftwaffe Feldkompanie

(AIR FORCE FIELD COMPANY)

After the winter of 1941, the army desperately needed spare air force personnel as reinforcements. Instead, Göring, head of the Luftwaffe (German Air Force) pledged to form 22 Luftwaffe Felddivisionen (Air Force Field Divisions), vowing that the reactionary army would never have his loyal National Socialist airmen. These divisions (still clothed in their air force blue uniforms!) fared badly, being poorly equipped and lacking all but the most rudimentary infantry training.

You can field your Grenadierkompanie as a Luftwaffe Feldkompanie. If you do this the number of points you have available to spend on your force increases as follows:

Normal Force	Luftwaffe Force
1000 points	1300 points
1500 points	1950 points
2000 points	2600 points

- Mortar Platoons may not be upgraded to 12cm sGW43 heavy mortars.
- Your force cannot contain Infantry Gun Platoons, Assault Troops, Heavy Assault Gun Platoons, or Assault Tank Platoons.

- You may only have one Anti-tank Platoon.
- You may have up to two Light Anti-aircraft Platoons.
- You may only have one Artillery Battery. This may be equipped with 12cm sGW43 mortars (actually 10cm NW 40 mortars) for -10 points per Gun Section, or 7.5cm leIG18 infantry guns (actually 7.5cm GebK15 mountain guns) for -35 points per Gun Section.

Heavy Tank Platoons, Tank-hunter Platoons, and Rocket Launcher Batteries remain Veteran, however their cost increases by +15 points for every 50 points or part thereof spent on them.

Motivation and Skill

The Luftwaffe Feldkompanie has only had the most basic infantry training. A Luftwaffe Feldkompanie is rated as **Confident Trained**.

Schnellschwadron

(RECONNAISSANCE INFANTRY COMPANY)

The divisional reconnaissance battalion was the only mobile reserve available to the divisional commander. It was often grouped with the anti-tank battalion to form a Schnellbataillon *or Fast* Battalion. *This tough force acted as an advance guard and a last-ditch reserve.*

You may field a Schnellschwadron, containing:

- a Company HQ, and
- 2 or 3 Schnell Platoons.

The Company HQ is organised like a Grenadierkompanie costing an additional +15 points to make it a reconnaissance platoon. Rather than a Mortar Section, it may have a Machine-gun Section with two HMG teams for +75 points.

Weapons platoons available to a Schnellschwadron are:

- an Infantry Gun Platoon equipped with 7.5cm leIG18 guns,
- any number of Anti-tank Gun Platoons,

- an Armoured Car Platoon, and
- a Pioneer Platoon.

All Weapons platoons taken must be motorised.

Support platoons available to a Schnellschwadron are:

- Divisional Support Platoons.

You may only have **one** Support Platoon attached to your company for each Schnell Platoon in your force.

Motivation and Skill

The reconnaissance troops are well-trained and sure of their abilities. A Schnellschwadron is rated as **Confident Veteran**.

2 or 3 Schnell Platoons

Platoon

HQ Section with:

3 Schnell Squads	200 points
2 Schnell Squads	145 points

Options

- Replace Command Rifle/MG team with Command Panzerknacker SMG team for +5 points.
- Replace all Rifle/MG and SMG teams with Assault Rifle teams for +15 points per squad.

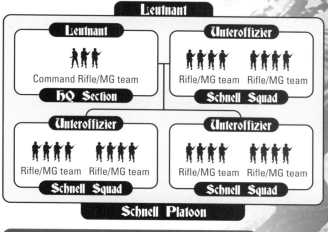

Schnell Platoons are Reconnaissance Platoons.

The *Schnellschwadron* (pronounced shnel-shvad-rone), or Fast Company, has all of its support weapons motorised instead of horse-drawn. In the attack it advances ahead of the division to seize key objectives before the enemy can react. In the defence it acts as the divisions mobile reserve.

0 to 1 Armoured Car Platoon

Platoon

Sd Kfz 223 with:

2 Sd Kfz 221	100 points
1 Sd Kfz 221	65 points
or	
1 captured BA-10	55 points

The division's three armoured cars operated with the *Schnellbataillon*.

Armoured Car Platoons are Reconnaissance Platoons.

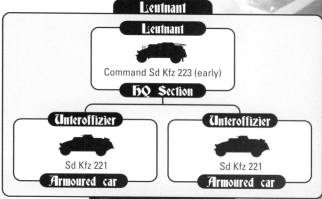

Pionierkompanie

(INFANTRY COMPANY)

Every division has a Pionierbataillon or Pioneer Battalion, and more are attached from the army reserves when needed for particularly difficult missions. At Stalingrad the pioneers led the final assaults on the factories, facing the stiffest opposition the German Army has yet faced. Despite the odds, they took their objectives, pushing the Soviets back to the Volga.

You may field a Pionierkompanie or Pioneer Company containing:

- a Company HQ, and
- 2 or 3 Pioneer Platoons.

The Company HQ is organised like a Grenadierkompanie. It may include:

- two Kfz 15 field cars for +15 points, and
- a Machine-gun Section with two HMG teams for +65 points. Add a 3-ton truck to the section for +5 points.

Weapons Platoons available to a Pionierkompanie are:

- an Assault Troop.

Support Platoons available to a Pionierkompanie are:

- any Divisional Support Platoons.

You may only have one Support Platoon attached to your company for each Pioneer Platoon in your force.

Motivation and Skill

Pioneers are highly professional. A Pionierkompanie is rated as **Confident Veteran**.

2 to 3 Pioneer Platoons

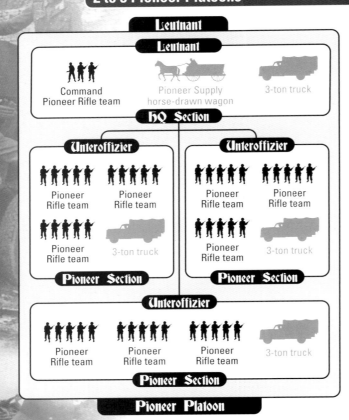

Platoon

HQ Section with:

3 Pioneer Sections	220 points
2 Pioneer Sections	155 points
1 Pioneer Section	90 points

Options

- Replace Command Pioneer Rifle team with Command Pioneer Panzerknacker SMG team for +5 points.
- Equip up to two Pioneer Rifle teams with a Goliath remote-control demolition carrier in addition to its normal weapons for +10 points per team.
- Add Pioneer Supply horse-drawn wagon for +20 points, or Pioneer Supply 3-ton truck or RSO tractor for +25 points.
- Add 3-ton trucks for +5 points per section.

'Black' pioneers perform all the specialist tasks that are required to get the army to the front. The divisional pioneers clear minefields, dig ditches and build roads and bridges. They also lead assaults against particularly tough enemy strong points.

You may replace up to one Pioneer Rifle team per Pioneer Squad with a Flame-thrower team at the start of the game before deployment.

Fallschirmjägerkompanie

(INFANTRY COMPANY)

"The Diving Eagle badge says everything that one needs to know about the Fallschirmjäger, the parachute troops. The eagle symbolises the German soldier, brave, strong, and alert. It flies like the eagle of the Luftwaffe, the air force of which they are part. Diving towards the earth, it represents the swift and ferocious descent of the parachutist on his land-bound foe. The wreath speaks of valour and deeds of courage. Only a veteran of six parachute jumps may wear that badge on their breast. Only the bravest and the best." —Hauptmann Hugo Sydow

A force based around a Fallschirmjägerkompanie must contain:

- a Company HQ, and
- two or three Fallschirmjäger Platoons.

Weapons Platoons available to a Fallschirmjägerkompanie are:

- two MG Platoons,
- a Mortar Platoon, and
- a Light Gun Platoon.

Support Platoons for a Fallschirmjägerkompanie can be:

- a Parachute Heavy Mortar Platoon,
- a Parachute Anti-tank Gun Platoon,
- a Parachute Anti-aircraft Platoon,
- a Glider Light Artillery Battery, or
- a Parachute Pioneer Platoon.

You may have up to **two** Support Platoons attached to your company for each Fallschirmjäger Platoon in it.

Motivation and Skill

All Fallschirmjäger are volunteers. They are put through rigorous selection examinations and hard training before they win their wings. A Fallschirmjägerkompanie is rated as **Fearless Veteran**.

Regular Army Support

The Fallschirmjäger were frequently supported by regular army units on the Eastern Front. A Fallschirmjägerkompanie may choose any **two** of the following platoons as Support Platoons:

- a Panzer Platoon
- a Motorised Artillery Battery,
- a Grenadier or a Panzergrenadier Platoon,
- an Armoured Car Patrol,
- an Artillery Battery,
- a Heavy Tank Platoon,
- an Assault Gun Platoon,
- a Heavy Anti-aircraft Gun Platoon, and
- a Rocket Launcher Battery.

Regular army support platoons retain their own Motivation and Skill ratings of **Confident Veteran**.

HEADQUARTERS

1 Company HQ

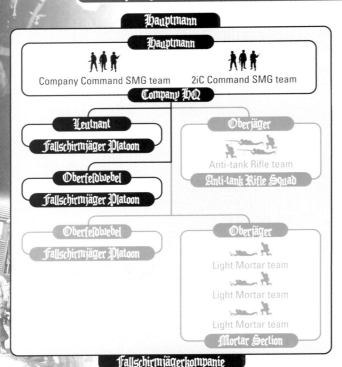

Headquarters

Company HQ	**55 points**

Options

- Replace Command SMG teams with Command Panzerknacker SMG teams for +5 points.
- Add an Anti-tank Rifle Squad with: an Anti-tank Rifle team for +30 points, a 2.8cm sPzB41 for +45 points or an 8.8cm RW43 (Püppchen) launcher for +50 points.
- Add a Mortar Section of up to three Light Mortar teams for +20 points per team, or up to three 8cm GW42 (Stummelwerfer) mortars for +30 points per mortar.

Fallschirmjäger used 5cm leGW36 light mortars and 7.92mm PzB39 anti-tank rifles in the Crete landings. Later the paratroops replaced their light mortars with more effective *Stummelwerfer* and adopted the heavy 2.8cm sPzB41 anti-tank rifle, and then the *Püppchen* rocket launcher.

COMBAT PLATOONS

2 or 3 Fallschirmjäger Platoons

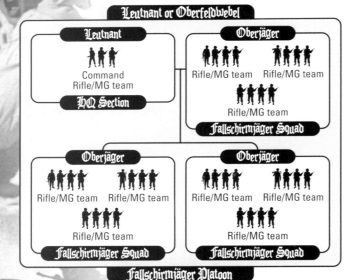

Platoon

HQ Section with

3 Fallschirmjäger Squads	**280 points**
2 Fallschirmjäger Squads	**195 points**

Option

- Replace Command Rifle/MG team with a Command Panzerknacker SMG team for +5 points.

The versatility of the Fallschirmjäger platoon makes it the core of the *Fallschirmjäger-kompanie*. Six MG34 machine-guns make them deadly in a firefight, but determination and hard training make them even more dangerous in an assault.

WEAPONS PLATOONS

0 to 2 Machine-gun Platoons

Platoon

HQ Section with

2 Machine-gun Sections	**175 points**
1 Machine-gun Section	**105 points**

Option

- Replace Command SMG team with a Command Panzerknacker SMG team for +5 points.

Machine-gun Platoons may make Combat Attachments to Combat Platoons.

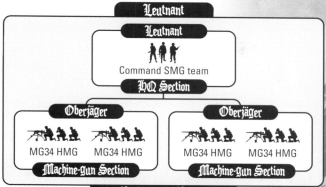

0 to 1 Mortar Platoon

Platoon

HQ Section with

2 Mortar Sections	**175 points**
1 Mortar Section	**100 points**

Options

- Replace Command SMG team with a Command Panzerknacker SMG team for +5 points.
- Replace all 8cm GW34 mortars with 8cm GW42 (Stummelwerfer) for -5 points per Mortar Section.

Mortars give the *Fallschirmjägerkompanie* its own artillery, able to deliver concentrated firepower anywhere along the company front.

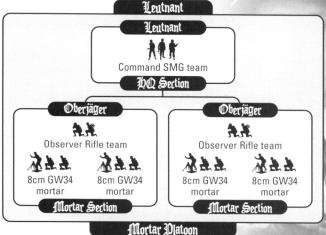

0 to 1 Light Gun Platoon

Platoon

HQ Section with

2 Light Gun Sections	**90 points**
1 Light Gun Section	**60 points**

Option

- Replace Command SMG team with a Command Panzerknacker SMG team for +5 points.

The recoilless 7.5cm LG40 light gun entered service just in time for four of them to be used in the battles on Crete. Since then, they have been issued throughout the airborne forces as battalion anti-tank weapons.

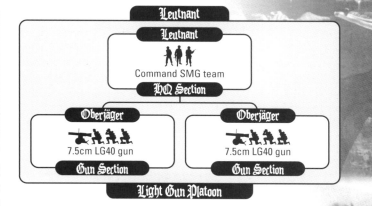

SUPPORT PLATOONS

0 to 1 Parachute Heavy Mortar Platoon

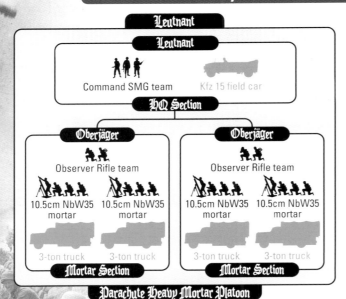

Platoon

HQ Section with

2 Mortar Sections	**215 points**
1 Mortar Section	**120 points**

Options

- Add Kfz 15 field car and 3-ton trucks to the platoon at no cost.

For ground operations heavy mortar platoons are often equipped with trucks to carry their weapons and equipment. The extra mobility makes them much handier in attacks since they can move rapidly to wherever their support is most needed.

0 to 2 Parachute Anti-tank Gun Platoons

Platoon

HQ Section with

3 Anti-tank Gun Sections	**125 points**
2 Anti-tank Gun Sections	**95 points**

Options

- Replace all motorcycles & sidecars with Kettenkrad tractors at no cost or Kfz 70 trucks for +5 points for the platoon.
- Equip all 3.7cm PaK36 guns with Stielgranate ammunition for +5 points per gun.
- Replace all 3.7cm PaK36 guns and motorcycles with 4.2cm PJK41 guns and Kfz 70 trucks for +10 points per section.
- Replace all 3.7cm PaK36 guns and motorcycles with 5cm PaK38 guns and Kfz 70 trucks for +15 points per section.
- Replace all 3.7cm PaK36 guns and motorcycles with 7.5cm PaK40 guns and 3-ton trucks for +60 points per section.
- You must add a Kfz 15 field car to any platoon equipped with Kfz 70 or 3-ton trucks for +5 points.

You may only have one Anti-tank Gun Platoon equipped with 4.2cm PJK41, 5cm PaK38, or 7.5cm PaK40 anti-tank guns.

The Diving Eagles are lightly equipped towing their anti-tank guns with motorcycle or *Kettenkrad* tractors. These are often replaced with Kfz 70 trucks for ground operations, making them a truly mobile force.

With no air assault operations in Russia the necessity for weapons to be air-transportable lessened and the paratroops gained small numbers of heavier anti-tank guns like the 4.2cm PJK41, 5cm PaK38 and the 7.5cm PaK40.

0 to 1 Parachute Tank Hunter Platoon

Platoon

4 Marder II	520 points
3 Marder II	390 points
2 Marder II	260 points

As ground operations became more common, the Fallschirmjäger were issued with more heavy weapons like self-propelled tank-hunters.

The heavy guns of the Marder tank-hunters can destroy any tank the enemy cares to send against them, although their light armour and lack of overhead protection make them very vulnerable to enemy fire.

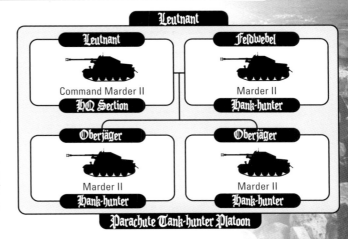

0 to 1 Parachute Anti-aircraft Platoon

Platoon

HQ Section with

4 Anti-aircraft Sections	135 points
3 Anti-aircraft Sections	110 points
2 Anti-aircraft Sections	85 points

Options

- Remove gun shields from all 2cm Flak38 guns for -5 points per gun.
- Replace all motorcycles and sidecars with Kettenkrad tractors at no cost or Kfz 70 trucks for +5 points for the platoon.
- You must add a Kfz 15 car to any platoon equipped with Kfz 70 trucks for +5 points.

Because of their intended role as airborne troops, the Fallschirmjäger only had light anti-aircraft guns.

Fighting as infantry, this proved less useful. However the light anti-aircraft guns in the right hands are sufficient to stop the Red Air Force.

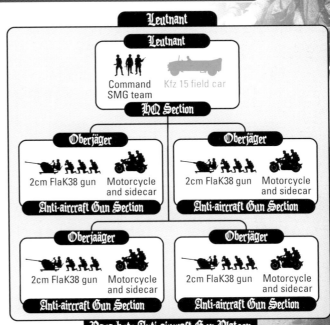

0 to 1 Light Artillery Battery

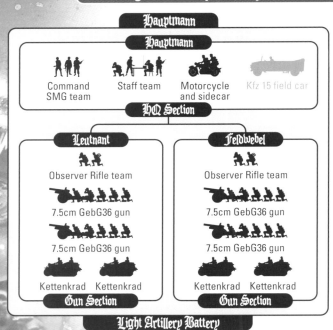

Hauptmann

Hauptmann

Command SMG team | Staff team | Motorcycle and sidecar | Kfz 15 field car

HQ Section

Leutnant

Observer Rifle team

7.5cm GebG36 gun

7.5cm GebG36 gun

Kettenkrad | Kettenkrad

Gun Section

Feldwebel

Observer Rifle team

7.5cm GebG36 gun

7.5cm GebG36 gun

Kettenkrad | Kettenkrad

Gun Section

Light Artillery Battery

Platoon

HQ Section with

2 Gun Sections	**315 points**
1 Gun Section	**180 points**

Options

- Replace motorcycle and sidecar with a Kfz 68 radio truck and add a Kfz 15 field car to HQ section for +5 points.
- Replace all Kettenkrad tractors with Kfz 70 trucks for +5 points per section.

Unusually, the crews of the light artillery batteries are equipped with two different artillery pieces, the conventional 7.5cm mountain gun and the newly-developed 10.5cm recoilless gun. Before an operation the *Fallschirmjäger* commander selects the most appropriate weapon for the mission.

You may replace all 7.5cm GebG36 guns with 10.5cm LG40 recoilless guns at the start of any game before deployment.

0 to 1 Parachute Pioneer Platoon

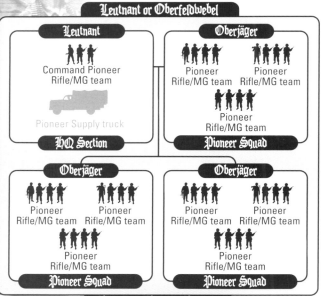

Leutnant or Oberfeldwebel

Leutnant

Command Pioneer Rifle/MG team

Pioneer Supply truck

HQ Section

Oberjäger

Pioneer Rifle/MG team | Pioneer Rifle/MG team

Pioneer Rifle/MG team

Pioneer Squad

Oberjäger

Pioneer Rifle/MG team | Pioneer Rifle/MG team

Pioneer Rifle/MG team

Pioneer Squad

Oberjäger

Pioneer Rifle/MG team | Pioneer Rifle/MG team

Pioneer Rifle/MG team

Pioneer Squad

Parachute Pioneer Platoon

Platoon

HQ Section with

3 Pioneer Squads	**360 points**
2 Pioneer Squads	**250 points**
1 Pioneer Squad	**140 points**

Options

- Add a Pioneer Supply truck for +25 points.

You may replace up to one Pioneer Rifle team per Pioneer Squad with a Flame-thrower team at the start of the game before deployment.

Fallschirmpionierkompanie

(PARACHUTE PIONEER COMPANY)

The *Fallschirmjäger* assault engineers formed the core of *Kampfgruppe Meindl* fighting in the north near Leningrad. To recreate their exploits you can form a Fallschirmpionierkompanie.

A force from a Fallschirmpionierkompanie contains:

* a Company HQ, and
* two to four Pioneer Platoons.

The Company HQ is organised like that of a Fallschirmjägerkompanie, but has no Mortar Section. Instead it may have a Machine-gun Section with one or two HMG teams for +35 points per team.

The weapons and support platoons available to a Fallschirmpionierkompanie are identical to those of a Fallschirmjägerkompanie, with the exception of heavy mortar platoons which are not available.

DEPLOYMENT OF FALLSCHIRMJÄGER COMBAT UNITS

Leningrad Front, September to December 1941

The unexpectedly high casualties suffered by the army in Operation Barbarossa meant that the Fallschirmjäger were thrown in to battle on foot as elite light infantry.

Regimental HQ, I, and III Battalions of Fallschirmjäger Regiment 1

Regimental HQ, I, II, and III Battalions of Fallschirmjäger Regiment 3

1. and 2. Companies of Fallschirmjäger Pioneer Battalion 7

1. and 3. Batteries of Fallschirmjäger Artillery Battalion 7

2. Company of Fallschirmjäger Panzerjäger Battalion 7

2. Company of Fallschirmjäger Machine-gun Battalion 7

II Battalion of the Luftlandesturmregiment

Leningrad Front, March to July 1942

In January they were withdrawn to rest and re-equip. Some units returned to the Leningrad sector.

Fallschirmjäger Regiment 2

1. Company of Fallschirmjäger Panzerjäger battalion 7

Moscow Front, September to December 1941

Like their comrades near Leningrad, Fallschirmjäger on the Moscow front saw intense fighting.

7. Company of Fallschirmjäger Regiment 2

Regimental HQ, and I Battalion of the Luftlandesturmregiment

Fallschirmjäger Machine-gun Battalion 7

Stalino, November 1941 to March 1942

While their comrades fought in the north, Fallschirmjäger were sent to Stalino in the south.

I and II Battalions of Fallschirmjäger Regiment 2

IV. Battalion of Luftlandesturmregiment

1. Company of Fallschirmjäger Panzerjäger Battalion 7

Fallschirmjäger Machine-gun Battalion 7

Smolensk and Rzhev, October 1942 to April 1943

7. Fliegerdivision was withdrawn from the Eastern Front in early 1942, but after training and rest in France it soon returned to the front.

The 7. Fliegerdivision returned to the Russian front in October 1942. They fought in the Rzhev pocket where they held off Marshal Zhukov's Operation Mars offensive in November and December. Some Fallschirmjäger units remained in the salient until April 1943.

Regimental HQ, I, II, and III Battalions of Fallschirmjäger Regiment 1

Regimental HQ, II, and IV Battalions of Fallschirmjäger Regiment 3

Regimental HQ and I Battalion of Fallschirmjäger Regiment 4

Fallschirmjäger Pioneer Battalion 7

Regimental HQ, and I Battalion of the Luftlandesturmregiment

Fallschirmjäger Regiment 1

Fallschirmjäger Panzerjäger Battalion 7

Fallschirmjäger Machine-gun Battalion 7

In the 1930's, Germany only had 35 infantry divisions. As war approached each division provided a cadre to form one or more divisions in a series of waves. As part of the eighth wave of this expansion in February 1940, *295. Infanteriedivision* (the 295th Infantry Division) formed in Magdeburg, Hanover, under command of *Generalmajor* Herbert Geitner. Its components came from parts of the Hanoverian *19., 31.,* and *71. Infanteriedivisionen* filled out with many new recruits. Later that year, while training in France, it was split itself to provide a cadre for *321. Infanteriedivision* as the army grew to its full strength of more than 200 divisions for its biggest undertaking, the invasion of the Soviet Union.

The division was part of *IV. Armeekorps* (4th Corps) of *17. Armee* (17th Army) in *Heeresgruppe Süd* (Army Group South) during the opening months of the invasion. It reached the Dnepr River in September and Poltava in October after marching over 300 miles (500 km) on foot. November saw the capture of Ivanovskoye in the Don Basin, just as the first snows of the worst winter in 50 years set in.

The division fought throughout the bitter winter of 1941 under a new general, *Generalmajor* Karl Gümbel after Geitner was severely wounded. In order to hold the town of Artemovsk

where the division was stationed, it took command of *204. Infanterieregiment* (204th Infantry Regiment) from *93. leichte Division* (93rd Light Division). Together, they held the line against heavy Soviet counter attacks, and finally in April 1942, the division began rebuilding in preparation for the summer offensive, *Fall Blau* (Case Blue) which would take them to the Volga River.

For *Fall Blau*, the division joined *LI Armeekorps* (51st Corps) of von Paulus' ill-fated *6. Armee* (6th Army), once again under a new general, *Generalmajor* Rolf Wuthmann. The division reached Stalingrad in August after marching more than 200 miles (320 km), once again all on foot.

On 14 September, the division launched its first major attack, capturing the Mamayev Kurgan, a burial mound dominating the city, breaking through to the Volga and splitting the Red Army in two. By 3 pm *295. Infanteriedivision* was the first to break through to the Volga in the centre of Stalingrad. The Red Army launched desperate counterattacks, regaining a foothold on the Kurgan. The battle raged on for two more months as the German Army slowly captured the factory areas.

When the Soviet offensive cut off *6. Armee* on 23 November,

295. Infanteriedivision (now under *Generalmajor* Dr Otto Korfes) was holding the river bank south of the Factory area. By 28 December, heavy casualties, the harsh winter and starvation rations had reduced the combat strength of the division to the point where it could no longer carry out offensive operations. It only had one weak battalion, and five worn-out battalions left, along with 36 artillery pieces, seven anti-tank guns, a weak pioneer battalion and no transport. Of the 21 divisions in the pocket, the only one still capable of attacking was *29. Infanteriedivision (mot)*, and even it only had one strong battalion, five moderate-strength battalions, and three weak battalions, 30 artillery pieces, and three anti-tank guns!

During the assault on Stalingrad, four members of the division won the *Ritterkreuz*, the Knight's Cross, Germany's highest decoration. They were: *Hauptmann* Wilhelm Herb (I/517 I.R.), *Hauptmann* Ernst Werner (III/516. I.R.), *Major* Richard Henze (II/518 I.R.) and *Oberfeldwebel* Hermann Fleischer (2./517. I.R.).

By the time the division surrendered on 31 January 1943, five more members had won the *Ritterkreuz*, including the division's commander. *295. Infanteriedivision* was immediately reformed in Germany and spent the rest of the war garrisoning Norway.

German Companies may have the following support platoons:

- Heavy Tank Platoons,
- Heavy Assault Gun Platoons,
- Assault Tank Platoons,
- Assault Gun Platoons,
- Tank-hunter Platoons,

- Heavy Anti-aircraft Platoons, and
- Rocket Launcher Batteries.

Motivation and Skill

Like the troops they support, the Divisional Support Platoons are experienced troops that know their worth. Divisional Support platoon are rated as **Confident Veteran**.

Air Support		
Aircraft	Priority Air Support	Limited Air support
Ju 87D Stuka	175 points	135 points
Ju 87G Stuka	175 points	135 points
Hs 129B	200 points	155 points
Bf 109E or FW 190F	165 points	130 points

0 to 1 Heavy Tank Platoon

Platoon

2 Tiger I E	770 points
1 Tiger I E	385 points

Options

- Add either: one or two Panzer III L or M tanks for +115 points per tank, one or two Panzer III N tanks for +105 points per tank, or one or two Tiger I E tanks for +385 points per tank.
- Add Schürzen side skirts to any Panzer III for +5 points per tank.

Remember to roll for your Tiger Ace Skills before each game.

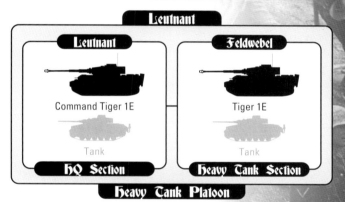

The arrival of the Tiger at the front lines signals the death of the Soviet resistance. The Bolshevists have nothing that can stand up to its mighty gun and have few weapons that can pierce its thick hide.

0 to 1 Heavy Assault Gun Platoon

Platoon

4 Ferdinand	1580 points
3 Ferdinand	1185 points
2 Ferdinand	790 points
1 Ferdinand	395 points

Armed with a powerful 8.8cm PaK43/2 gun the Ferdinand heavy assault gun is capable of destroying any Bolshevist tank that crosses its path.

0 to 1 Assault Tank Platoon

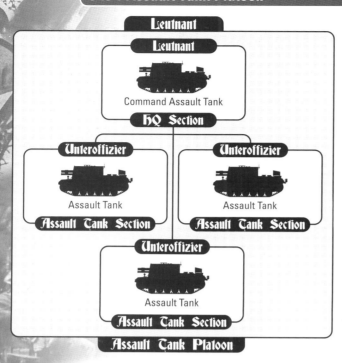

Leutnant

Leutnant

Command Assault Tank

HQ Section

Unteroffizier — Assault Tank — **Assault Tank Section**

Unteroffizier — Assault Tank — **Assault Tank Section**

Unteroffizier — Assault Tank — **Assault Tank Section**

Assault Tank Platoon

Platoon	
4 StuIG33B	400 points
3 StuIG33B	300 points
2 StuIG33B	200 points
4 Brummbär	460 points
3 Brummbär	345 points
2 Brummbär	230 points

Option

- Add Schürzen side skirts to any Brummbär assault tanks for +5 points per tank.

The StuIG33B and *Brummbär* both mount heavy 15cm guns. Known as *Stupa* (short for *Sturmpanzer*), they demolish the strongest Bolshevist fortifications with ease.

0 to 1 Assault Gun Platoon

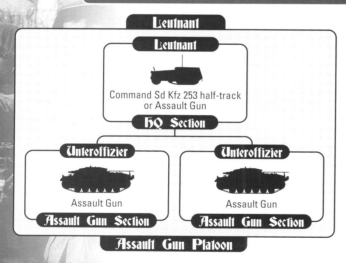

Leutnant

Leutnant

Command Sd Kfz 253 half-track or Assault Gun

HQ Section

Unteroffizier — Assault Gun — **Assault Gun Section**

Unteroffizier — Assault Gun — **Assault Gun Section**

Assault Gun Platoon

Platoon	
Sd Kfz 253 and 2 StuG D/E	225 points
Sd Kfz 253 and 1 StuG D/E	125 points
3 StuG F	460 points
2 StuG F	305 points

Options

- Upgrade any or all StuG F assault guns to StuG F/8 or G assault guns or StuH42 assault howitzers for +25 points per gun.
- Add Schürzen side skirts to any StuG F/8 or G assault guns or StuH42 assault howitzers for +5 points per gun.

0 to 1 Tank-hunter Platoon

Platoon

4 Marder I	365 points
3 Marder I	280 points
2 Marder I	195 points

Options

- Upgrade all Marder I to:

  Marder II for +15 points per tank hunter,

  Marder III (7.62cm) for +10 points per tank hunter,

  Marder III H for +15 points per tank hunter,

  Marder III M for +10 points per tank hunter,

  or Hornisse for +80 points per tank hunter.

- Downgrade all Marder I to Panzerjäger I for -40 points per tank-hunter.

Leutnant

Tank-Hunter Platoon

Tank-Hunter Section — Leutnant — Command Tank-hunter / Tank-hunter

Tank-Hunter Section — Unteroffizier — Tank-hunter / Tank-hunter

Panzerjäger I and Marder I tank-hunters were normally found supporting the *Grenadier* divisions while the more powerful Marder II and III, and Hornisse tank hunters operated with both *Grenadier* divisions and the more mobile *Panzer* and *Panzergrenadier* divisions

0 to 1 Heavy Anti-aircraft Platoon

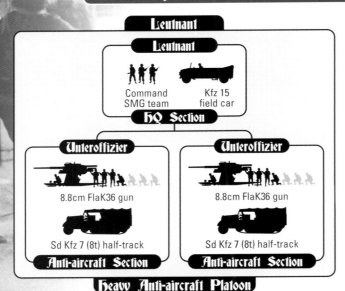

Platoon

HQ Section with:

2 Anti-aircraft Sections	**280 points**
1 Anti-aircraft Section	**150 points**

Option

- Model 8.8cm FlaK36 guns with eight or more crew and increase their ROF to 3 for +10 points per gun.
- Replace all 8.8cm FlaK36 guns and Sd Kfz 7 half-tracks with Sd Kfz 7/2 3.7cm self-propelled anti-aircraft guns at a cost of -90 points per gun.
- Add a third Sd Kfz 7/2 3.7cm self-propelled Anti-aircraft gun for +55 points.

The Luftwaffe are often called upon to provide heavy anti-tank support for the Grenadier-kompanie. Their 8.8cm FlaK36, or Acht-Acht, is the same gun as in the Tiger heavy tank. No Soviet tank or aircraft can stand up to its deadly fire.

0 to 1 Rocket Launcher Battery

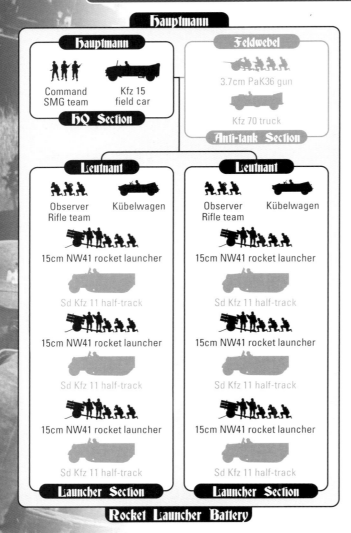

Platoon

HQ Section with:

2 Launcher Sections	**280 points**
1 Launcher Section	**150 points**

Option

- Replace three 15cm NW41 rocket launchers and Sd Kfz 11 half-tracks in each section with four Panzerwerfer 42 (Maultier) rocket launchers for +100 points per section.
- Add Anti-tank Section for +35 points.
- Equip 3.7cm PaK36 gun with Stielgranate ammunition for +5 points.
- Replace 3.7cm PaK36 gun with 5cm PaK38 gun for +15 points.
- Replace Kfz 70 truck with Sd Kfz 10 half-track for +5 points.

In German Nebelwerfer means Fog Launcher as it was intended for chemical warfare. However they are equally good firing high-explosive shells.

Rocket launcher batteries demoralize the enemy with smashing rocket salvos, and lay covering smoke screens. Their only drawback is that rockets leave long smoke trails in the sky, making the battery easy to locate.

JATKOSOTA
FINNISH FORCES

Winter War

The Finnish Army first came to world attention in 1939 in the famous Winter War or *Talvisota*, when it faced an invasion by a Soviet Army of nearly one million men. The invasion had followed failed peace talks in 1939 when Stalin had demanded Finland cede key territory, bases and mines. Facing a massive Soviet army, the Finnish defender's fought a heroic David vs. Goliath struggle for four months.

During one of the harshest winter's seen in the Arctic Circle for a hundred years, the brave and stoic defenders used the –30°C to –40°C tempera tures to advantage as they first stopped and then destroyed attacking Soviet columns. They skilfully used the lakes and heavily forested terrain of their homeland to channel their attackers vastly superior numbers. The Finns earned a reputation as fearless and skilled fighters. But promised Allied aid did not arrive in time to prevent defeat. A second Soviet offensive finally forced Finland to sue for peace. Still, as one Soviet general is reported to have said 'we won nearly enough land to bury our dead'.

Uneasy Peace

Finland had defended courageously and inflicted losses of over 250,000 on the Soviet Army. Yet many Finns felt aggrieved by the outcome of the Winter War and the harsh treaty conditions imposed on them by the Soviets. The loss of Viipuri and Finnish territory in Karelia saw about 400,000 Finns displaced from their homes.

Continued Soviet meddling in Finnish affairs indicated Stalin still had a desire to subjugate Finland and the Western Allies were increasingly siding with the Soviet Union against Germany, many considered a renewed invasion by the Russians to be inevita ble. For the whole of 1940 and 1941, the fully-mobilised Finnish Army remained on duty and prepared for a second invasion.

Against this backdrop Germany began to court the Finnish Government, offering modern arms in return for transition rights for *Wehrmacht* troops through Finland to reinforce its army in Norway. Feeling alone and vulner able, Finland grasped this offered straw, hoping that the presence of German troops would dissuade the Russians from any hasty actions.

Continuation War

On 22 June 1941 Germany launched Operation *Barbarossa*, the invasion of the Soviet Union. This included attacks by Germany made from Finnish territory in a drive to capture the vital Soviet seaport of Murmansk. Finland was aware of these attacks and sanctioned the use of their territory but did not actually declare war on the Soviets themselves.

This state of semi-peace was short lived, shattered by the drone of Soviet bombers as they sought retribution on the cities in northern Finland. On 25 June 1941 Finnish President Risto Ryti informed his people in a speech from parliament that a state of war existed between Finland and the Soviet Union although Finland did not sign a formal alliance with Germany. For the Finns this struggle became

known as the Continuation War or *Jatkosota*, reflecting their view that it was part of a continuing struggle for national survival. Britain declared war on Finland whilst America did not but neither country took part in hostilities against Finland.

Operation Silver Fox *(Silberfuchs)*
The first fighting was Operation *Silberfuchs* in the far north involving the German Mountain Corps (2nd and 3rd Mountain Divisions). It made a successful attack to recapture the Petsamo nickel mines. Pushing towards Murmansk it was stopped on the Litsa River by Soviet defence and a long supply line.

Further south at Salla the German 36th Corps, consisting of *SS-Nord* Division, 69th Division, Panzer Battalion 40 and 211, and the Finnish 6th Division, tried to cut the railway line to Murmansk but the attempt soon stalled. Finnish troops remained under Finnish command and cooperation between the two forces was poor. The Finnish 3rd Division then attacked and reached Kestenga but then it too was stopped.

Not wishing to force the hand of the Western Allies, the Finnish High Command issued secret orders to halt the offensive. By September 1941 it had been abandoned.

Karelian Isthmus Offensive
On 30 June 1941 the veteran Finnish forces moved onto the offensive in the south, advancing to sweep their old enemy from the Karelian Isthmus. This narrow strip of land between Leningrad and Finland, a key

defensive position, had been Finnish territory before the Winter War.

The Isthmus had been the scene of the heaviest fighting in the Winter War and three Finnish Corps attacked it, including the 2nd, 4th, 8th, 10th, 12th, 15th and 18th Divisions. A pincer offensive was launched which retook Viipuri by the end of August, trapping three Soviet divisions at Porlammi. By December 1941 Finnish forces had regained all of the Isthmus and dug in on a new defensive line. The Germans wanted them to continue and capture Leningrad, but they refused.

East Karelia Offensive
In July 1941 he Finnish Commander, Marshal Mannerheim, launched what was to become Finland's most successful offensive of the war—the drive to take back the rich farming area of Karelia east of Lake Ladoga. This involved two corps including the Finnish 1st, 5th 6th, 11th, and 14th Divisions, and the German 163rd Division in Group Oivonen. Most of the captured Soviet tanks were combined with 1st *Jääkäri* Brigade into Group Lagus—the future Finnish *Panssari* Division—to lead the attack.

The 5th Division quickly achieved a break through at Korpiselkä on 10 July. The offensive soon recaptured the Finnish town of Sortavala and pressed on, trapping two Soviet Divisions against Lake Ladoga. By the end of September 1941 it had recovered all lost Finnish territory. However, Marshal Mannerheim ordered the offensive to capture the rest of Soviet East Karelia. This would result in a

shorter, more defensible front line. In October the 4th and 8th Divisions were transferred from the Karelian Isthmus to reinforce the advance. The spearhead swung south and within three days Group Lagus reached a secure defensive position along the Syväri (Svir) River between Lake Ladoga and Lake Onega. Petroskoi on the shores of Lake Onega fell on 1 October 1941. On Independence Day, 6 December 1941, the areas lost in the Winter War were declared as rejoined to Finland and the refugees displaced by the Winter War began the slow repopulation of their homes. The Finnish Army had lost 26,000 men recovering their lands.

Shifting to Defence
Not wishing to incur the wrath of the United States, Marshal Mannerheim and President Ryti decided not to continue the offensive to the White Sea, leaving the vital supply port of Archangelsk in Soviet hands and ensuring the continued flow of American and British lend-lease equipment to the Red Army. Battles continued until January 1942 to mop up the last pockets of Soviet resistance, but by then the front line was largely set. Strong defensive lines of field fortifications and earthworks were established across the Karelian Isthmus, along the Syväri river running between the southern ends of Lake Ladoga and Lake Onega and across the Maaselkä Isthmus north of Lake Onega. Further north the line was thinly held by ski patrols.

With the war lasting longer than anticipated the country began to feel the shortage of manpower and many of the older generation of soldiers were released from active service to return to important home front tasks like farming and industry. Five divisions were disbanded and only enough men for defence were kept in the line.

Soviet Counterattacks
Early in 1942 the Soviet Union launched the first of several counter attacks, striking with several divisions and naval brigades at the eastern-most part of the Finnish lines in the area of Kriv on the Maaselkä Isthmus. The Finnish 3rd Brigade was quickly moved from their position on the Karelian Isthmus to reinforce the line and the Soviet offensive driven back,

suffering heavy losses.

In early January 1942 the Red Army took Suursaari Island in the Gulf of Finland. Major General Aaro Pajarit's Combat Unit P launched a surprise attack across the ice to retake the island in March. Strongly supported by the Finnish Air Force, they were successful.

On several occasions in early January the Soviets attempted to establish a foothold on the western side of the White Sea Canal north of Lake Onega and to retake the towns of Poventsa and Karhumäki. They met strong resistance from the veteran Finnish 1st *Jääkäri* Brigade, who where able to repulse the attacking force of two rifle regiments and a ski brigade. The Soviets suffered heavy losses leading the Finns to dub the area *Tapponiemi* (Slaughter Cape).

The largest Soviet offensives occurred in April 1942. At the Syväri River three Soviet corps, including large formations of KV-1 tanks, breached the defences. However a Finnish counterattack by four divisions, including the 3rd and 6th *Panssari Komppania*, was highly successful. The Soviet spearhead was cut off and destroyed. By June 1942 the defensive line on the Syväri River had been re-established. Meanwhile at Kestenga in the north several Soviet divisions attacked the Finno-German corps. They made little progress in the rugged terrain, and the attack soon stalled.

During July the fiercest battle on the Karelian Isthmus occurred over the possession of Sevastopol, a Finnish base located in the sector controlled by the 7th Infantry Regiment. Both sides suffered losses but the Finn defence held firm. About this time a brigade of Soviet partisans infiltrated behind the Finnish lines under cover provided by the heavy forests in the area. Within a few days the Finns had killed or captured much of this brigade with relatively little damage being done.

Stalemate

For the remainder of 1942 and 1943 there were no large-scale operations conducted and the area settled down to relative quiet. In the south, from Lake Onega to the Karelian Isthmus, both sides adopted tactics of static trench warfare. However in the north the long frontier, forests and lack of roads all combined to make trench lines impractical. Borders were patrolled regularly and there were many small-scale skirmishes. Reconnaissance operations continued to capture prisoners for intelligence or to scout defensive positions. A number of small scale raids captured strategic features. Several small bases changed hands frequently during this time. Attacks on village populations caused deep resentment among the Finns. Soviet and Finnish patrols continued to probe the lines and in eastern Karelia, where the earthworks gave way to expanses of wooded wilderness.

Securing Peace

As the war dragged on and Germany's fortunes waned, Finland sought peace. However, Stalin demanded unconditional surrender, a price Finland was not prepared to pay. As a result of the negotiations, Germany's support for Finland also soured and Hitler withdrew crucial arms supplies.

In June 1944, the Soviets started an all-out offensive with two Guards Tank Armies, quickly smashing through the Finnish defensive lines on the Karelian Isthmus. Marshal Mannerheim made a personal plea to Hitler who relented and rushed vital anti-tank weapons to the front line. However, the Soviet advance continued until, in forests north of Viipuri, the two armies clashed in the mighty battle of Tali-Ihantala, the largest ever seen on Nordic soil. After a week of intense and bloody fighting the Soviet advance was halted by Finnish troops using new German artillery, assault guns and Panzerfaust rockets. Further fierce battles at Viipurinlahti, Vuosalmi, Siiranmäki and Äyräpää, also stopped Soviet attacks. Then the Red Army then turned its attention to Poland and the Balkans and the front once more stabilised. However, Finland was weary of the war and Stalin needed to free up his forces, so peace was negotiated.

The war with the Soviet Union was over. Finland had secured its independence.

Finnish Special Rules

Self Sufficient

The Finnish Army is composed of farmers and hunters, used to an outdoor lifestyle and making their own decisions. Their training emphasised this self-sufficiency.

> *Finnish Platoons use the German Mission Tactics special rule from the rule book.*

Ski-equipped

Skiing is the national sport in Finland, as well as a necessity for travelling cross-country. Finnish platoons are ski-equipped, increasing their mobility during winter.

> *Finnish Infantry and Man-packed Gun teams treat deep snow as Cross-country Terrain, allowing them to move At the Double.*

Bitter Enemies

The Finns are a stubborn people used to adversity. The survival of their country is at stake. All Finnish troops are prepared to fight at close quarters if needed to see off the invading Red Army.

> *Finnish forces gain the British Bulldog special rule when fighting against any Soviet force.*

Using 'Motti' tactics of divide and conquer the Finns attack a vulnerable Soviet supply column.

Anti-tank rifles easily silence light tanks.

Soviet equipment is captured and turned on its former owners.

The Finns are fearless in the defence of their very homes.

Finns rely on fighting prowess over technology.

Captured Maxim HMG's cut swathes through the Soviet infantry hordes.

Lauri Allan Törni was born in Viipuri in 1919 where his family had a large home. He learned from an Olympic boxing champion and already had a reputation as a tough, disciplined fighter and a fine skier before he joined the Finnish Army in 1938. During the Winter War he proved a brilliantly effective soldier in *Sissi* ski-guerilla units. By the end of the Winter War he had earned the rank of Sergeant.

Despite this, his home in Viipuri was part of the Finnish territory lost to the Soviet Union. This only added to Törni's hatred of communism.

After the Winter War, Törni was determined to continue the fight against the Soviet Union, and travelled to Germany to train with the *Waffen-SS*. In Operation Barbarossa, Törni again proved an excellent soldier, and was decorated with the Iron Cross Second Class. After Finland declared war on the Soviet Union again in the Continuation War, he returned home and re-enlisted in the Finnish Army.

During the Continuation War (1941-1944) Törni proved an excellent combat leader, first with armour and then with light infantry, and was promoted to Captain. His long-range missions were so successful that the Red Army put a price of 3 million Finnish Marks on his head. In 1944 he was transferred to the Karelian Isthmus, scene of the final Soviet offensive. He led a *Jääkäri* unit which made a decisive counterattack and helped stabilise the line after the Soviet breakthrough. He was awarded the Mannerheim Cross, Finland's highest medal for bravery.

Torni's life in the military did not end there. After the war he journeyed to the United States, became a citizen and enlisted in the US army as Larry Thorn. He served with US Special Forces and led missions in places ranging from Iran to Vietnam, being decorated several times. He served two tours in Vietnam before being killed in Laos in 1965.

He was the basis of the character played by John Wayne in the movie *Green Berets*.

Characteristics

Captain Lauri Törni is a Warrior and Command team rated as **Fearless Veteran**.

Lauri replaces the Command team of a Jääkäri Platoon for a cost of +50 points. Lauri counts as a Recce team.

He is armed with a Suomi SMG and Satchel Charges with the following ratings:

Range: 4"/10cm, **ROF:** 3, **Anti-tank:** 1, and **Firepower:** 6.

Like an SMG team, Lauri fires at full ROF when moving and with Satchel Charges counts as having **Anti-tank: 3** in assaults.

Special Rules

Implacable: Lauri and the Jääkäri platoon he is leading pass all Motivation Tests on a 2+.

Skilled Soldier: Lauri and the Jääkäri platoon he is leading may re-roll any failed Skill Tests, applying the new result instead.

Panssarikomppania

(TANK COMPANY)

The Finnish army now has enough captured tanks to assign you the command of a complete Panssari komppania *(pronounced pahns-sahr-ee-komp-pahn-ee-ya) or Tank Company. You will be at the forefront of the offensive to recapture Finnish territory taken in the Soviet invasion. Your men have had time to become familiar with their tanks and are now expected to operate with the same high degree of efficiency as our infantry.*

A force based around a Panssarikomppania must contain:

* a Company HQ, and
* two or three Panssari Platoons.

Weapon platoons available to a Panssari-komppania are:

* two Jääkäri Platoons.

Support platoons for a Panssarikomppania can be:

* an Armoured Anti-aircraft Platoon, and

* Divisional Support Platoons.

You may have up to **one** Support Platoon for each Panssari Platoon in the Company.

Motivation and Skill

The Finnish tank units have spent the time since the end of Winter War in 1940 in constant training. The bitter lessons of the Winter War have been well learned and with some of the hardest fighting of autumn 1941 behind them the tank troops are rated as **Fearless Veteran.**

HEADQUARTERS

1 Company HQ

Headquarters

Company HQ	100 points

Soviet T-26 tanks that have been repaired and put back into Finnish use formed the bulk of Finnish armoured companies. The tanks are obsolete by current standards, but aggressive tactics and skilful use means good results can still be obtained from them. The commanders are drawn from the ranks of the pre-war Finnish armoured company, and from *Jääkäri* units used in offensive operations.

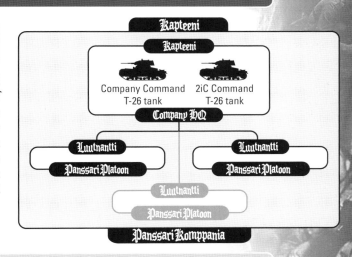

Kapteeni

Kapteeni

Company Command
T-26 tank

2iC Command
T-26 tank

Company HQ

Luutnantti — Panssari Platoon

Luutnantti — Panssari Platoon

Luutnantti — Panssari Platoon

Panssari Komppania

Mixed Model T-26 Tanks

The Finn's captured T-26 tanks of every model, from the early model 1931 to the later model 1939 and everything in between.

Most of the T-26 tanks were refurbished and standardised, to represent this in your force you may field any mix of T-26 models in your platoons, but they all count as being the later T-26 obr 1939.

The History Of The Finnish Hakaristi

The blue Finnish hooked cross (*Hakaristi*) was originally the symbol of luck of the family of Count von Rosen, who donated his first plane to the Finnish 'White Army', in 1918 during the War of Independence.

It was adopted as the official national marking of the Finnish Air Forces and later on, the Army. Only after the Nazis adopted a similar hooked cross as their emblem did this ancient symbol acquire political significance. In other words, the Finnish hooked cross had nothing to do with the Nazi party, Nazi ideology or fascism in general.

COMBAT PLATOONS

2 or 3 Panssari Platoons

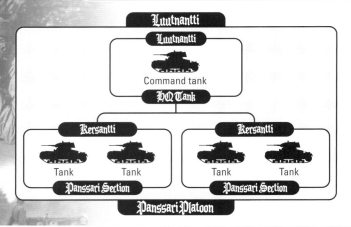

Platoon	
5 T-26	250 points
4 T-26	200 points
3 T-26	150 points

Captured Soviet armour has been used to equip the Finnish tank battalions. We have managed to press 167 tanks into service, unfortunately mostly obsolete T-26 light tanks of various models.

Captured Tanks

The Finnish army was vastly under-equipped in the face of the mighty Red Army and had to press into service any piece of equipment they could capture or find. Although the tank forces were primarily made up of the light Soviet T-26 tank, other captured Soviet tanks appeared in some formations.

Instead of the normal organisation you may field your Panssarikomppania as either the 3rd Tank Company or the 6th Tank Company, but not both in the same force.

3rd Tank Company

The Finnish 3rd *Panssarikomppania* had 3 T-34 tanks that were purchased from the Germans and some T-28 tanks captured from the Soviet Union.

One Panssari Platoon is equipped with 3 T-34 tanks for 475 points and one Panssari Platoon is equipped with 4 T-28's for 310 points. The remaining Panssari Platoon is equipped with T-26 light tanks as shown above.

6th Tank Company

The Finnish 6th *Panssarikomppania* had 2 KV-1 tanks and 4 T-28 tanks captured from the Soviet Union.

One Panssari Platoon is equipped with 2 KV-1 tanks for 420 points and one Panssari Platoon is equipped with 4 T-28's for 310 points. The remaining Panssari Platoon is equipped with T-26 light tanks as shown above.

WEAPONS PLATOONS

0 to 2 Jääkäri Platoons

This is organised and equipped like the Jääkäri Platoon shown on page 76.

SUPPORT PLATOONS

0 to 1 Armoured Anti-aircraft Platoon

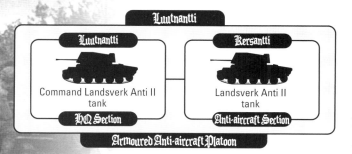

Platoon	
2 Landsverk Anti II	180 points

Finland purchased six *Landsverk Anti II* anti-aircraft tanks from Sweden, and formed a Armour AA-Battery in May 1942 as part of the *Panssari Divisioona*, the Armoured Division. They were highly effective both in air-defence and in support of ground operations.

Jalkaväkikomppania

(INFANTRY COMPANY)

The main strength of the Finnish army remains its well-trained and skilfully-led Jalkaväkikomppania (pronounced yahl-kah-vae-kee-komp-pahn-ee-ya) or infantry company, now well tested in battle. These are now fully equipped with heavy weapons, thanks to some purchased from abroad, and many others captured from the Soviets. Earlier losses from the Winter War and the demands of the wartime economy mean that manpower is in short supply, so companies now only have three rifle platoons each. But that should still be enough to stop any invader.

A force based around a Jalkaväkikomppania must contain:

* a Company HQ, and
* two or three Jalkaväki Platoons.

Weapon platoons available to a Jalkaväkikomppania are:

* a Jääkäri Platoon,
* two Machine-gun Platoons, and
* a Mortar Platoon.

Support platoons for a Jalkaväkikomppania can be:

* a Panssari Platoon, and
* Divisional Support Platoons.

You may have up to **one** Support Platoon for each Jalkaväki Platoon in the Company.

Motivation and Skill

The Finns fight hard against a numerically and technologically superior enemy, much to the dismay of the Soviet Red Army. The Finnish Jalkaväki are rated as **Fearless Veteran**.

HEADQUARTERS

1 Company HQ

Headquarters

Company HQ	50 points

Options

* Add Close-defence Squad for +25 points per team.
* Replace all Close-defence Rifle teams with Lhati anti-tank rifle teams at no cost.

A *Kapteeni* (Captain) leads an infantry company of three platoons. Finnish infantry companies are organised along German lines. A cadre of Finnish field officers fought as a *Jäger* battalion in the German Army in World War One. They returned to teach German *Jäger* tactics to all of our officers. As a result Finnish field officers are very well trained and after three years of war, highly experienced. Finnish infantry companies are well-balanced teams with infantry, *Jääkäri* units, and machine-guns and mortars able to see off any enemy infantry assault. With the attachment of divisional assets such as anti-aircraft and anti-tank platoons, and perhaps even some captured *Panssari*, they have made the forests of Finland a death trap for enemy tanks. In attack their superior fieldcraft gives our troops the ability to advance quickly and use *'motti'* tactics—first encircling and then assaulting and destroying the enemy.

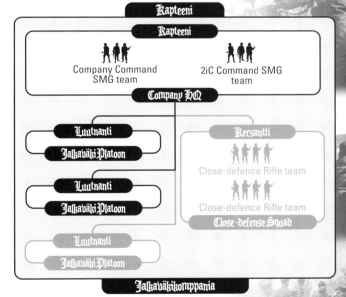

COMBAT PLATOONS

2 to 3 Jalkaväki Platoons

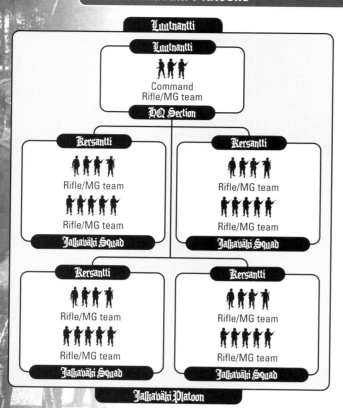

Platoon

HQ Section with:

4 Jalkaväki Squads	**215 points**
3 Jalkaväki Squads	**165 points**
2 Jalkaväki Squads	**115 points**

Options

- Replace the Command Rifle/MG team with a Command Close-defence SMG team for +5 points.

Jalkaväki platoons are the strength of the Finnish Army. The troops were not regular soldiers but all had reserve training before the war. Now three years of combat has made them unmatched fighters. There can be no question of retreat, for they are fighting for their very homes. No other infantry defend better than dug-in *Jalkaväki* as the Soviets have discovered to their cost. In attack they are not afraid to take on any foe, even hunting down the invaders' tanks.

WEAPONS PLATOONS

0 to 1 Jääkäri Platoon

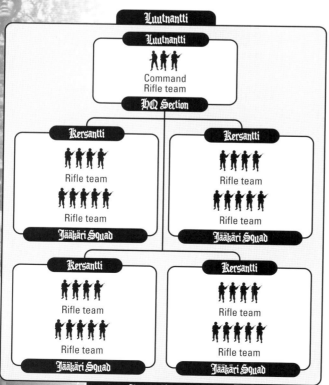

Platoon

HQ Section with:

4 Jääkäri Squads	**225 points**
3 Jääkäri Squads	**175 points**
2 Jääkäri Squads	**125 points**

Options

- Replace the Command Rifle team with a Command Close-defence SMG team for +10 points.
- Replace all Rifle teams with SMG teams for +20 points per Jääkäri Squad.

The *Jääkäri* (yay-kah-ree, or hunters) scout ahead and provide flank security. Many Finnish soldiers are hunters and woodsmen, familiar with the country and completely at home in it. Their ability to advance silently and undetected is remarkable. They are aggressively led and their role is as much assault as reconnaissance.

A Jääkäri Platoons are Reconnaissance Platoons

0 to 2 Machine-gun Platoon

Platoon
HQ Section with:

2 Machine-gun Sections	155 points
1 Machine-gun Section	90 points

Heavy machine-guns are the mainstay of Finnish defences against enemy infantry. The Finns use the Soviet Maxim with the bulky gun shield removed. It is a reliable weapon that will keep firing until the job is done and Soviet companies contain plenty of targets.

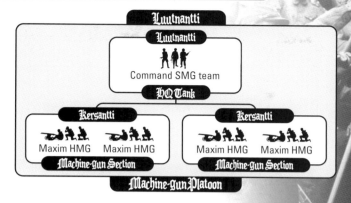

0 to 1 Mortar Platoon

Platoon
HQ Section with:

3 Mortar Sections	125 points
2 Mortar Sections	95 points

Every Finnish battalion has a light mortar unit to provide immediate fire support to front-line infantry. They can fire smoke to assist in attack and there rapid-fire missions break up the enemy in defence. Their light weight enables them to be brought forward quickly to keep up with an advance.

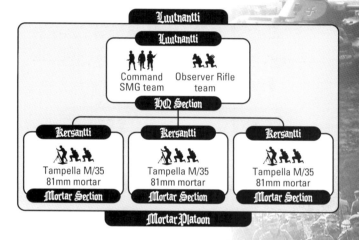

SUPPORT PLATOONS

0 to 1 Panssari Platoon

This is organised and equipped like the Panssari Platoons shown on page 74. This includes the variant Panssari Platoons of the 3rd and 6th Tank Companies.

Any Panssarikomppania or Jalkaväki Komppania may have the following Support Platoons:

- an Anti-aircraft Platoon,
- Anti-tank Platoons,
- an Armoured Car Platoon,
- an Assault Gun Platoon
- Field Artillery Platoons,
- a Heavy Mortar Platoon, and
- a Pioneer Platoon

Motivation and Skill

Like the troops they support, the Divisional Support Platoons are hardened from battle and show the fervour of a people defending their country and way of life. Divisional Support Platoons are rated as **Fearless Veteran**.

Air Support

You may request Sporadic Air Support at a cost of +90 points. Sporadic Air Support will provide you supporting Fokker CX ground-attack aircraft.

0 to 1 Anti-aircraft Platoon

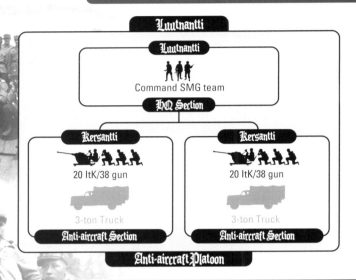

Platoon

HQ Section with:

2 Anti-aircraft sections	**80 points**

Options

- Replace both 20 ItK/38 (2cm FlaK 38) anti-aircraft guns with two 40 LtK/38 (40mm Bofors) anti-aircraft guns for +15 points.
- Add one 3-ton truck to each Anti-aircraft Section for +5 points for the platoon.

Every division now has integral anti-aircraft platoons, armed mainly with the 40mm Bofors imported from Sweden or 20mm guns purchased from Germany. These protect the troops against the swarming Red Air Force.

0 to 2 Anti-tank Platoons

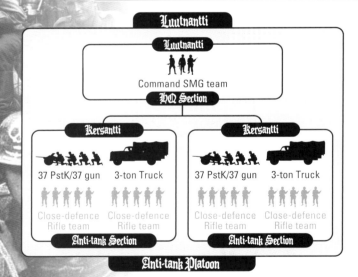

Platoon

HQ Section with:

2 Anti-tank Sections	**90 points**

Options

- Add up to two Close-defence Rifle teams per section, for +25 points per team.
- Replace all 37 PstK/37 (3.7cm PaK36) anti-tank guns with 45 PstK/37 (45mm obr 1937) anti-tank guns for +10 points for the platoon, with 50 PstK/38 (5cm PaK 38) anti-tank guns for +30 points for the platoon, with 75 PstK/97-38 (7.5cm Pak 97/38) anti-tank guns for +40 points for the platoon, or with 75 PstK/40 (7.5cm PaK 40) anti-tank guns for +115 points for the platoon.

Your force may not contain more than one Anti-tank Platoon armed with 75 PstK/40 (7.5cm PaK 40) anti-tank guns, even if it has more than one Panssarikomppania or Jalkaväkikomppania.

Anti-tank guns are precious. In addition to the 37mm and 45mm anti-tank guns, there are now a few heavy 50mm and 75mm guns purchased from Germany. Finland still does not have enough however, and close-defence teams equipped with satchel charges continue to be used to bolster anti-tank defences.

0 to 1 Armoured Car Platoon

Platoon	
3 BA-10	180 points
2 BA-10	120 points

Some of the many Soviet armoured cars captured in the Winter War are now used for reconnaissance in both *Jalkaväki* and *Panssari* units. The BA-10 is the preferred model, with the lighter Soviet vehicles being discarded.

An Armoured Car Platoon is a Reconnaissance Platoons

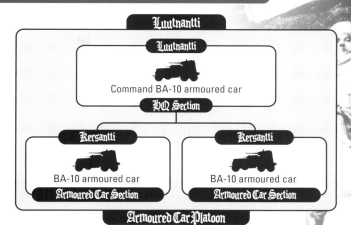

0 to 1 Assault Gun Platoon

Platoon	
3 BT-42	220 points
2 BT-42	145 points

Our forces captured many Soviet BT-7 tanks in the Winter War and 1941 offensive that were too lightly armoured for service as tanks. Instead they have had howitzers added to form the BT-42, our first assault gun! The conversion has proved a little unwieldy for tank combat, but they are useful for infantry support.

Field Artillery Platoon

Platoon
HQ Section with:

2 Gun Sections	190 points
1 Gun Section	115 points

Options
* Replace all 76mm K/02 guns with 105 H/33 (10.5cm leFH18) howitzers for +35 points per Gun Section.
* Add horse-drawn limbers to each Gun Section and a horse-drawn wagon to the HQ Section at no cost.
* Replace all horse-drawn vehicles with 3-ton trucks for +5 points per Gun Section.

Reorganised under the brilliant General Vilho P Nenonen, Finnish artillery is now very capable. It is well trained, no longer suffers from the ammunition shortages which plagued it in the Winter War, and has been re-equipped with captured Soviet field guns and modern German howitzers.

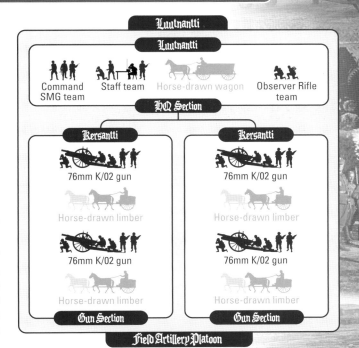

0 to 1 Heavy Mortar Platoon

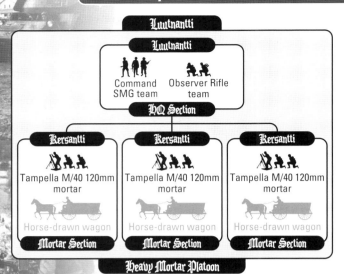

Platoon

HQ Section with:

3 Mortar Sections	180 points
2 Mortar Sections	130 points

Options

- Add one horse-drawn wagon to each Mortar Section at no cost.
- Replace all horse-drawn wagons with 3-ton trucks for +5 points for the platoon.

The Tampella 120mm mortar put into production after the Winter War, and plenty of captured Soviet weapons ensure that each infantry regiment now has a company of these excellent infantry support weapons.

0 to 1 Pioneer Platoon

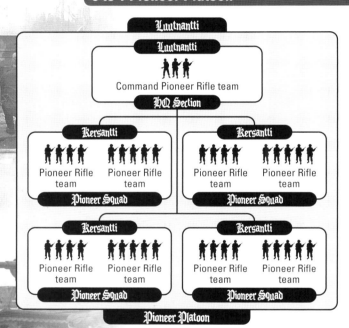

Platoon

HQ Section with:

4 Pioneer Squads	235 points
3 Pioneer Squads	185 points
2 Pioneer Squads	135 points

Options

- Replace the Command Pioneer Rifle team with a Command Pioneer SMG team for +5 points.

The large number of foresters in the Finnish army means there is no shortage of soldiers familiar with explosives and engineering equipment. These units are now amongst the best trained in the whole army, and have the full range of pioneer abilities, as well as satchel charges for use against fortifications or tanks.

You may replace up to two Pioneer Rifle teams with Flame-thrower teams at the start of the game before deployment.

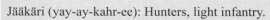

Finnish Terminology

Jääkäri (yay-ay-kahr-ee): Hunters, light infantry.

Jalkävakikomppania (yahl-kah-vae-kee-komp-pahn-ee-ya): Infantry company.

Jatkosota (yaht-koh-soh-tah): 1941-1944 Continuation War.

Kapteeni (kap-te-ee-nee): Captain.

Kersantii (kerr-sahn-tee): Corporal.

Lahti (lahh-tee): Finnish armaments manufacturer.

Landsverk (lahnds-vehrk): Swedish armaments manufacturer.

Luutnantii (loo-oot-nahn-tee): Lieutenant.

Panssarikomppania (pahn-sahr-ee-komp-pahn-ee-ya): Tank company.

Talvisota (tahl-vee-soh-tah): 1939-1940 Winter War.

Tampella (tahm-pehl-lah): Finnish armaments manufacturer.

HONVÉD
HUNGARIAN FORCES

Hungary entered the war for territorial reasons. It had been punished for its role in the First World War by the loss of territory to their neighbours, and wanted it returned.

Operation Barbarossa

Hungary joined the German invasion of the Soviet Union when the cities of Kassa and Munkács were bombed on 26 June 1941, allegedly by the Soviet Union.

The Carpathian Army Group was formed from units stationed on Soviet frontier. For the invasion the Mobile Corps (1st and 2nd Motorised, and 1st Cavalry Brigades) was added.

The attack began on 27 June. From July to November 1941 the Mobile Corps led the Hungarian advance. They moved from their positions in the Carpathians to Mecsebelovka, just to the south of Kharkov, engaging in a major battle at Nikolayev on 12 August.

The Mobile Corps thwarted Soviet attempts to form bridgeheads over the Dnepr around Nikopol in August and September. On 12 October, the Mobile Corps crossed the Dnepr River in support of the German advance on Izyum. On 11 November the Corps was withdrawn back to Dneperpetrovsk.

A New Army

Having achieved his war aims, Admiral Horthy, Hungary's leader, decided to limit his country's involvement in further operations in Russia to a minimum. After much wrangling between Berlin and Budapest it was decided the Hungarians would contribute an army of 220,000 men in three corps: III Corps (6th, 7th and 9th Light Divisions), IV Corps (10th, 12th and 13th Light Divisions), VII Corps (19th, 20th and 23rd Light Divisions), and the 1st Armoured Field Division

Between 11 April and 27 July the Hungarian 2nd Army slowly arrived at the front and took up positions within Army Group Weichs, along with the German 2nd Army and 4th Panzer Army

As the new Hungarian army was being moved to the front the Germans launched Code Blue, the advance to Stalingrad and the Caucasus, on 28 June 1942. The Hungarian units that took part in the initial attack were from the III Corps (7th and 9th Light Divisions. Hungarian troops took Staryi Oskol on 4 July and by 7 July III Corps' leading units had reached the Don River.

The Battles for Uryv

The Hungarians had barely dug into positions behind the Don when the Soviets launched attacks across the river to establish bridgeheads at Uryv, Karotyak and Stutye. The Hungarians counterattacked with the 1st Armoured

Field Division. They pushed the Soviets out of Uryv in to a small bend in the Don River north of the town. The Hungarian tankers in their T-38 and Panzer IV tanks had learned well from their German instructors. They waited until the Soviet T-34 tanks fired, knowing the crew would be temporarily blinded by smoke then moved around the flanks, shooting at their weaker side armour. The Hungarian armoured troops accounted for 21 T-34 tanks during the First Battle of Uryv (27 July). Unfortunately the attack had to be called off when ammunition ran low due to the failure of the Germans to resupply them.

The Hungarian III Corps attacked again on 10 August, but Soviet resistance proved tough. After taking high casualties they were forced to withdraw, but they had proven their mettle to their German allies.

A third attempt was made on the Uryv bridgehead on 9 September. This time the Germans planned the attack. Taking part were the Hungarian 7th 12th, 13th and 20th Light Divisions, supported by 1st Armoured Field Division and one German division from XXIV Panzer Corps. After five days of heavy fighting the attack was broken off, both sides taking substantial casualties. The Hungarian troops were left to fortify the position and seal up the Soviet bridgehead.

The Battles for Karotyak

The task of clearing the Karotyak bridgehead fell to Hungarian IV Corps. They attacked on 7 August with support of the 1st Armoured Field Division and by evening the 12th Light Division and 1st Armoured Field Division had reached the Don at the northern outskirts of the town. They were continually harassed by Soviet aircraft, but had little to counter them, as the Corps' anti-aircraft guns were still moving to the front. The armour was recalled back to the III Corps at Uryv on 8 August, leaving the left flank of the 12th Light Division dangerously exposed.

The Soviets quickly took advantage of the opportunity and thrust through the gap against the 4th Heavy Artillery Battalion. The artillery unit was forced to deploy most of their men as infantry, leaving minimal crews to man the guns. With the aid of German reinforcements the artillerymen were able to halt the attack before it reached their gun positions.

On 3 September the attack on Karotyak began again. With better support from the armour, and their Germans allies, they finally took the bridgehead.

Winter 1942-43

By mid-September 1942 the 2nd Army had settled into defensive positions along the Don River. A lack of supplies and labour meant only the areas immediately around the bridge heads could be fortified.

Supply problems plagued the 2nd Army. The Germans viewed their allies as a secondary priority and the Hungarian Government withheld equipment and supplies needed for home defence.

The weather also played a role as armoured troops complained that their T-38 tanks needed time to warm-up in the cold, and that if stationed too close to the front lines any breakthrough couldn't be stopped if the tanks weren't already running.

The German 168th Infantry Division (including 559th Anti-tank Battalion), and the 429th Infantry Regiment were initially moved into the area to support the Hungarians. Then after the neighbouring Romanian army was crushed by a Soviet offensive, the Germans sent further reinforcements in the form of the 700th Army Panzer Unit (equipped with obsolete Panzer 38(t) tanks) and the 26th Infantry Division (including the 190th Assault gun battalion). These units combined with the 1st Armoured Field Division and the 168th Infantry Division to form Corps Cramer as the army reserve.

The Soviet Attack

On 3 January, 1943 the Soviets launched several probing attacks against the 2nd Hungarian and 8th Italian Armies, but these attacks were successfully fended off.

The storm broke over the 2nd Hungarian Army on 12 January. The 40th Soviet Army launched an attack from the Uryv bridgehead into the 7th Light Division and the German 429th Infantry Regiment. The 35th Infantry Regiment of 7th Light Division held their positions, but the 4th Infantry Regiment was overrun. On this first day the Soviets were able to drive a six kilometre wide gap between III and IV Corps.

13 January saw Soviet attacks concentrate on the 20th Light Division to the north of Uryv. The 20th Light Division were supported by the remnants of the 7th Light Division and 429th Infantry Regiment. However, at dawn both corners of the Uryv bulge still held.

Four battalions of III Corps reserves supported by the German 700th Army Panzer Unit counterattacked the next day. By the end of the day the Germans had just four tanks remaining and the Hungarian troops engaged had been smashed by unrelenting Soviet attacks.

The German commander of the 429th Infantry Regiment wrote in his report: 'the Hungarian troops had fought very well, and that the cause for the failure of the attempt lay with the helplessness of the Hungarian units against enemy armour and the freezing weather.'

Soviet Breakthrough

After two days of fighting, the gap in the Hungarian lines was now 10 kilometres wide. On 14 January the Soviet offensive got into full swing and thrusts were made from Stutye and Kantemirovka while the Soviet 18th Rifle Corps smashed through the 12th Light Division and moved towards Ostrogosk.

The release of the German 168th Infantry Division from reserves on 15 January slowed the Soviet advance on the southern flank, but to the north a continuous flow of Soviet troops poured through the widening breach in the Hungarian lines.

The remnants of III Corps now faced south, their western flank exposed. All along the front the Hungarian divisions were under pressure. The 7th and 12th Light Division had been destroyed and the 2nd Army was quickly running out of men.

On 16 January it was the 13th Light Division at Karotyak's turn to come under pressure from the Soviet 40th Army. After heavy fighting they withdrew to Ostrogosk where they and the 10th Light Division and German 168th Infantry Division were surrounded, losing the artillery of the 10th Light Division because of a lack of horses to withdraw the guns.

The same day Corps Cramer launched an attack, that stalled the advance of the Soviet 18th Rifle Corps. However, the attack had to be called off when the 1st Armoured Field Division's flanks became dangerously exposed.

The Soviets also worked their way behind the positions of VII Corps and

the 2nd Army were forced to retreat before their position became too exposed.

Resistance by III Corps in the north continued with German reinforcements on 17 January. Lead elements of the Soviet 40th Army reached the airfield at Ilovskoye around noon, but fierce resistance from Hungarian Air Force ground crew forced them to withdraw. IV Corps was ordered to retreat on Ostrogosk. By evening all communications with the 2nd Army HQ were cut.

Collapse

On 18 January Hitler declared Ostrogosk a fortress, inside were the remainder of the 10th and 13th Light Divisions, the German 168th Infantry Division, and corps troops from the III and IV Corps.

VII Corps was withdrawing when it encountered the left wing of the Soviet 18th Rifle Corps. When Soviets

tanks appeared to the south their retreat rapidly became a rout. The Soviets occupied Alexeyevka, but a counterattack by the 1st Armoured Field Division pushed the Soviets out. The Hungarian armour then joined the defence of Ilovskoye to the north.

On 19 January the defence of Alexeyevka, Ilovskoye and Ostrogosk continued, and the following day the Soviet 40th Army turned its attention to the German 2nd Army to the north, leaving the 18th Rifle Corps and 3rd Tank Army to finish off the Hungarian 2nd Army.

Counterattacks on 21 January re-established contact with Ostrogosk and the last German and Hungarian troops were withdrawn to Novyi Oskol. Meanwhile the 1st Armoured Field Division tenaciously held off continued attempts to take Alexeyevka. The remaining Hungarian troops in the Ostrogosk-Alexeyevka area were grouped together under Corps Cramer, and on 22 January they started withdrawing towards Budyenny and on to Novyi Oskol.

That same day the Hungarian 2nd Army ceased functioning as a command unit and was moved to the rear to reorganise. Those units still capable of fighting (barely 12,000 Hungarian troops) remained with Corps Cramer, under German command. As the front stabilised Hungarian units were sent to the rear where they began their reorganisation.

After the mauling of January 1943, the Hungarians wouldn't see any serious fighting again until 1944.

The tanks and men of the Hungarian Honvéd fought many battles against Soviet bridgeheads over the Don in 1942.

The Csaba armoured cars fighting along side motorised infantry and T-38G's of the 1st Armoured Field Division.

The little T-38G confronts a mighty foe.

The Nimrod, an excellent anti-aircraft vehicle, was often pressed into action again Soviet tanks and infantry.

Steadfast Hungarian riflemen storm into the Soviet positions.

Small anti-tank guns easily take on light armour.

Hungarian Terminology

Alhadnagy (ol-hod-nodya): Junior platoon leader.

Botond (bot-ond): Mace-wielder. Hungarian armaments manufacturer.

Csaba (choh-boh): Shepherd. Name of armoured car.

Ezred (ez-red): Regiment.

Felderito (feld-ehr-i-toh): Scout.

Föhadnagy (fer-hod-nodya): Senior platoon leader.

Gépkocsizó Lövész Század (gaep-koh-chiz-oe ler-vaess ssoz-od): Motorised infantry company.

Hadnagy (hord-nodya): Platoon leader.

Hadosztály (hoh-dos-tah-lee): Division.

Harckocsizó Század (horts-kots-iz-oe ssoz-od): Tank company.

Honvéd (hon-vaed): Hungarian Army.

Huszar (hoo-ssarr): Hussar.

Nimrod (nim-rrod): Ancient warrior king. Name of anti-aircraft tank.

Ormester (orr-mesh-terr): Squad leader.

Puskás Század (poosh-karsh ssoz-od): Rifle company.

Szakasz (soh-kos): Platoon.

Százados (ssar-zod-osh): Company commander.

Páncélvadász (Pahn-tsal-vadahs): Tank destroyer.

Toldi (tol-dee): 14th Century knight. Name of light tank.

Zászlóalj (zahs-loe-oh-lya): Battalion.

Hungarian Special Rules

Hussar

Descended from Magyar horsemen, Hungary has a strong cavalry tradition. Hungarian knights often stood alone against the Ottoman Turks as the defenders of Europe and during the 17th to 19th Centuries they supplied the Habsburg Empire's elite light cavalry. Hungarian mobile troops are famed for their aggression and wide sweeping movements.

Any Hussar Platoon with a Command team may attempt a Hussar move at the start of the Shooting Step instead of shooting. If a platoon attempts to make a Hussar move, it may not shoot even if it fails to make a Hussar move.

Roll a Skill test for each platoon:

- *If the test is successful, the platoon may move another 4"/10cm,*
- *Otherwise the platoon cannot move this step.*

All normal rules apply for this movement. Platoons cannot make Hussar moves if they are Pinned Down or have moved At the Double. Bogged Down or Bailed vehicles cannot make Hussar moves.

Stoic Service

The Hungarians came to Russia to get a job done. Hungarian infantry are willing to take their part in any offensive and will assault enemy positions, but will not unnecessarily take risks by over extending themselves.

Only Hussar Platoons may make a Breakthrough Assault after winning an assault, all other platoons must always Consolidate.

Preparing for the Coming Storm

The Hungarians' job is to hold their section of the Don while the Germans fight for Stalingrad. They make sure defensive positions are well prepared and ready for any Soviet attacks.

Hungarian platoons may re-roll failed Skill Tests to Dig In.

Harckocsizó Század

(TANK COMPANY)

The men of Hungary's 1st Armoured Field Division are as good as those of any armoured division anywhere. Unfortunately, the same cannot be said of our tanks. Our Harckocsizó Század (pronounced horts-koh-chee-zoe ssoz-od) or Tank Company has only a handful of modern tanks with which to fight. Still, as we must prevail, they will have to be enough.

—Föhadnagy Nagy Laszlo

A force based around a Harckocsizó Század must contain:

- a Company HQ, and
- two to four Harckocsizó Platoons.

Weapon Platoons available to a Harckocsizó Század are:

- a Heavy Harckocsizó Platoon.

Support Platoons available to a Harckocsizó Század are:

- a Light Harckocsizó Platoon,
- an Armoured Car Platoon,
- a Motorcycle Scout Platoon,
- Self-propelled Anti-aircraft Platoons,
- Motorised Puskás Platoons,
- Divisional Support Platoons,
- an allied German Grenadier Platoon,

- an allied German Anti-tank Gun Platoon,
- an allied German Motorised Artillery Battery
- an allied German Tank-hunter Platoon, and
- an allied German Panzer Platoon equipped with Panzer III M, or Panzer III N tanks.

You may have **two** Support Platoons for each Tank Platoon you field.

Motivation and Skill

The 1st Armoured Field Division is the elite of the Hungarian 2nd Army. All the tank crews have undergone extensive training with the Germans in tank warfare. In the winter of 1942 they proved themselves again and again against the overwhelming odds of the Soviet break through. A Harckocsizó Század is rated as **Confident Veteran**.

HEADQUARTERS

1 Company HQ

Headquarters

Company HQ	135 points

The Harckocsizó Század commander controls the Hungarian mobile battle, supporting the motorised infantry clearing bridgeheads, and fighting with the 1st Armoured Field Division as the army's mobile reserve.

Hungary has a long and proud cavalry tradition, and the armoured commanders carry on this in their tanks. Motivating their platoons in the face of the enemy they can be found leading from the front.

The Company HQ is a Hussar Platoon

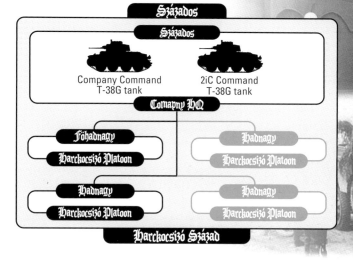

Százados

Százados

Company Command T-38G tank

2iC Command T-38G tank

Comapny HQ

Föhadnagy — Harckocsizó Platoon

Hadnagy — Harckocsizó Platoon

Hadnagy — Harckocsizó Platoon

Hadnagy — Harckocsizó Platoon

Harckocsizó Század

COMBAT PLATOONS

2 to 4 Harckocsizó Platoons

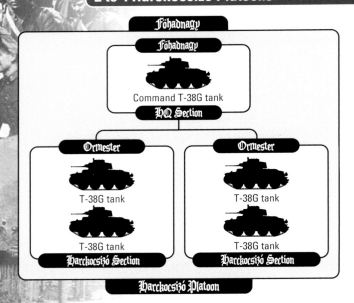

Platoon	
5 T-38G tanks	330 points
4 T-38G tanks	265 points
3 T-38G tanks	200 points

The Hungarians had been developing their own tank industry, but were unable to produce sufficient medium tanks in 1942, so the Germans supplied 108 T-38G tanks to the Hungarian 1st Field Armoured Division. The T-38G was the up-armoured last production model of the Panzer 38(t), still produced by the Germans in 1942 and supplied to her allies on the Russian Front.

Despite its light armament the Hungarian tankers were able use the T-38G with great daring and success in battle.

Harckocsizó Platoons are Hussar Platoons.

WEAPONS PLATOONS

0 to 1 Heavy Harckocsizó Platoon

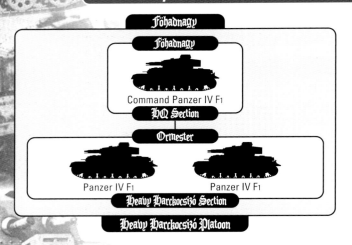

Platoon	
3 Panzer IV F_1	280 points

Option

• Upgrade any or all tanks to Panzer IV F_2 for +55 points per tank.

Upon its deployment to the Don the 1st Field Armoured Division's heavy companies were equipped with 22 Panzer IV F_1 tanks. To replace front-line losses the Germans later supplied ten Panzer IV F_2 models.

The Heavy Harckocsizó Platoon is a Hussar Platoon.

SUPPORT PLATOONS

0 to 1 Light Harckocsizó Platoon

Platoon	
5 Toldi I	240 points
4 Toldi I	190 points
3 Toldi I	140 points

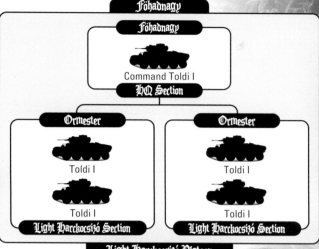

The *38M Toldi I* is a Hungarian-built light tank based on the Swedish L-60. Due to its light armour and armament, the vehicle is only used for reconnaissance and light support roles.

A Light Harckocsizó Platoon is a Hussar Platoon and a Reconnaissance Platoon.

0 to 1 Armoured Car Platoon

Platoon	
3 Csaba	130 points
2 Csaba	85 points

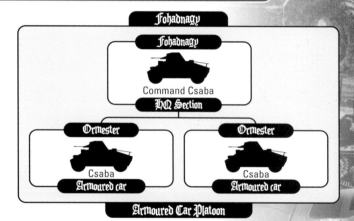

The *38M Csaba* is a Hungarian-built armoured car. It is a very effective design initially intended for the British Army. The war intervened and the Csaba has been pressed into Hungarian service for reconnaissance duties.

An Armoured Car Platoon is a Hussar Platoon and a Reconnaissance Platoon.

0 to 1 Self-propelled Anti-aircraft Platoons

Platoon	
2 Nimrod	160 points

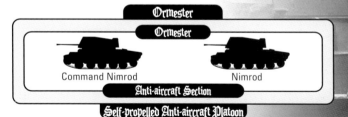

The *40M Nimrod* has been pressed into service in a dual anti-tank/anti-aircraft role where it proved successful.

A Self-propelled Anti-aircraft Platoon is a Hussar Platoon.

0 to 1 Motorcycle Scout Platoon

Motorcycle Scout Platoons are organised the same as Scout Platoons, see page 93, but are equipped with a motorcycle team for each Rifle/MG team for +5 points per team. Motorcycle Scouts are **Confident Trained**.

0 to 2 Motorised Puskás Platoons

Motorised Puskás Platoons are organised the same as Puskás Platoons on page 91, but are transported by a 1.5-ton Botond truck per Puskás Squad for +5 points per squad and must be upgraded to Rifle/MG teams. Motorised Infantry are **Confident Trained**.

HUNGARIAN

Puskás Század

(INFANTRY COMPANY)

Our Puskás Század (pronounced Poosh-karsh ssoz-od) marched and marched across an endless plain, chasing the fleeing Russians. At last they stopped on the Don River. There we fight them as we must protect our homes, but we are too few for this vast land. So we dig trenches and hold what we have, waiting for more men, more guns, and more ammunition to finish this war.

—Ormester Cseri Botond

A force based around a Puskás Század must contain:

- a Company HQ, and
- two or three Puskás Platoons.

Weapon Platoons available to a Puskás Század are:

- a Heavy Weapons Platoon,
- a Machine-gun Platoon, and
- a Mortar Platoon.

Support Platoons available to a Puskás Század are:

- an Anti-tank Platoon,
- a Scout Platoon,
- a Regimental Gun Platoon,
- Divisional Support Platoons,
- an allied German Grenadier Platoon,
- an allied German Anti-tank Gun Platoon,
- an allied German Tank-hunter Platoon,
- an allied German Assault Gun Platoon,
- an allied German Motorised Artillery Battery, and
- an allied German Panzer Platoon equipped with Panzer 38(t) tanks.

You may have **two** Support Platoons for each Puskás Platoon you field.

Motivation and Skill

Many of Hungary's experienced soldiers were kept in Hungary as part of the 1st Army watching the Romanian border, so the 2nd Army at the front was made up of a hard core of professionals and veterans from 1941, with the addition of many raw recruits. Many of these recruits were sent to the front with minimal training and no weapons. They were expected to finish their training in the trenches. A Puskás Század is rated as **Confident Trained**.

HEADQUARTERS

1 Company HQ

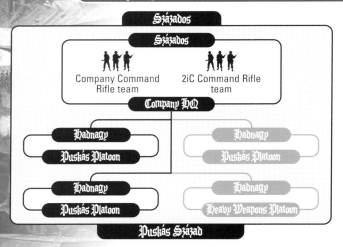

Headquarters

Company HQ	25 points

Option

- Replace either or both Command Rifle teams with Command Páncélvadász Rifle teams for +5 points per team.

A Hungarian infantry commander knows that his troops are not the best equipped but has faith in their fighting spirit. Dug in on the Don they hold the line while their German allies complete the conquest of Stalingrad that will surely see the red tide recede.

COMBAT PLATOONS

2 or 3 Puskás Platoons

Platoon

HQ Section with:

3 Puskás Squads	**120 points**
2 Puskás Squads	**85 points**

Option

- Replace Command Rifle team with a Command Páncélvadász Rifle team for +5 points.
- Upgrade all Rifle teams to Rifle/MG teams for +15 points per Puskás Squad.

As the upholders of European civilisation in the east the Hungarian riflemen are ready and willing to do their part to hold back Bolshevism. Training has been brief, but experienced veterans in their midst will show them the way of war against the Soviets.

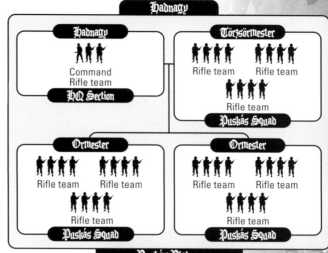

WEAPONS PLATOONS

0 to 1 Heavy Weapons Platoon

Platoon

HQ Section with:

3 Machine-gun Sections	**80 points**
2 Machine-gun Sections	**60 points**

Option

- Add Light Mortar Section for +30 points.
- Add Anti-tank Rifle Section for +30 points.

The fourth platoon of every *Puskás Század* supplies the heavy firepower of the company, especially on defence.

Heavy Weapons Platoons may make Combat Attachments to Combat Platoons.

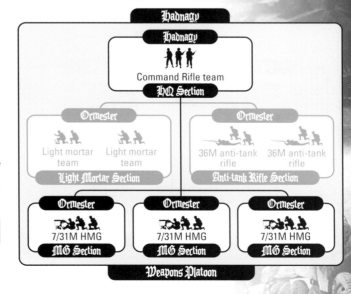

HUNGARIAN

0 to 1 Machine-gun Platoon

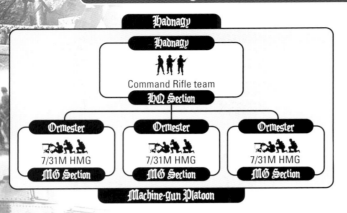

Platoon

HQ Section with:

3 MG Sections	80 points
2 MG Sections	60 points

The *Schwarzlose* 7/31M machine-guns from the battalion's medium machine-gun company provide addition support in the defensive line, able to offer interlaced lanes of fire to fend off even the most determined Soviet attack.

0 to 1 Mortar Platoon

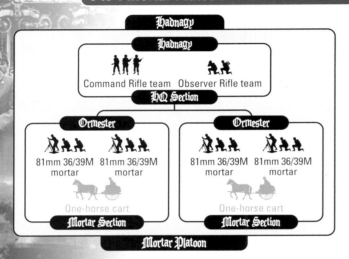

Platoon

HQ Section with:

2 Mortar Sections	105 points
1 Mortar Section	60 points

Option

• Add one-horse carts at no cost.

The mortar platoon provides on call fire support. Against any enemy advance in the open it can provide just the firepower to turn an enemy attack. Mortars also provide smoke screens to mask the Hungarian infantry's movements when on attack.

SUPPORT PLATOONS

0 to 1 Anti-tank Platoon

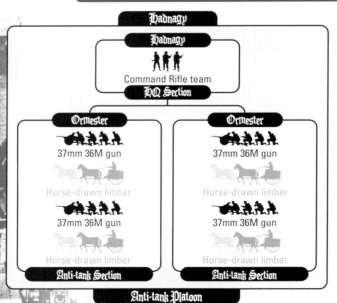

Platoon

HQ Section with:

2 Anti-tank Sections	90 points
1 Anti-tank Sections	50 points

Option

• Add horse-drawn limbers at no cost.

• Replace horse-drawn limbers with Botond 38M 3-ton trucks for +5 points per truck.

• Replace all 37mm 36M (3.7cm PaK36) guns with 40mm 40M guns for +5 points per section, with 50mm 38M (5cm PaK38) guns for +20 points per section, or with 75mm 97/38M (7.5cm PaK 97/38) guns for +25 points per section.

0 to 1 Scout Platoon

Platoon

HQ Section with:

3 Scout Squads	140 points
2 Scout Squads	100 points

Every light division had available both bicycle infantry companies and Hussar squadrons for reconnaissance duties, both usually performed front line reconnaissance on foot.

A Scout Platoon is a Reconnaissance Platoon.

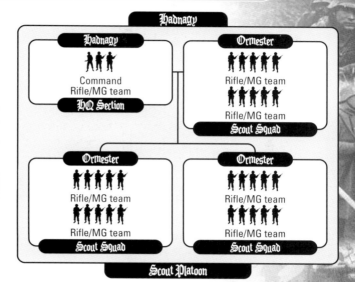

0 to 1 Regimental Gun Platoon

Platoon

HQ Section with:

2 Gun Sections	70 points

Option

• Add horse-drawn limbers at no cost.

Every Hungarian infantry regiment had a battery of four 80mm 5/8M guns as part of its formation. The guns were parcelled out along the line to give the infantry some heavy support in case of a Soviet attack.

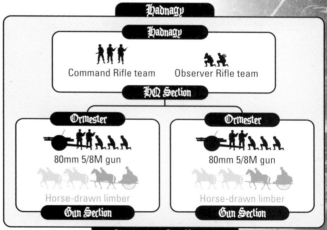

HUNGARIAN

Gépkocsizó Lövész Század

(MOTORISED INFANTRY COMPANY)

For a country with as few trucks as Hungary, the Gépkocsizó Lövész Század (pronounced Gaep-koh-chi-oe loo-vaes ssoz-od) or Motorised Company, the infantry of the 1st Armoured Field Division are extremely fortunate. Rather than walking into battle they ride in trucks. They are further blessed with tank support and the heaviest anti-tank guns in the Hungarian arsenal, making them perhaps the best troops in the Honvéd.

Hungarian motorised infantry is organised the same way as Puskás Század with the addition of trucks for transport and different support options.

- The Company HQ must be equipped with a 1.5-ton Botond truck for +5 points.
- All Puskás Platoons must be upgraded to Rifle/MG teams and equipped with a 1.5 ton Botond truck per Puskás Squad for +5 points per squad.
- Mortar Platoons must add one 3-ton truck to each section apart from the HQ Section for +5 points per truck.
- Heavy Weapons Platoons must add two 3-ton trucks for +10 points.
- Machine-gun Platoons must add one 3-ton truck for +5 points.
- The anti-tank Platoon may replace all of its 37mm 36M (3.7cm PaK36) guns with 75mm 40M (7.5cm PaK40) guns for +75 points per anti-tank section.

Weapon Platoons available to a Gépkocsizó Lövész Század are:

- a Heavy Weapons Platoon,
- a Machine-gun Platoon, and
- a Mortar Platoon.

Support Platoons available to a Gépkocsizó Lövész Század are:

- an Anti-tank Platoon,
- a Motorcycle Scout Platoon,
- a Self-propelled Anti-aircraft Platoon,
- up to two Harckocsizó Platoons,
- a Heavy Harckocsizó Platoon,
- a Light Harckocsizó Platoon,
- Divisional Support Platoons,
- an allied German Grenadier Platoon,
- an allied German Anti-tank Gun Platoon,
- an allied German Tank-hunter Platoon,
- an allied German Assault Gun Platoon,
- an allied German Motorised Artillery Battery, and
- an allied German Panzer Platoon equipped with Panzer 38(t) tanks.

You can have no more than three Harckocsizó platoons of any type (Harckocsizó, Heavy Harckocsizó or Light Harckocsizó) supporting your company.

You may have **two** Support Platoons for each Rifle Platoon you field.

Motivation and Skill

A Gépkocsizó Lövész Század is rated as **Confident Trained**

Hungarian Companies have the following support platoons:

- a Light Anti-aircraft Platoon
- an Artillery Battery
- an Assault Pioneer Platoon

Motivation and Skill

Divisional support platoons are rated as **Confident Trained**.

Air Support

You may request Sporadic Air Support at a cost of +100 points. Sporadic Air Support will provide you supporting Junkers Ju87 ground-attack aircraft.

0 to 1 Light Anti-aircraft Platoon

Platoon

HQ Section with:

2 Anti-aircraft Sections	**65 points**

The Swedish 40mm 36M Bofors gun was the standard light anti-aircraft gun of the Hungarian army, but only six were available to each division. The improved anti-tank round they share with the 40mm 40M anti-tank gun makes them a handy asset against light armour breakthroughs.

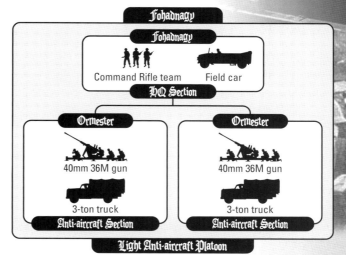

0 to 1 Artillery Batteries

Platoon

HQ Section with:

2 Gun Sections	**130 points**
1 Gun Section	**75 points**

Option

- Replace all 80mm 5/8M (75/27) guns with 100mm 14M (100/17) guns for +15 points per Gun Section, with 105mm 37M (10.5cm leFH18) guns for +20 points per Gun Section.
- Add horse-drawn limbers at no cost.
- Replace horse-drawn limbers with Hansa-Lloyd (Sd Kfz 11) half-tracks in 105mm 37M Gun Sections for +10 points per Gun Section and add a 3-ton truck to the HQ Section for +5 points.

Each infantry light division had one light field gun battery (80mm 5/8M) and three light howitzer batteries (100mm 14M) available.

The 1st Field Armoured Division had six light howitzer batteries available armed with the new German 105mm 37M howitzer.

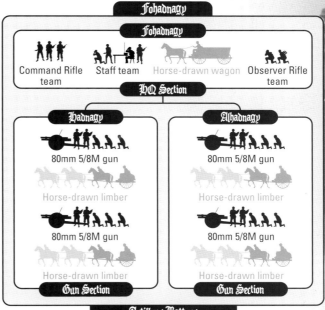

0 to 1 Assault Pioneer Platoons

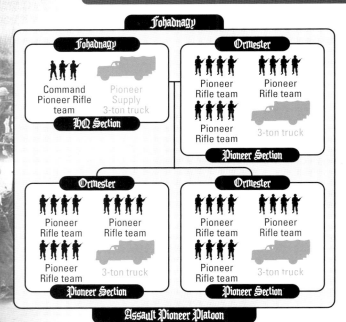

Fohadnagy

Fohadnagy

Command Pioneer Rifle team

Pioneer Supply 3-ton truck

HQ Section

Ormester

Pioneer Rifle team

Pioneer Rifle team

Pioneer Rifle team

3-ton truck

Pioneer Section

Ormester

Pioneer Rifle team

Pioneer Rifle team

Pioneer Rifle team

3-ton truck

Pioneer Section

Ormester

Pioneer Rifle team

Pioneer Rifle team

Pioneer Rifle team

3-ton truck

Pioneer Section

Assault Pioneer Platoon

Platoon

HQ Section with:

3 Pioneer Sections	**170 points**
2 Pioneer Sections	**120 points**
1 Pioneer Sections	**70 points**

Option

- Upgrade all Pioneer Rifle teams to Pioneer Rifle/MG teams for +10 points per Pioneer Section.

- Add 3-ton trucks for +5 points per section.

- Add a Pioneer Supply 3-ton truck to the HQ Section for +25 points.

The light divisions and 1st Armoured Division all had a compliment of combat engineers used to clear and lay mines, help in the preparation of defences, to perform demolition work and to provide specialist assault infantry to take prepared positions.

Excerpt from the diary of sottotenente Eugenio Braida, LXI gruppo artiglieria, 30° raggruppamento artiglieria di corpo d'armata, la Pasubio.

14 December 1942
It is coming soon. The Generals say that the Communists don't have enough men for another offensive, that the worst is past, but they said that before too. This storm which has engulfed the Germans at Stalingrad and swept away the Rumanians to the south is coming for us. Antonini lead a raid against the Communists opposite our positions here at Abrosimono. The Byelorussians who we had become acquainted with have been replaced by Uzbeks and Tartars. Fresh divisions, descendants of the Golden Horde of Mongolia. I do not think this will be like our little diversion in Yugoslavia. Oh for the bright days of Summer.

15 December 1942
A quiet day today. Maybe I was wrong. Very cold but sun shining weakly. Back on duty. Must go.

16 December 1942
Only time for a brief note, they came today, little warning. We are holding, flinging shell after shell from our old cannoni into the swarms of tanks and floods of men. We are not firing now, but I can hear the locomotive rumble as the army's cannoni da 149/40 and obici da 210/22 fire over us. Il signor maggiore Bellini tells us that things are bad, but that ARMIR is holding on, that we are doing Italia proud.

19 December 1942
Three days! Orders came today for la Pasubio, along with the rest of XXXV corpo d'armata, to pull back to Meshkov. We have held with honour, but the Hungarians to the north have failed, as did the Rumanians before them. Niente benzina, no diesel for the Fiats. We will have to leave many of the guns.

21 December 1942
We were joined by white-clad Germans today. Many trucks and sleighs, lots half empty, but I could not get a ride. Even wounded Italians could not get rides. Nothing to eat and water is from sucking snow, my socks are wet and I'm cold.

22 December 1942
We have finally stopped in Arbuzov and the vecchi, the veterans, are already calling this the Valley of Death. We have been hemmed in by the Communists and are freezing to death. If only we hadn't left behind all of the guns, we could return some of the fire. I have heard that Manstein is coming for us with his Panzers, I am sure they will come soon.

23 December 1942
With a cry of 'Savoia' we charged the Russians with our bayonets. Each man had only a few bullets, many less than a

full charge for their musket, but the Communists fell back before us! The Germans fell behind as we took the fore yelling 'avanti!' We broke through their lines, and out of that valley of suffering. Now we continue the retreat, past the shattered hulks of the Communist tanks.

26 December 1942
We arrived in Chertkovo today. The German 298th Division have taken up positions around the perimeter. The town is surrounded on three sides, but is open to the west, but we cannot go on. Today I saw the wings of our planes, the wings of home, the Patria, the wings of home. Our pilots risk everything, flying low to drop us supplies. I hear la Julia are coming. The alpini will get us out of here.

1 January 1943
Happy New Year! Sleep was difficult at 20 degrees below zero. My blanket was stiff as corrugated steel. We keep hay for the wounded. The cold is atrocious. Today I covered my head with my blanket and my balaclava was covered in ice, so all I could see was the beaten snow at my feet. Nearly hit by a Katyusha. I dived to the ground and prayed to Madonna as 16 shells landed in a straight line like hail.

4 January 1943
They came in waves again today. Their cries of 'Urrah' were met by the cries of 'Savoia!'. The chatter of our old Revelli 'knucklebuster', our only machine-gun, kept time for us as we fired into their mass and drove them off. Afterwards one of the men asked me 'Signor tenente, how much longer must we wait to break through them?' I found some potatoes. Put them in my pocket for later.

16 January 1943
I do not write as there is nothing to write. Cold, Communists, marching, death and dying. I had delirium on the march. I thought I was at a Swiss hotel and was about to lie down on the shiny white floor and sleep. We fought a battle against tanks today. The T-34's came out of a balka and the Katyushas dropped their presents among us. We fought back, our arditi cracking their tanks with grenades until a wave of picchiatelli arrived, the Germans call them Stuka. How we cheered! The picchiatelli dive-bombers swarmed in the sky, diving down and smashing the Communists, one after another they nose-dived down. We must be near our lines!

17 January 1943
We have made it! Broken out of the Russian encirclement! I hear that no-one made it out of the German pockets, but there were no Italians in those! I am waiting here at Streltsovka waiting for the trucks which will take us to Belvodsk and then to Starobelsk. Then home on warm trains, back to the Patria, back to Italia!

THE EXPEDITION TO RUSSIA

When Mussolini learned of the German attack on the Soviet Union, he quickly pledged Italian help in Hitler's 'crusade against Communism'. This aid took the form of the *Corpo di Spedizione Italiano in Russia (CSIR)*, the Italian Expeditionary Corps in Russia, of three divisions.

This force took part in numerous battles in 1941 and generally acquitted itself well. However, the winter of 1941/42 was bitterly cold and the Italians were as ill-prepared for it as their German allies. Soviet attacks combined with the sub-zero temperatures to cause heavy casualties.

By the Spring of 1942, it was obvious that the war in Russia would not be as easy a victory as the dictators had hoped, and that more troops would be needed. Italy reinforced the *CSIR* to form its Eighth Army, the *Armata Italiana in Russia, (ARMIR)* in the Ukraine in June 1942. *ARMIR* took part in the victorious drive to the Don River north of Stalingrad, defeating numerous Soviet forces en route.

As the German Sixth Army bogged down in Stalingrad, *ARMIR* went on the defensive covering a huge front between the Third Rumanian and Second Hungarian Armies. Divisional frontages were far too wide, but the lack of German forces to aid them meant that they had to be held with fewer men. On the Don River *ARMIR* faced and defeated several strong Soviet diversionary attacks as the weather worsened to another winter.

Disaster struck in late November 1942, when the Soviet Operation Uranus broke through the Rumanian lines to surround the German Sixth Army in Stalingrad. The gaping hole left in the German front line could only be filled by abandoning the Sixth Army and pulling Army Group B out of the Caucasus before the Soviets cut them off completely.

The Soviets had no intention of letting this happen and launched their follow-up Operation Little Saturn on 16 December 1942, smashing against the thinly-stretched Italian Army with waves of massed tank and infantry forces. Within days the Italian defence was broken through as lightly-equipped and immobile infantry divisions faced off against massed Soviet tanks. With no German Panzer divisions available to restore the line, there was little alternative but retreat.

Marching through deep snow in sub-zero temperatures, pursued by tanks, *ARMIR* disintegrated. By the time the lines stabilised in March, *ARMIR* had ceased to exist and the survivors returned to Italy. The needs of the war in North Africa and the subsequent invasion of Italy itself prevented any further Italian commitment to the Eastern Front.

The forces sent to Russia with *ARMIR* were largely infantry. The core of the force were the five infantry divisions. These were organised as normal with three rifle platoons per company and comparatively well supplied with motorised transport and artillery.

Unfortunately the absence of an Italian armoured division in the composition of *ARMIR* limited their direct tank support to the fifty-odd L6/40 light tanks of *LXVII battaglione corazzato* and the nineteen Semovente 47/32 self-propelled guns of the *Cavalleggeri di Alessandria*. The German *27. Panzerdivision*, equipped with a single battalion of outdated Panzer 38(t) tanks, could do little to remedy this deficiency.

However, at least one T-34 was captured in an operational state by the Italians and may have been used in combat. You could field this as part of a Compagnia Fucilieri by taking a Looted Panzer Platoon from page 86 of *Stalingrad*

In the field of anti-tank guns, the forces in Russia were actually better supplied than their comrades in the desert. Each division in Russia was issued six ex-German 7.5cm PaK38/97 anti-tank guns to protect them from Soviet tanks. In addition, several German anti-tank companies were assigned to the Italian divisions to increase their anti-tank power even further.

What they gained here, they lost out in heavy anti-aircraft weapons though.

The entire anti-aircraft arsenal of *ARMIR* was older 75mm guns, unsuitable for anti-tank work, and kept in the rear areas. None of the towed or self-propelled 88mm and 90mm guns that proved so devastating for anti-tank work in the desert were provided to the forces on the Eastern Front.

Despite its limitations in equipment, *ARMIR* proved itself capable of taking on and repeatedly beating Soviet infantry forces. Its anti-tank guns and artillery were enough to stop limited Soviet tank attacks. However no army lacking in medium and heavy tanks could reasonably be expected to halt an entire Soviet Tank Army, and such a force will prove a challenge on the tabletop as well.

The Italian Army In Russia, 1942-1943
ARMIR—Armata Italiana In Russia (Italian Army In Russia)

Unit	Battalions and Regiments
Raggruppamento Truppe Cavallo	3 Cavalry 'Savoia Cavalleria', 5 Cavalry 'Lancieri di Novara', 3 Horse Artillery
27. Panzerdivision (German)	
Corpo d'Armata Alpino (Alpine Corps)	
2ª Divisione Alpina 'Tridentina'	5 ('Morbegno', 'Tirano', 'Edolo'), 6 ('Verona', 'Vestone', 'Valchiese'), 2 Artillery ('Bergamo', 'Vicenza', ' Valcamonica')
3ª Divisione Alpina 'Julia'	8 ('Tolmezzo', 'Gemona', 'Cividale'), 9 (' L'Aquila', 'Vicenza', 'Val Cismon'), 3 Artillery ('Conegliano', 'Udine', 'Val Piave')
4ª Divisione Alpina 'Cuneense'	1 ('Ceva', 'Pieve di Teco', 'Mondovì'), 2 ('Borgo San Dalmazzo', 'Dronero', 'Saluzzo'), 4 Artillery ('Pinerolo', 'Mondovì', 'Val Po')
II Corpo d'Armata	
Raggruppamento CCNN '23 Marzo'	'Leonessa' (XIV, XV), 'Valle Scrivia' (V, XXXIV)
3ª Divisione da Montagna 'Ravenna'	37, 38, 11 Artillery
5ª Divisione Fanteria 'Cosseria'	89 & 90 'Salerno', 37 Artillery
XXXV Corpo d'Armata	
Raggruppamento CCNN '3 Gennaio'	'Montebello' (VI, XXX), 'Tagliamento' (LXIII, LXXIX)
9ª Divisione Autotrasportabile 'Pasubio'*	79 & 80 'Roma', 8 Artillery
298. Infanteriedivision (German)	
XXIX Armeekorps (German)	
3ª Divisione Celere	
'Principe Amedeo Duca d'Aosta'*	3 Bersaglieri (XIV, XXII), 6 Bersaglieri (VI, XIII), XLVII Motociclisti, LXVII Armoured Bersaglieri (L6/40), XIII 'Cavalleggeri di Alessandria' (Semovente 47/32), 120 Artillery, Croat Legion
2ª Divisione da Montagna 'Sforzesca'	53 & 54 'Umbria', 17 Artillery
52ª Divisione Autotrasportabile 'Torino'*	81, 82, 52 Artillery

* *Originally part of CSIR.*

Regiments are shown in Arabic numerals (1, 2, 3, etc.). Battalions are shown in Roman numerals (I, II, III, etc.). Unless noted a regiment bears the same name as its parent division. Most infantry regiments have two battalions (I and II) and a weapons battalion (III) unless otherwise noted.

raggruppamento = regiment, divisione = division, alpini = alpine, autotrasportabile = truck transportable, bersaglieri = light infantry, celere = fast, fanteria = infantry, montagna = mountain, truppe cavallo = cavalry troops, CCNN, camice nere = black shirts, fascist militia

Positioned between the Hungarians and the Rumanians, the Italian forces help push the Soviet forces back to the Don river.

The brave Italians defeat several Soviet diversionary attacks...

The Soviet forces kicked off Operation Little Saturn in December to smash through the Italian defences.

...While the Rumanian forces on the right flank are overwhelmed, and the German army at Stalingrad is surrounded, the Italians fight on.

With the lines stretched thin the under-equipped Italian forces disintegrate and the survivors head back to Italy.

Italian Special Rules

The Regio Esercito, the Royal Army, was unprepared for war in 1940, despite Mussolini's call for an army of '8 million bayonets'. The resulting force is very uneven—some officers are excellent, while others are simply abysmal, and the training of their soldiers and these special rules reflect this.

Avanti!

The Italian Army learned many lessons from the First World War. From the Germans they took the concept of speed and mobility in breakthrough operations. From the French they gained the techniques of methodical destruction of the enemy defences. The resulting doctrine emphasised mobile warfare and demanded rapid movement into contact with the enemy before bringing massive firepower to bear to open a gap and allow manoeuvre once more.

Any Italian platoon with a Command team may attempt an Avanti move at the start of its Shooting step instead of shooting. If a platoon attempts to make an Avanti move, it may not shoot even if fails to make an Avanti move.

Roll a Skill test for each platoon:

- *If the test is successful, the platoon may move another 4"/10cm,*
- *Otherwise the platoon cannot move this step.*

All of the normal rules apply for this movement. Platoons cannot make Avanti moves if they are Pinned Down or moved At the Double. Bogged Down or Bailed Out vehicles cannot make Avanti moves.

8 Million Bayonets

Mussolini demanded an army eight million strong to create his new Roman Empire. The rapid expansion needed for this led to reservist officers being recalled to the colours with little extra training. After 20 years of civilian life, some were still good soldiers, however most were not!

To reflect the variable quality of Italian officers, Italian platoons are rated as Regular, Elite, or Artillery. After deployment, but before the first turn, roll a die for each platoon and its attached teams and consult the 8 Million Bayonets table to determine their Training and Motivation characteristics.

Heroism

The Italian Army's lack of modern equipment gave its officers plenty of opportunities to display extreme *eroismo*, heroism, usually in extremis. Because these great deeds were usually fatal to the hero, it was impossible to know in advance who the heroes were, though if their comrades survived, their deeds would be enshrined in heroic prose and a medal sent to their dearest.

When your company first has a Command team Destroyed by the enemy, roll a Motivation test for that Command team. This test can never be re-rolled for any reason.

- *If they pass the Motivation test, the officer shrugs off his wounds, shouts encouragement to his men and a challenge to the enemy and fights on as an Unknown Hero.*
- *On any other roll, the Command team is Destroyed as normal and you roll again to discover your hero the next time a Command team is Destroyed.*

Once you have found your Unknown Hero, stop rolling. There can only be one Unknown Hero in your company in each game.

If the Unknown Hero is an Infantry team, bring the team back into play. If the Unknown Hero was a Tank team, the hero transfers to any other tank in his platoon that is within Command Distance making that the Platoon Command team. If no suitable tank is within Command Distance, the Unknown Hero is out of the battle and removed from the game.

An Unknown Hero and any platoon led by him always passes all Motivation tests on a roll of 2+. If the Unknown Hero is Destroyed while leading a platoon, the platoon will continue to take Motivation tests as if led by the Unknown Hero, although all other penalties for being Out Of Command still apply.

8 Million Bayonets

Roll	Regular	Elite	Artillery	CCNN
1	Reluctant Trained	Confident Trained	Confident Trained	Confident Conscript
2	Reluctant Trained	Confident Trained	Confident Veteran	Confident Conscript
3	Reluctant Trained	Confident Veteran	Confident Veteran	Confident Conscript
4	Confident Trained	Confident Veteran	Confident Veteran	Fearless Conscript
5	Confident Trained	Confident Veteran	Confident Veteran	Confident Trained
6	Fearless Conscript	Fearless Veteran	Fearless Veteran	Fearless Trained

Compagnia Fucilieri

(INFANTRY COMPANY)

Mussolini has called for 8 Million Bayonets and my countrymen you have answered. The strength and traditions of the fucilieri run in your veins as well as the admiration of your country. The eyes of the world are upon you. Sons of Italy make us proud!
—Colonello Carlo Stormo

A force based around a Compagnia Fucilieri must contain:

- a Company HQ,
- one to three Fucilieri Platoons.

Weapons Platoons available to a Compagnia Fucilieri are:

- a Machine-gun Platoon, and
- a Light Mortar Platoon.

Support Platoons for a Compagnia Fucilieri can be:

- two Mortar Platoons,
- a Regimental Gun Platoon,
- an Anti-tank Platoon,
- a Light Tank Platoon,
- a Self-propelled 47/32 Platoon,
- a Bersaglieri Platoon,
- a Light Anti-aircraft Platoon,
- Artillery Batteries,
- Demolisher Platoons,
- Alpini Platoons,
- an allied German Grenadier Platoon,
- an allied German Panzergrenadier Platoon,
- an allied German Anti-tank Gun Platoon,
- an allied German Artillery Battery.

You may have up to **two** Support Platoons attached to your company for each Fucilieri Platoon you field.

Motivation and Skill

The fucilieri, the riflemen, are the backbone of the Royal Army. They are not volunteers. They don't want to be heroes. They just want to win this war and return to their farms and villages. The combat and weapons platoons of a Compagnia Fucilieri are rated as **Regular**. Support platoons have the rating shown in their descriptions.

Air Support

You may request Sporadic Air Support at a cost of +100 points. Sporadic Air Support will provide you supporting Junkers Ju87 ground-attack aircraft.

HEADQUARTERS

1 Company HQ

Headquarters

Company HQ	25 points

Option

- Add Solothurn anti-tank rifles for +15 points per team.

A *capitano dei fucilieri* has a strong role to play in commanding his company-sized portion of the '8 million bayonets' demanded by Mussolini.

As the leader of your company it is up to you to show your men the way. To lead them into danger and out the other side to victory. Your courage and leadership at the critical point on the battlefield makes the difference between glorious victory and ignoble defeat.

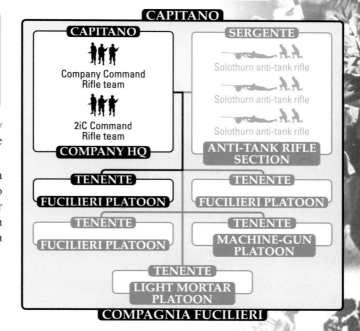

ITALIAN

COMBAT PLATOONS

1 to 3 Fucilieri Platoons

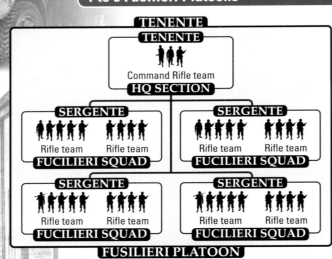

TENENTE
TENENTE
Command Rifle team
HQ SECTION

SERGENTE
Rifle team — Rifle team
FUCILIERI SQUAD

SERGENTE
Rifle team — Rifle team
FUCILIERI SQUAD

SERGENTE
Rifle team — Rifle team
FUCILIERI SQUAD

SERGENTE
Rifle team — Rifle team
FUCILIERI SQUAD

FUSILIERI PLATOON

Platoon

HQ Section with:

4 Fucilieri Squads	95 points
3 Fucilieri Squads	75 points
2 Fucilieri Squads	55 points

Options

- Arm all Rifle teams with Passaglia bombs for +5 points per team.
- Upgrade all Rifle teams to Rifle/MG teams for +5 points per Fucilieri Squad.

Armed with the old Carcano 91 rifle and a few new Breda 30 machine-guns, the *fucilieri* must rely on their courage more than on technology.

WEAPONS PLATOONS

0 to 1 Machine-gun Platoon

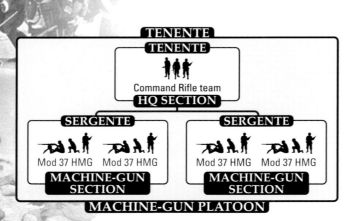

TENENTE
TENENTE
Command Rifle team
HQ SECTION

SERGENTE
Mod 37 HMG — Mod 37 HMG
MACHINE-GUN SECTION

SERGENTE
Mod 37 HMG — Mod 37 HMG
MACHINE-GUN SECTION

MACHINE-GUN PLATOON

Platoon

HQ Section with:

2 Machine-gun Sections	95 points
1 Machine-gun Section	55 points

The *8mm Breda modello 37* machine gun laid down an impressive 450 rounds a minute, a big improvement over the old unreliable FIAT-Revelli *modello 35* (nicknamed the 'knuckle-buster' for its exposed recoil mechanism!)

In the hands of an adept gunner, a withering hail of fire could be maintained to support the advancing *fucilieri*.

0 to 1 Light Mortar Platoon

Platoon

HQ Section with:

3 Mortar Sections	175 points
2 Mortar Sections	120 points
1 Mortar Section	65 points

The *45mm Brixia modello 35* light mortar is designed to provide covering fire for the *fucilieri* right up to the point of assault. Unlike machine-guns and medium mortars that have to cease firing early to avoid hitting their own troops, the Brixia fires its small grenades over the attacking infantry allowing it to keep firing until the last few seconds before the assault. This makes the Brixia perfect for supporting infantry assaults.

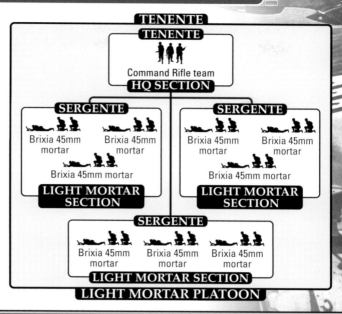

SUPPORT PLATOONS

0 to 2 Mortar Platoons

Platoon

HQ Section with:

3 Mortar Sections	80 points
2 Mortar Sections	60 points

Rated as Regular.

The long-ranged *Mortaio da 81/14 modello 35* is available in sufficient numbers to give the fucilieri excellent close artillery support. This mortar is great at breaking up attacks and pinning down enemy defenders making them welcomed by all *fucilieri* company commanders.

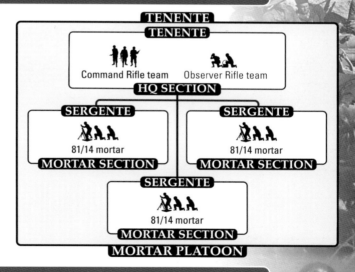

0 to 1 Regimental Gun Platoon

Platoon

HQ Section with:

2 Gun Sections	85 points
1 Gun Section	50 points

Options

• Add Gun shields to all 65/17 guns for +5 points per Gun Section. 65/17 guns with Gun shields are Heavy guns rather than Light guns.

Rated as Regular.

The *Cannone da 65/17 modello 13* was originally a mountain gun, able to be broken into small loads for transport. Now it is an infantry gun to give the *fucilieri* close-up fire support.

ITALIAN

0 to 1 Anti-tank Platoon

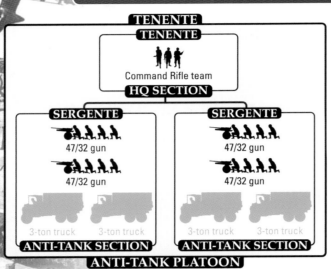

TENENTE
TENENTE
Command Rifle team
HQ SECTION

SERGENTE
47/32 gun
47/32 gun
3-ton truck   3-ton truck
ANTI-TANK SECTION

SERGENTE
47/32 gun
47/32 gun
3-ton truck   3-ton truck
ANTI-TANK SECTION

ANTI-TANK PLATOON

Platoon
HQ Section with:

2 Gun Sections	115 points
1 Gun Section	65 points

Options
- Replace all 47/32 guns with 75/39 (German 7.5cm PaK97/38) guns and add 3-ton trucks for +20 points per Gun Section.

You may not field more than one Anti-tank Platoon equipped with 75/39 guns in any force.

Rated as Regular.

While most units had the Italian 47/32 gun, less fortunate ones made do with the German 37/45 guns. On the Russian front these were backed by heavier German 75/39 anti-tank guns.

0 to 3 Light Tank Platoons

TENENTE
TENENTE
Command L6/40 tank   L6/40 tank
HQ SECTION

SERGENTE
L6/40 tank   L6/40 tank
LIGHT TANK SECTION

SERGENTE
L6/40 tank   L6/40 tank
LIGHT TANK SECTION

LIGHT TANK PLATOON

Platoon

6 L6/40	200 points
5 L6/40	165 points
4 L6/40	130 points
3 L6/40	95 points

Rated As Elite.

The 6-ton L6/40 light tank was produced in 1940 as the successor to the old L3/35 tankette. The small L6/40 was armed with a 20mm gun with a coaxial 8mm gun making it ideal for reconnaissance groups where mobility matters more than firepower.

0 to 1 Self-propelled 47/32 Platoon

Platoon

4 Semovente 47/32	195 points
3 Semovente 47/32	145 points
2 Semovente 47/32	95 points

Option

- Arm any or all Semovente 47/32 assault guns with an AA MG for +5 points per assault gun.

Rated as Elite.

The *Semovente da 47/32* is a mobile infantry-support weapon, perfect for knocking out machine-gun nests holding up the infantry advance. The semovente is also useful as an anti-tank weapon against light tanks.

0 to 1 Bersaglieri Platoon

Platoon

HQ Section with:

3 Bersaglieri Squads	150 points
2 Bersaglieri Squads	105 points

Options

- Arm all Rifle/MG teams with Passaglia bombs for +5 points per team.

Rated as Elite.

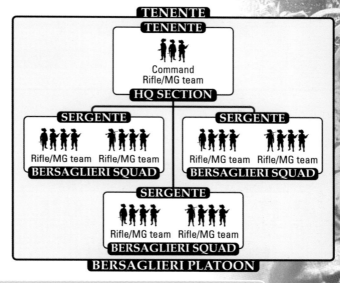

General Rommel said 'The German soldier impressed the world, the Italian bersaglieri impressed the German soldier!'

The platoon is armed with Breda machine-guns, *bombe Passaglia*, and *bottiglia incendiaria*, Molotov Cocktails, but the absolute dedication of his men is a greater asset to the Tenente.

You may upgrade your Bersaglieri Platoon to a Motociclisti Platoon. If you do so you may add a fourth Bersaglieri squad for +40 points. All Motociclisti Rifle/MG teams must be equipped with motorcycles for +5 points per teams. This makes them into Cavalry teams except that Motociclisti mounted on motorcycles cannot Launch an Assault, and they move as a Jeep team rather than a Cavalry team.

0 to 1 Light Anti-aircraft Platoon

Platoon

HQ Section with:

2 Gun Sections	75 points

Rated as Artillery

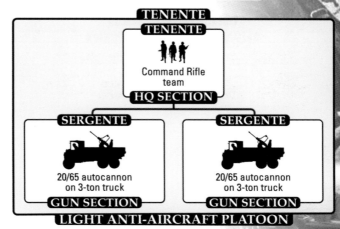

The anti-aircraft company keeps enemy aircraft at bay, protecting the vulnerable artillery and tanks, allowing them to destroy the enemy undisturbed.

In mobile operations the guns fire from the back of their trucks, but dismount in static battles.

Artillery Batteries

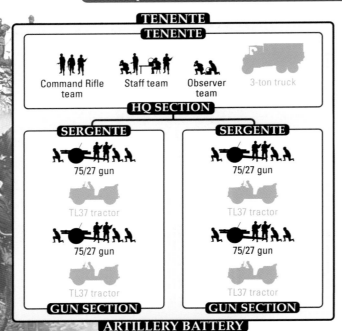

Platoon

HQ Section with:

2 Gun Sections	190 points
1 Gun Section	110 points

Options

- Replace all 75/27 guns with 100/17 howitzers for +20 points per Gun Section.
- Add 3-ton truck and TL37 tractors to the platoon at no cost.

Rated As Artillery

The *artiglieria*, artillery, of the Second World War used the guns that their fathers fired in the First World War. These guns are still the equal of any artillery in the world. The Italian *artigliere* tenaciously fights to the last to preserve the good name of Italy.

Demolisher Platoon

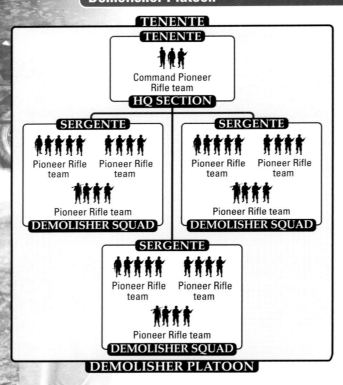

Platoon

HQ Section with:

3 Demolisher Squads	250 points
2 Demolisher Squads	175 points
1 Demolisher Squad	100 points

Options

- Upgrade all Rifle teams to Rifle/MG teams for +5 points for the HQ Section and +10 points per Demolisher Squad.

Rated As Elite

The traditions of the *Arditi del Genio*, the assault engineers of the First World War, were resurrected in the Second World War under the honoured name *Guastatori*, demolishers, used since the time of Napoleon.

Organised into companies with names like *Valanga* (vah-lahn-gah, Avalanche), the *Guastatori* led assaults against fortified positions in every theatre. Their battle cry was '*Varco!*', 'Passage!'.

> You may replace up to one Pioneer Rifle team per Demolisher Squad with a Flame-thrower team at the start of the game before deployment.

Compagnia Alpini

(MOUNTAIN COMPANY)

A Compagnia Alpini is based on a Compagnia Fucilieri with the changes listed below. Because the Alpini are rated as **Elite** rather than **Regular**, the cost of each platoon previously rated as **Regular** increases by +10 points for a Company HQ or HQ Section and +10 points for each Squad or Section in the platoon.

A force based around a Compagnia Alpini must contain:

- a Company HQ.
- two to three Alpini Platoons. These are identical to the Fucilieri Platoons. However, they must be upgraded to Rifle/MG teams.

Weapons Platoons available to a Compagnia Alpini are:

- a Machine-gun Platoon, and
- a Light Mortar Platoon.

Support Platoons for a Compagnia Alpini can be:

- a Mortar Platoon (note this is fewer than allowed in a Compagnia Fucilieri),
- a Regimental Gun Platoon (may have a Packhorse team per gun at no cost),
- up to two Anti-tank Platoons,
- Bersaglieri Platoons

- a Light Tank Platoon,
- a Self-propelled 47/32 Platoon
- a Light Anti-Aircraft Platoon. The 3-ton trucks may be replaced by horse-drawn limbers for -10 points per platoon.
- Artillery Batteries. Trucks may not be added to 75mm guns, but Packhorse teams may be used at no additional cost. Treat these as horse-drawn limber teams.
- a Demolisher Platoon

A Compagnia Alpini may have **two** Support Platoons attached for each Alpini Platoon you field.

Motivation and Skill

The Alpini embody a distinguished fighting tradition, proudly maintained by the hand-picked and well-trained troops that comprise its ranks.

Officers who have served in the Alpini often wear the distinctive headgear for the rest of their careers, even when commanding other units. The platoons of a Compagnia Alpini are rated as **Elite,** unless they are rated as Artillery.

Alpine Elite

The Alpini developed considerable skill in dealing with mountainous terrain and even the support weapons in their divisions were designed to be carried by hand or pack animals into and over precipitous terrain. Even pack howitzers could be dismantled, transported via winches and ropes and put together again with astonishing speed.

Alpini Infantry teams and Gun teams carried by Packhorse teams can attempt to cross Impassable cliffs and similar obstacles. To do so they must start their Movement step adjacent to the obstacle and not be Pinned Down. Roll a Skill Test for each team instead of moving in the Movement step.

- If the test is successful the team crosses the obstacle, halting on the other side.
- If the team failed the test it remains where it was.

A team that attempts to cross an Impassable obstacle this way cannot shoot this turn, though it can assault.

ITALIAN

(INFANTRY COMPANY)

A Centuria CCNN (Black Shirt Century) is organized the same as the Compagnia Fucilieri.

Motivation and Skill

You can either field them as one of the better 'M' Battalions using the normal **Regular** rating on the 8 Million Bayonets table or as one of the more enthusiastic, but less trained battalions using **CCNN** rating.

Miniatures and Uniforms

The CCNN can be easily fielded using the Fucilieri Miniatures with no modifications. Just paint any exposed shirts black rather than light grey-green.

Instead of the bustina side cap, it was common for CCNN troops to be issued with a black fez. Officers often wore a black bustina.

Trousers or pantaloons often had a narrow black stripe running down the sides.

Italian Terminology

Alpini (ahl-pee-nee): Mountain troops.

ARMIR, Armata Italiana In Russia (ahrr-meerr): Italian Army in Russia, the Italian 8th Army.

Artiglieria (ahr-tee-yearr-ee-ah): Artillery.

Avanti Savoia (ah-vahn-tee sah-voi-ah): Forward Savoy! Savoy is the royal house of Italy.

Bersaglieri (bearr-sah-yearr-ee): Elite light infantry renowned for marching at the run.

Bombe Passaglia (bohm-beh pahs-sah-yee-ah): Anti-tank grenade designed by Passaglia, an engineer officer. Basically a minestrone tin full of explosives ignited by a hand grenade.

CA,'Corpo d'Armata (korr-poh dahrr-mah-tah): Army corps.

ca, Contraerea (kohn-trah-eh-reh-ah): Anti-aircraft.

cc, Controcarro (kohn-troh karr-roh): Anti-tank.

CCNN, Camice Nere: (kah-mee-cheh neh-reh): Black Shirts, the armed forces of the Fascist Party.

Capitano (kah-pee-tah-noh): Captain.

Compagnia (kom-pan-yee-ah): Company.

CSIR, Corpo Spedizione In Russia (chee-seerr): Expeditionary Corps In Russia in 1941.

Divisione Autotrasportabile (dee-vee-see-ohn-eh ow-toh-trahs-porr-tah-bee-leh): Infantry division ready for truck transport.

Divisione Celere (dee-vee-see-ohn-eh cheh-leh-reh): Fast or cavalry division.

Divisione Fanteria (dee-vee-see-ohn-eh fahn-teh-ree-ah): Infantry division.

Divisione da Montagna (dee-vee-see-ohn-eh dah mohn-tah-nyah): Mountain division.

Fantaccino (fahn-tah-chee-noh): Nickname for rifleman.

Fascio (fah-shoh): Fasces. Bundle of sticks and an axe. Symbol of Italian Fascist Party. Previously symbol of the power of a Roman senator carried by his lictor.

Fucilieri (foo-chee-lyearr-ee): Riflemen.

Guastatori (gwah-stah-torr-ee): Demolishers. Assault engineers.

I Mussolini (ee moos-soh-lee-nee): The Mussolinis. Disparaging name for CCNN 'M' battalions.

Il novantuno (eel noh-vahn-too-noh) The Ninety-one. Nickname for standard Carcano model 1891 rifle.

Italia (Ee-tah-lee-ah): Italy.

Lanciafiamme (lahn-chee-ah-fee-ahm-meh): Flame-thrower.

Mitraglieri (mee-trah-yearr-ee): Machine-gun.

Modello (moh-dehl-loh): Model.

Mortaio (morr-tai-oh): Mortar.

Picchiatello (peek-kee-ah-tehl-loh): Nutter. Nickname for Ju87 dive bomber playing on the Italian word for diver.

Raggruppamento (rahg-groop-pah-mehn-toh): Artillery group.

Semovente (say-moh-ven-teh): Self-propelled gun.

Solothurn (soh-loh-toornn): Maker of anti-tank rifle.

Tenente (teh-nehn-teh): Lieutenant.

ARMATA REGALĂ ROMÂNĂ
ROMANIAN FORCES

Background

During the 1930's, Rumania boasted a huge but obsolescent army, firmly tied to the doctrines that had evolved from the First World War, particularly those of her close ally, France. King Carol of Romania embarked on modest programmes of reform, but the army remained poorly equipped, particularly in terms of motor transport, communications equipment, and anti-tank weapons.

In 1940, the situation changed dramatically. France fell, the Soviet Union occupied the Romanian province of Bessarabia and land was also lost to Hungary and Bulgaria. King Carol abdicated and hard-line General Ion Antonescu became *Conducator* or Leader. Romania saw its best means of survival being allegiance with Germany. A German training mission was sent in October 1940 in an effort to modernise the Romanian Army and met with some success with the Romanian infantry, but resistance from other branches, particularly the artillery.

The core of the army lay in 18 infantry divisions and one Guard and one Frontier division, each comprising three infantry and two artillery regiments, plus signals, engineer and reconnaissance troops.

Each infantry regiment had three (later reduced to two) infantry battalions, plus support in the form of cavalry, mortars and a very modest allocation of anti-tank weapons. Regiments were numbered 1 to 33 and 81 to 96, with the former group bearing the traditional honorific *Dorobanti*. Some divisions contained *Vanatori* rifle regiments, these being identical in organisation to the infantry regiments.

The cavalry and mountain brigades were expanded to full divisions in March 1942, while the single armoured brigade became the nucleus for an armoured division.

Barbarossa

On 22 June 1941, the German Army launched Operation *Barbarossa*, the invasion of the Soviet Union. Seeing an opportunity to regain lost territory, Romania declared war on the Soviet Union and the army's best units were committed to the campaign.

Romanian divisions served with the German 11th, 30th and 54th Corps in the German 11th Army, as well as forming the separate Romanian 3rd and 4th Armies. These forces took part in Operation *München*, which began on 2 July.

Romanian and German forces advanced rapidly driving the Soviet forces out of Bessarabia and Northern Bukovina within a mônth at the cost of over 4,000 dead, 12,000 wounded

and 5,500 missing. Rumania had succeeded in its limited war aims.

Odessa

Germany, however, demanded further Romanian assistance and Romanian troops were committed to the capture of the vital Black Sea port of Odessa. By 13 August, Odessa had been isolated on its landward side, but assaulting Romanian troops made slow progress. The Soviet garrison swelled to over 86,000 men by early October and the attacking Romanian 4th Army required heavy reinforcement.

The besieging force eventually involved 17 infantry divisions, a reserve division, the armoured division, and Guards, Frontier and cavalry as well as several German units. Steady pressure saw the Romanians capture Odessa on 16 October, rounding up 7,000 stragglers following a skilful Soviet naval evacuation of the bulk of the garrison.

This significant feat of arms in storming a Soviet 'Hero City' was almost entirely a Romanian operation, but came at a heavy cost, with total losses of 17,729 dead, 63,345 wounded and 11,471 missing. However serious deficiencies in tactics and equipment had been exposed.

Crimean Operations

While the Romanian 3rd Army was deployed to assist German 11th Army,

engaged in operations up to the Dnepr, the 3rd Army's Cavalry Corps and the Mountain Corps assisted in the assault on the Crimea.

Having secured most of the Crimea, Romanian units were outflanked by a Soviet landing at Feodosiya in January 1942 which created a substantial bridgehead in the Kerch Peninsula. Additional units from VII Corps were committed to contain the Kerch bridgehead, finally wiping it out in May.

X Mountain Corps then participated in the assault on Sevastopol in June 1942, with the 1st Mountain Division taking the crucial Sugar Loaf position and 4th Mountain Division capturing over 10,000 prisoners at Balaclava.

Stalingrad Campaign

While the fighting in Crimea contin ued, German pressure for Romanian troops to remain at the front saw VI Corps placed under the command of the German Army Group South from January to April 1942.

In May, while preparing for their own offensive, the 1st and 4th Divisions of VI Corps were hit by a new Soviet offensive south of Kharkov. They were badly shaken by the heavy Soviet tanks against which they had no answer, but held the line until a German Panzer counterattack restored the situation.

The corps then formed part of 4th Panzer Army for the summer offensive toward Stalingrad, before engaging in heavy fighting as the southern flank of the German defensive line around the city in September. There they were joined by VII Corps to form a new 4th Army making the Romanian contribution to the Axis third largest behind Germany and Italy.

In October 1942, the 3rd Army with newly reorganised and re-equipped divisions, veterans of the Odessa Campaign, moved into the line in the open steppe along the Don River, north of Stalingrad. There they repulsed numerous Soviet attacks throughout the month. However, lacking motorised transport, they were desperately short of ammunition and supplies including barbed wire and mines.

To the Black Sea

While most of the army advanced to the Don, the Cavalry Corps operated with German forces along the coast of the Sea of Azov, reaching the Black Sea on 12 September 1943, captur ing the port of Anapa and trapping the Soviet 47th Army.

The 10th and 19th Infantry Divisions and 2nd and 3rd Mountain Divisions then crossed the straits from Crimea and Mountain Division, capturing the city of Nalchik, taking 7,000 Soviet prisoners in the process.

Disaster on the Don

3rd Army was hit by a massive Soviet assault on 19 November 1942, as several Soviet guards and tank armies sought to outflank Stalingrad. Romanian resistance proved stronger than the Soviets had planned on and their losses were high. Despite this, Soviet armoured spearheads broke through the 9th, 14th and 13th Divisions, surrounded the 5th, 6th, 13th, 14th and 15th Divisions, and forced others to fall back.

A counterattack by the 1st Armoured division could not stop the massive Soviet offensive, but did protect several other divisions from encirclement. The surrounded Romanian pocket held out until 25 November before finally surrendering for the loss of 27,000 men. Despite this setback, 1st Armoured and 7th Cavalry Divisions with the remnants of the 14th and 15th Divisions stabilised the front on the Chir River, staving off further disaster.

Meanwhile, 4th Army to the south of Stalingrad was assaulted on 20 November, losing the 1st and 4th Divisions overrun at heavy cost in Soviet tanks. The remnants of these divisions withdrew with the 2nd and 18th Divisions, covered by the superb 8th Cavalry Division. However the 20th Infantry Division remained trapped with the German 6th Army in Stalingrad.

Romanian and German units counter attacked on 12 December to relieve Stalingrad, but on 18 December, Soviet armour broke through the Italian 8th Army, surrounding and

destroying I Corps. VI and VII Corps began to disintegrate under the pressure of the new Soviet offensive, and the survivors were withdrawn to Rumania in February 1943.

The disaster on the Don cost Rumania two-thirds of its field army. Romanian bravery (three generals were killed leading bayonet charges) had proved unable to compensate for a lack of appropriate equipment.

Kuban Bridgehead

The Stalingrad disaster forced a retreat from the Caucasus into the Kuban bridgehead around the Taman Peninsula. Morale in the infantry divisions fell and they were dispersed among German units, but the cavalry and mountain formations remained effective and were regarded as good troops. The 80,000 Romanian troops in the Kuban suffered heavy losses before being withdrawn to the Crimea in October 1943.

Their respite was brief for the Crimea was cut off in November 1943. In hard fighting the 6th Cavalry and 3rd Mountain Divisions wiped out a Soviet naval landing on the Kerch Peninsula, taking over 2,000 prisoners. However Soviet forces broke through the main defensive lines on 14 April 1944. 60,000 Romanian troops were evacuated from Sevastopol, leaving over 20,000 men and all of their heavy equipment behind.

Changing Sides

Soviet forces now pushed into Romanian territory, pushing German and Romanian defenders back, and while Romanian units resisted strongly, the situation became untenable. Rumania defected, with Antonescu being arrested on 23 August and war declared on Germany on 25 August.

Fierce fighting broke out and operations to clear Romania proved effective, capturing or eliminating over 61,000 Germans for the loss of 8,586 Romanians. Soviet forces (including the 'Tudor Vladimirescu' Division consisting of Romanian ex-prisoners of war) flooded into Rumania and by September, had joined Romanian forces along the Hungarian and Yugoslavian borders.

For the remainder of the war, Romanian forces passed under Soviet control and were often poorly treated, but fought hard against Hungarian and German forces, with over 538,536 Romanians fighting against the Axis, a contribution ranking fourth behind the USSR, USA and Great Britain. Casualties were very heavy, over 160,000 before the final peace in May 1945.

Timoshenko's counterattack crashes into the Romanian lines in the Ukraine.

The infantry face tanks with their bare hands.

R-2 tanks (and a captured T-26) counterattack to drive off the Soviets.

Romanian combined arms attacks break into the Soviet position.

T-4 tanks cannot halt the Red hordes.

The counterattacking Soviet T-34 tanks are unstoppable, driving the infantry back.

Peasant Army

Romania's huge army was drawn from the rural peasant class, officered by the aristocratic upper class, and disciplined by NCO's using 18th century style corporal punishment. Men were regularly beaten for minor breaches in regulation and discipline. The separation of men, NCO's, and officers even went as far as meals that were supplied in three qualities, with officers, naturally, getting the best. The officers were also responsible for the training of their own units, this lead to a great variation in the quality of troops combat preparedness. The distant relationship between the officers and their largely illiterate men combined with the harsh conditions of army life, and sometimes poor training, lead to mixed level of performance and morale in the field.

> *To reflect the variable quality of the men and officers' relationship and performance, Romanian platoons are rated as Regular or Elite. After deployment, but before the first turn, roll a die for each platoon and its attached teams and consult the Peasant Army table to determine their Training and Motivation characteristics.*

Peasant Army Table

Roll	Regular	Elite
1	Reluctant Trained	Reluctant Trained
2	Reluctant Trained	Reluctant Veteran
3	Reluctant Veteran	Reluctant Veteran
4	Confident Trained	Confident Trained
5	Confident Trained	Confident Veteran
6	Confident Veteran	Confident Veteran

Defend the Homeland

Though the Romanian infantryman may have mixed treatment from his officers and NCO's once in the thick of the fighting he would often fight tenaciously when confronted by the enemy. They were not interested in invading Russia or conquering the world, but to simply fight stubbornly to defend what they already have.

> *Romanian platoons use the British Bulldog special rule.*

French Doctrine

The Romanian troops are trained in the French doctrine of trench warfare. Their operational plan is to make a short deliberate advance under cover of massed artillery fire, then fortify their position to hold it while the artillery comes up to repeat the process. While the advance is slow, it is sure and will eventually result in the defeat of the enemy.

Once entrenched, Romanian infantry set up crossfire positions for every weapon allowing them to take any attack in enfilade.

> *When entrenched in Foxholes or Gun Pits, Romanian Gun teams can shoot over any Romanian Infantry team in Foxholes or Trenches, whether it shoots or not, when conducting Defensive Fire*

Central Fire Control

Like the US Army, the Romanians were great followers of French doctrine during the 1920's and 1930's and their artillery methods reflect this.

When a Romanian Observer places a request for fire, the artillery battalion fire direction centre assesses its priority and assigns all available artillery batteries to fire the mission. This ensures that the battalion's artillery resources are used in the most efficient manner. However, everything must go through the proper channels with properly trained officers directing the artillery fire.

> *Romanian Company Command teams cannot act as spotting teams for artillery bombardments.*
>
> *Romanian Artillery Batteries use the US Hit 'em With Everything You've Got special rule.*

AC, Aruncatoare (ah-roon-kah-toh-ahr-eh): Mortar.

Armata Regală Română (ahr-mah-tah reh-gah-ler roh-muhn-er): Royal Romanian Army.

Capitan (kah-pee-tahn): Captain.

Cari de Lupta (kah-ree deh loop-tah): Battle wagon, tank.

Companie Cari de Lupta (kohm-pahn-ee kah-ree deh loop-tah): Tank company.

Companie Puscasi (kohm-pahn-ee pooss-kahs-see): Rifle company.

Companie Vanatori de Munte (kom-pahn-ee vah-nah-tor-ee deh moon-teh): Mountain infantry company.

Companie Vanatori Motorizata (kom-pah-nee vah-nah-tor-ee moh-toh-ree-zah-tah): Motorised infantry company.

Locotenent (loh-koh-teh-nehnt): Lieutenant.

Malaxa (mah-lahks-ah): Romanian armaments manufacturer.

Sergent (sehr-gehnt): Sergeant.

Sublocotenent (soob-loh-koh-teh-nehnt): Second lieutenant.

TAC, Tun Anticar (toon ahn-tee-kahr): Anti-tank gun.

Vanator de Care (vah-nah-torr deh kahr-eh): Tank-hunter.

Vanatori (vah-nah-tor-ee): Hunter, light infantry.

Companie Cari de Lupta

(TANK COMPANY)

A force based around a Companie Cari de Lupta must contain:

- a Company HQ, and
- two to five Cari de Lupta Platoons

Support Platoons available to a Companie Cari de Lupta are:

- an Armoured Car Platoon,
- a Motorised Anti-tank Platoon,
- Vanatori Motorizata Platoons,
- Divisional Support Platoons,
- an allied German Grenadier Platoon,
- an allied German Anti-tank Gun Platoon,

- an allied German Motorised Artillery Battery, and
- an allied German 1942 Panzer Platoon.

You may have **two** Support Platoons for each Cari de Lupta Platoon you field.

Motivation and Skill

The armoured troops of the Romanian army, while not always equipped with the best, were always well motivated and trained. A Companie Cari de Lupta is rated as **Elite**.

HEADQUARTERS

1 Company HQ

Headquarters

Company HQ	45 points

Option

- Replace R-2 (Panzer 35(t)) tank with T-3 (Panzer III N) tank for +40 points, or T-4 (Panzer IV G, early) tank for +80 points.

You must have at least one Cari de Lupta platoon equipped with the same type of tank as the Company HQ.

The Tankers are ably supported by armoured cars to find the gaps in the defences, motorized infantry to hold the gaps created and to rapidly move to support the tankers, and motorised anti-tank gunners who can quickly get to where they are needed to support the attack.

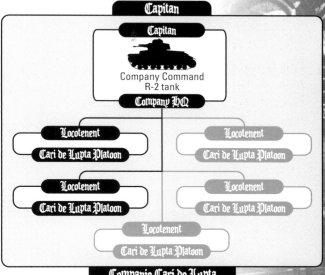

Capitan

Capitan

Company Command
R-2 tank

Company HQ

Locotenent — Cari de Lupta Platoon

Locotenent — Cari de Lupta Platoon

Locotenent — Cari de Lupta Platoon

Locotenent — Cari de Lupta Platoon

Locotenent — Cari de Lupta Platoon

Companie Cari de Lupta

COMBAT PLATOONS

2 to 5 Cari de Lupta Platoons

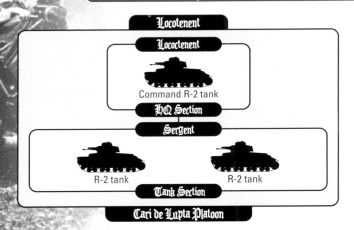

Locotenent

Locotenent

Command R-2 tank

HQ Section

Sergent

R-2 tank

R-2 tank

Tank Section

Cari de Lupta Platoon

Platoon

3 R-2	140 points

Option

- Replace all R-2 (Panzer 35(t)) tanks with T-3 (Panzer III N) tanks for +120 points per platoon, or T-4 (Panzer IV G, early) tanks for +225 points per platoon.

  You may not equip more than three platoons with T-3 or T-4 tanks

Romanian tankers are equipped with a hundred Czech-designed R-2 tanks backed up by the heavy firepower of a company each of excellent German-supplied T-3 (Panzer III N) and T-4 (Panzer IV G) tanks.

SUPPORT PLATOONS

0 to 1 Armoured Car Platoon

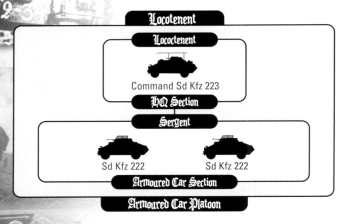

Locotenent

Locotenent

Command Sd Kfz 223

HQ Section

Sergent

Sd Kfz 222

Sd Kfz 222

Armoured Car Section

Armoured Car Platoon

Platoon

Sd Kfz 223 (radio) with:

2 Sd Kfz 222	100 points
1 Sd Kfz 222	65 points

An Armoured Car Platoon is a Reconnaissance Platoon.

Armed with modern light armoured cars supplied by the Germans these elite troops stealthily probe the Soviet front line looking for gaps for their tankers to exploit.

0 to 1 Motorised Anti-tank Platoon

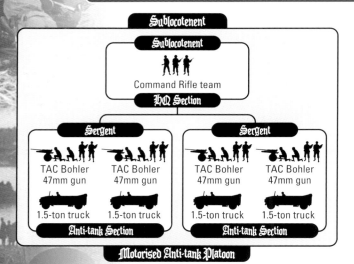

Sublocotenent

Sublocotenent

Command Rifle team

HQ Section

Sergent

TAC Bohler 47mm gun

TAC Bohler 47mm gun

1.5-ton truck

1.5-ton truck

Anti-tank Section

Sergent

TAC Bohler 47mm gun

TAC Bohler 47mm gun

1.5-ton truck

1.5-ton truck

Anti-tank Section

Motorised Anti-tank Platoon

Platoon

HQ Section with:

2 Anti-tank Sections	130 points
1 Anti-tank Section	70 points

Options

- Replace all TAC Bohler 47mm (47/32) guns to TAC 938 50mm (5cm PaK38) guns for +15 points per Anti-tank Section.
- Replace all 1.5-ton trucks with Malaxa (Renault UE) carriers for +5 points per Anti-tank Section.

Motorised anti-tank platoons tow their TAC Bohler 47 mm guns with modern trucks, so they can easily keep up with the fast moving tanks.

(INFANTRY COMPANY)

A force based around a Companie Vanatori Motorizata must contain:

- A Company HQ, and
- two or three Vanatori Motorizata Platoons.

Weapon Platoons available to a Companie Vanatori Motorizata are:

- two Motorised Machine-gun Platoons, and
- a Motorised Mortar Platoon.

Support Platoons available to a Companie Vanatori Motorizata are:

- two Cari de Lupta Platoons,
- two Motorised Anti-tank Platoons,
- Divisional Support Platoons,

- an allied German Grenadier Platoon,
- an allied German Anti-tank Gun Platoon, and
- an allied German Motorised Artillery Battery

You may have **two** Support Platoons for each Vanatori Motorizata Platoon you field.

Motivation and Skill

The vanatori of the Armoured Division are the best and most experienced troops in the Royal Army. Having acted as a fire brigade, racing from crisis to crisis whenever the infantry cannot handle the situation alone. A Companie Vanatori Motorizata is rated as **Elite**.

HEADQUARTERS

1 Company HQ

Headquarters

Company HQ	35 points

Options

- Replace any or all Command Rifle teams with Command Vanator de Care Rifle team for +5 points.
- Add 60mm Brandt mortars to Company HQ for +25 points each.

A Romanian Companie Puscasi has lots of firepower to pound and pulverise the Soviets, supported by light to heavy mortars and lots of crack artillery. And when the Russians' attack gets close to our infantry the well dug in HMG's will provide crossfire support. Any Soviet tanks will think twice about coming near our ace anti-tank gunners, while their aircraft steer clear of the anti-aircraft support we have.

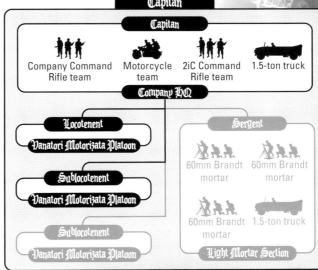

COMBAT PLATOONS

2 or 3 Vanatori Motorizata Platoons

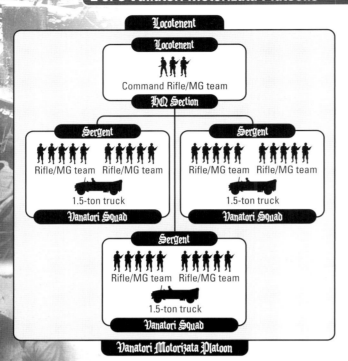

Platoon

HQ Section with:

3 Vanatori Squads	130 points
2 Vanatori Squads	95 points

Options

- Replace Command Rifle/MG team with a Command Vanator de Care Rifle/MG team for +5 points.
- Replace all 1.5-ton trucks with a motorcycle and sidecar team per Rifle/MG team for +5 points per Vanatori Squad.

Elite motorized infantry will to hold the positions taken by the tanks, as well as rapidly moving to support them. They ferret out the Russian anti-tank guns and deal with them. Highly motivated they will attack on the move, almost before their trucks have even stopped.

WEAPONS PLATOONS

0 to 2 Motorised Machine-gun Platoons

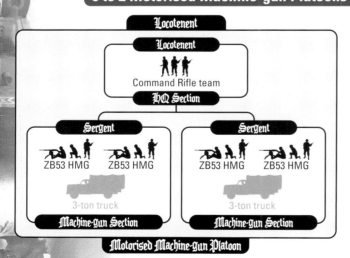

Platoon

HQ Section with:

2 Machine-gun Sections	125 points
1 Machine-gun Section	70 points

Option

- Add 3-ton trucks for +5 points per section.

Motorised Machine-gun Platoons may make Combat Attachments to Combat Platoons.

The motorised machine-guns give the *vanatori* fire support, pinning the enemy down as they attack. In defence, their high rate of fire mows down massed Soviet attacks.

0 to 1 Motorised Mortar Platoon

Platoon

HQ Section with:

2 Mortar Sections	125 points
1 Mortar Section	70 points

Option

- Add 3-ton trucks at no cost.

The motorised infantry's own artillery, their mortars are always on call for instant artillery support. While less effective than artillery in prolonged bombardments, the mortars get their rounds on target quicker, making them more useful in hasty attacks.

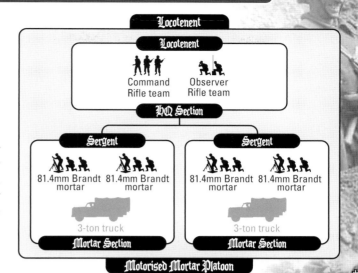

Companie Vanatori de Munte

(MOUNTAIN INFANTRY COMPANY)

A Companie Vanatori de Munte is organised the same way as a Companie Vanatori Motorizata, except that they are not motorised. Remove all trucks reducing the cost by -5 points per truck.

A Companie Vanatori de Munte may only have one Cari de Lupta Platoon. It must be equipped with T-38 (Panzer 38(t)) tanks instead of R-2 (Panzer 35(t)) tanks at the same points cost.

You may want to model your artillery battery's horse-drawn limbers as Packhorse teams.

...Gyorgy Popelscu, 20th Infantry Division, Stalingrad 1942...

I remember the cold, that terrible bitter cold. The harshest of winters back home in Plodvia couldn't compare to a Russian winter. I thought I had known cold. That was before I set foot inside this blasted country. We sit frozen rigid behind our hastily prepared barricades at the back of a bombed out bakery. The snow lazily cascades upon us from the dark night sky, eerily beautiful in a city as damned as this.

'Here they come again!' I don't recognise the voice but the warning is all too familiar-tanks. The hard frozen ground beneath my feet begins to tremble ominously. My stomach knots tight with the all-knowing familiarity of what is about to occur. The worst agony is the waiting-hearing the deep rumbling of engines, the clatter of tank tracks crushing their way towards our positions and knowing that they are bearing down upon you. Tanks make a man feel more human than ever-small and insignificant.

'Where are they coming from this time?' asks Gigi, his voice tinged with anticipation and dread. Then they are upon us. Tanks and hordes of Russian soldiers swarm into our perimeter. We duck as fire explodes around our ears, showering us in shards of broken glass and splinters of timber. To my left Ganea and Filipescu's machine-gun is spitting fire. Ilea throws down his rifle and disappears through the ruined bakery. Nobody tries to stop him. Tank fright affects each man differently. I just grit my teeth and keep firing.

Suddenly a black shape looms from the darkness-a dirty Russian tank has closed on our position. I shout a warning to the others in my section. Then the great beast levels its barrel and fires. The concussion washes over me like a raging torrent, my legs buckle as my helmet and rifle are torn away from me. Dirt, earth and glass fall all about us. Dimitriu has vanished. I taste blood upon my lips.

'Gyorgy, Gyorgy!' Ganea's voice sounds very distant, 'We have to move now-Ivan is overrunning us. We have orders. We have orders!' Adrianu helps me to my feet and half drags me from the bakery. The Russians have broken through. I am numb. I can feel nothing, no pain. But we are still alive. We will fight again.

ROMANIAN

Companie Puscasi

(INFANTRY COMPANY)

A force based around a Companie Puscasi must contain:

- A Company HQ, and
- two or three Puscasi Platoons.

Weapon Platoons available to a Companie Puscasi are:

- Machine-gun Platoons,
- a Mortar Platoon, and
- an Anti-tank Platoon.

Support Platoons available to a Companie Puscasi are:

- a Regimental Mortar Platoon,
- a Hunter Platoon,
- any Divisional Support Platoons,
- an allied German Grenadier Platoon,
- an allied German Anti-tank Gun Platoon, and

- an allied German Motorised Artillery Battery

You may have **two** Support Platoons for each Puscasi Platoon you field.

Motivation and Skill

Romania has three armies on the Russian Front, contributing more men to the conflict than any other Axis power except Germany. Romania is still an agrarian peasant society much as Russia had been before the revolution and the aristocratic officers rule over their men with an iron fist through their NCO's. Discipline is kept by using harsh punishment, much to the detriment of initiative. A Companie Puscasi is rated as **Regular**.

HEADQUARTERS

1 Company HQ

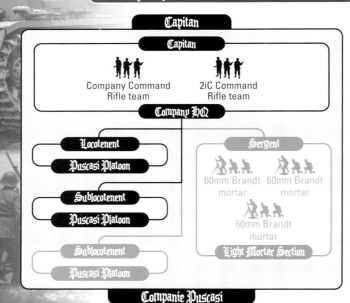

Headquarters

Company HQ	25 points

Options

- Replace any or all Command Rifle teams with Command Vanator de Care Rifle team for +5 points.
- Add 60mm Brandt mortars to Company HQ for +20 points each.

A Romanian Companie Puscasi has lots of firepower to pound and pulverise the Soviets, supported by light to heavy mortars and lots of crack artillery. And when the Russians' attack gets close to our infantry the well dug in HMG's will provide crossfire support. Any Soviet tanks will think twice about coming near our ace anti-tank gunners, while their aircraft steer clear of the anti-aircraft support we have.

COMBAT PLATOONS

2 or 3 Puscasi Platoons

Platoon
HQ Section with:

4 Puscasi Squads	105 points
3 Puscasi Squads	85 points
2 Puscasi Squads	65 points

Options

- Replace Command Rifle team with a Command Vanator de Care Rifle team for +5 points.
- Upgrade Rifle teams to Rifle/MG teams for +10 Points per Rifle squad.

The Romanian Peasant soldier knows how to fight and is very courageous in the defence of his Homeland. They are well-trained using old, well tried methods to defend their homeland from the plundering Soviets.

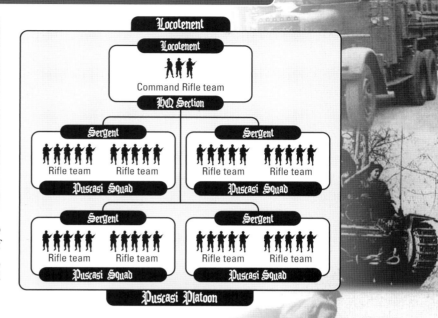

WEAPONS PLATOONS

0 to 2 Machine-gun Platoons

Platoon
HQ Section with:

2 Machine-gun Sections	105 points
1 Machine-gun Section	60 points

Machine-gun Platoons may make Combat Attachments to Combat Platoons.

Our gallant ZB53 gunners lay down a well set out hail of bullets that will stop any attack. They provide covering fire during assaults and then move quickly to captured positions and dig in expertly and hold off any counter attack.

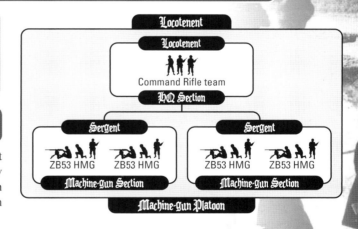

0 to 1 Mortar Platoon

Platoon
HQ Section with:

2 Mortar Sections	100 points
1 Mortar Section	60 points

Option

- Add two one-horse carts to each Mortar Section at no cost.

Close by the mortar platoon places accurate fire on the enemy positions in advance of the assaulting infantry, often combined with smoke to shield the advancing troops. The mortar section uses the effective 81.4mm mortars to rain death on the Soviets from above.

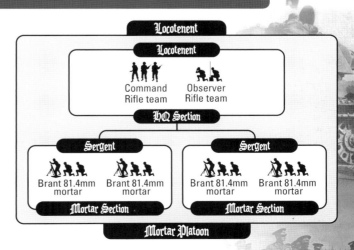

ROMANIAN

0 to 1 Anti-tank Platoon

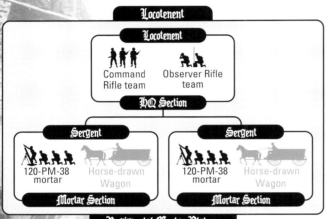

Sublocotenent
Sublocotenent
Command Rifle team
HQ Section
Sergent
TAC 37mm gun — horse-drawn limber — TAC 37mm gun — horse-drawn limber
Anti-tank Section
Anti-tank Platoon

Platoon
HQ Section with:

1 Anti-tank Section	50 points

Option
• Add horse-drawn limbers at no cost.

These light 37 mm anti-tank guns protect the infantry from the marauding Bolshevik light tanks. Easy to move and quick to fire, the infantry look to them for protection.

SUPPORT PLATOONS

0 to 1 Regimental Mortar Platoon

Locotenent
Locotenent
Command Rifle team — Observer Rifle team
HQ Section
Sergent — **Sergent**
120-PM-38 mortar — Horse-drawn Wagon — 120-PM-38 mortar — Horse-drawn Wagon
Mortar Section — **Mortar Section**
Regimental Mortar Platoon

Platoon
HQ Section with:

2 Mortar Sections	80 points

Option
• Add horse-drawn wagons at no cost.

Using captured 120mm mortars theses platoons return the explosives back to the Russians. So good are these mortars that Romanian manufactured large numbers as well. Even the Soviet tanks thought twice about driving through the hail of 120mm shells.

0 to 1 Hunter Platoon

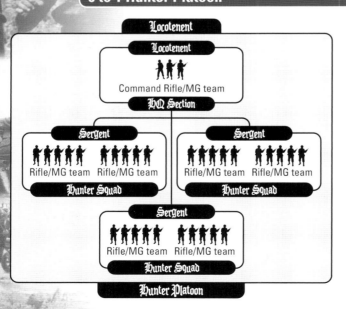

Locotenent
Locotenent
Command Rifle/MG team
HQ Section
Sergent — **Sergent**
Rifle/MG team — Rifle/MG team — Rifle/MG team — Rifle/MG team
Hunter Squad — **Hunter Squad**
Sergent
Rifle/MG team — Rifle/MG team
Hunter Squad
Hunter Platoon

Platoon
HQ Section with:

3 Hunter Squads	145 points
2 Hunter Squads	105 points

Options
• Replace Command Rifle/MG team with a Command Vanator de Care Rifle/MG team for +5 points.
• Replace all Rifle/MG teams with SMG teams at no cost.

A Hunter Platoon is a Reconnaissance Platoon.

A well trained reconnaissance infantry unit able to locate Soviet formations to bring in artillery and other supporting troops to deal with them. They are happily to use captured Soviet PPSh-41 submachine-guns on their previous owners.

Romanian Companies may have the following support platoons:

- a Light Anti-aircraft Platoon,
- Pioneer Platoons,
- Artillery Batteries,
- Cavalry Platoons, and
- Divisional Anti-tank Platoons,

Motivation and Skill

Divisional support platoons are rated as **Regular** or **Elite** as indicated in each platoon.

Air Support

You may request Sporadic Air Support at a cost of +100 points. Sporadic Air Support will provide you supporting Junkers Ju87 ground-attack aircraft.

0 to 1 Light Anti-aircraft Platoon

Platoon

HQ Section with:

2 Anti-aircraft Sections	**50 points**

Options

- Equip all Mitral 20mm guns (2cm FlaK38) with Gun Shields for +5 points per section.
- Add one 3-ton truck per Anti-aircraft Section for +10 points for the platoon.

Rated as Regular.

With their excellent Mistral 20 mm anti-aircraft guns these troops will send any Soviet aircraft from the skies. Thus they provide excellent protection for their own troops from any marauding Russian aircraft.

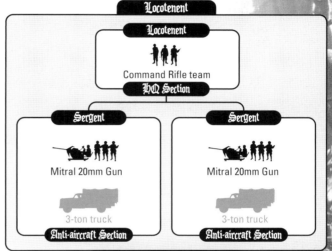

0 to 1 Pioneer Platoon

Platoon

HQ Section with:

3 Pioneer Squads	**130 points**
2 Pioneer Squads	**95 points**

Options

- Replace all Pioneer Rifle teams with Pioneer Rifle/MG teams for +10 points per Pioneer Squad.
- Replace all Pioneer Rifle teams with Pioneer SMG teams for +10 points per Pioneer Squad.
- Add one 3-ton truck per Pioneer Squad for +5 points per truck.
- Add Pioneer Supply 3-ton truck for +25 points.

Rated as Elite.

You may replace up to one Pioneer Rifle team with a Flame-thrower team at the start of the game before deployment.

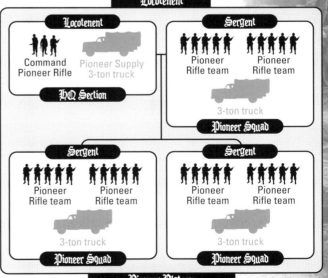

0 to 3 Artillery Batteries

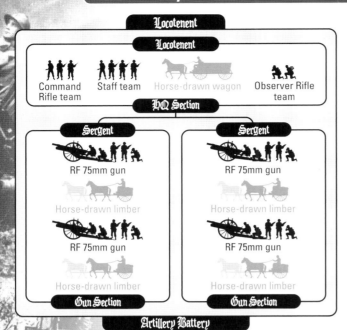

Platoon

HQ Section with:

2 Gun Sections	120 points
1 Gun Section	70 points

Option

- Replace all RF 75mm (76K/02) guns with Skoda 100mm (100/17) howitzers for +20 points per Gun Section.
- Add horse-drawn transport at no cost.
- Replace all horse-drawn vehicles with 3-ton trucks or Stalinets tractors for +10 points per Gun Section.

Rated as Regular.

The Artillery platoon can provide lots of accurate fire just in front of the advancing infantry keeping enemy pinned. The gunners are very adept at using the French techniques of artillery engagement developed during and after World War 1.

0 to 2 Cavalry Platoons

Platoon

HQ Section with:

3 Cavalry Squads	155 points
2 Cavalry Squads	110 points

Option

- Replace Command Rifle/MG team with a Command Vanator de Care Rifle/MG team for +5 points.

Rated as Elite.

These are the best of the best with their specially trained horses and they love nothing better than to exploit any breakthrough other troops have made in the Soviet lines. They are very mobile, highly trained and very motivated both on their horses and as dismounted infantry. You would want these troops in any army you field.

0 to 2 Divisional Anti-tank Platoons

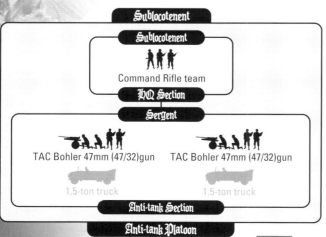

Platoon

HQ Section with:

1 Anti-tank Section	60 points

Options

- Add 1.5-ton trucks for +10 points for the platoon.
- Replace all TAC Bohler 47mm (47/32) guns with TAC 938 75mm (7.5cm PaK 97/38) guns for +20 points for the platoon.
- Replace all 1.5-ton trucks with Malaxa (Renault UE) carriers for +5 points for the platoon.

Rated as Regular

THE RED ARMY
SOVIET FORCES ON THE EASTERN FRONT

Formed amidst the turmoil of the Great Patriotic War, forged in the red heat of battle, and tempered by the fierce Russian winter, 3-y Mechanizirovanniy Korpus, the 3rd Mechanised Corps, fought against the Nazi invaders from the gates of Moscow to the ruins of Berlin.

The Last Blitzkrieg

The Great Patriotic War (as the Soviet Union called their part of the Second World War) began on 22 June 1941, when Hitler launched his battle-hardened army against an unprepared *RKKA* (Workers and Peasants Red Army) in Operation *Barbarossa*, the invasion of the Soviet Union. Using their blitzkrieg tactics perfected in the first two years of the war, the German Panzers raced east across the vast expanses of the Soviet Union with unprecedented speed. The armoured spearheads struck deep into Soviet territory encircling and destroying whole armies.

Amongst the massive casualties suffered by the RKKA in the face of the German onslaught were their poorly trained and led tank and motorised divisions. Although the Red Army had the world's biggest tank force, many were unservice-able when the war began, and most obsolete. The divisions were further hamstrung by shortages of trucks, radios, and experienced officers (tank officers had suffered badly in Stalin's pre-war purge).

Desperate Days

Stalin rebuilt the almost destroyed Red Army, desperately seeking to stem the German tide. Tank divisions were out of the question—the few armoured vehicles left were shuffled into small tank brigades instead. If large tank forces were difficult, motorised divisions were simply impossible. The few trucks available were desperately needed to supply the tank forces. Instead, there was a resurgence of the cavalry forces to provide mobile infantry. More than eighty new cavalry divisions were formed, with many composed of the dashing Cossacks—renowned horse warriors of a previous age.

Miraculously, the hastily scraped

127

together forces held. In early December 1941, the German Army finally ground to a halt in the outskirts of Moscow.

General Winter

The onset of the cruelest Russian winter in fifty years saved the devastated Red Army, freezing the advancing Germans in their tracks. With 'General Winter' on their side the *RKKA* undertook counter-offensives that were partially successful in pushing the invaders back, but at the cost of almost all of their hastily scraped together mobile forces.

A New Beginning

The spring of 1942 saw both sides rebuilding their exhausted forces. The Red Army realised that it needed strong armoured formations on the German model if it was to go back on the offensive. The resulting tank corps combined three tank brigades into one concentrated force.

As spring turned to summer, the Red Army struck first in June 1942 with offensives against the Rzhev pocket in front of Moscow and out of the Izyum bridgehead in the south. The new tank corps were committed, and being untrained and inexperienced, were devastated by German counter-attacks, leaving the cavalry isolated behind German lines.

With Soviet forces weakened, the German Army resumed the offensive, this time concentrating their efforts in the south. The Panzer divisions punched down the Don River smashing tank corps thrown in their path and captured Voronezh in July 1942. German forces swept into the oil-rich Caucasus. On the flanks of

this advance the ferocious battle for Stalingrad, the city named in honour of the Soviet leader himself, began in early September.

Soviet tank corps were thrown into battle against the flanks of the German thrust, aiming to relieve the city, but their handling was still inept and they were destroyed time and again by the Panzer veterans. Stalingrad was near to falling.

Mechanised Corps

The lack of infantry and artillery support in the Soviet tank corps had been cruelly exposed in the summer battles. In response the Peoples' Commissariat for Defence added support units to the tank corps and ordered the creation of eight new mechanised corps. The third of these, *3-y Mechanizirovanniy Korpus*, was formed in September 1942 from the shattered remnants of several tank corps. Placed under the command of General M E Katukov, a renowned tank commander, the Corps was assigned to *22-ya Armiya*, the 22nd Army, for the winter offensives.

Uranus and Mars

With Stalingrad about to fall, the only option open to the RKKA was to attack. The winter offensives of 1942 were based around the twin spheres of Operations Uranus and Mars. General Vasilevsky's Operation Uranus was intended to surround the 6th Army of the German General Von Paulus in the ruins of Stalingrad. In Operation Mars, Marshal Zhukov's forces were to attempt a similar encirclement of General Model's 9th Army, in the Rzhev salient north of Moscow.

Operation Uranus saw the more

balanced tank and mechanised corps allied with their old comrades, the cavalry corps. Together they smashed through the Rumanian 3rd and 4th Armies in mid-November 1942, encircling Stalingrad in a matter of days. They then turned to defeat the Panzer forces sent to break their stranglehold. It was the first real victory of the Red Army in the war.

The Rzhev Meat Grinder

Meanwhile in the north, amidst snowstorms and fog, Operation Mars began on 25 November. With more than 800,000 men and 2000 tanks available and simultaneous attacks in three sectors, the plan looked foolproof.

In the east, *20-ya Armiya*, at huge cost, established a bridgehead across the Vazuza River. The mobile group, *6-y Tankovy Korpus* (6th Tank Corps) and *2-y Gvardeyskiy Kavaleriyskiy Korpus* (2nd Guards Cavalry Corps), pushed though the breach only to be cut off and destroyed piecemeal. Only *20-ya Gvardeyskiy Kavaleriya Diviziya*, the 20th Guards Cavalry Division, survived, spending forty days behind German lines before returning.

On the western flank of the salient, *41 ya Armiya* smashed through the front-line and led by *1-y Mechanizirovanniy Korpus*, 1st Mechanised Corps, struck deep into German-held territory. However, the bulk of the army quickly become bogged down in a fruitless assault upon the heavily-fortified town of Belyi. Again the penetration was eventually cut off and the encircled forces destroyed.

In the most successful of the 3 sectors, *3-y Mechanizirovanniy Korpus* formed the spearhead of the drive by *22-ya Armiya* eastward along the Luchesa valley. For the first two days the Corps swept aside all opposition as they pushed towards their objective of the Olenino–Belyi road. Against the on-rushing Soviets the Germans threw the grenadiers of the famed *Grossdeutschland Division*. Heavy fighting ensued around the village of Starukhi, resulting in a stalemate that the steadily weakening ranks of *3-y Mechanizirovanniy Korpus* could not break.

As the Soviet offensive stalled, Zhukov, unwilling to concede defeat, issued orders to keep attacking at all costs, pouring his reserves into the 'Rzhev Meat Grinder' in an attempt to make a decisive breakthrough. By 15 December Soviet casualties had reached enormous levels, nearly 500,000 men and 1,700 tanks in total, and Stalin intervened to cancel the operation. Like most of the units involved, *3-y Mechanizirovanniy Korpus* had been nearly destroyed.

Little Saturn

With the ailing Mars operation finally cancelled, focus switched to Operation Saturn, designed to exploit the success of Uranus around Stalingrad. Saturn was to destroy all German forces in the Caucasus. General Vasilevsky was forced to revise this plan to counter German attempts to relieve 6th Army trapped inside an ever-tightening circle around Stalingrad. The revised Little Saturn, launched on 16 December 1942, parried the German relief attempt then went on to retake Kursk, Kharkov and Rostov in January and February 1943. As the Soviet thrust ran out of steam, the Germans counterattacked retaking Kharkov in March, forming a bulge in the Soviet front line around Kursk.

Operation Citadel

In early 1943 *3-y Mechanizirovanniy Korpus* was totally rebuilt, along with most of the virtually destroyed Soviet tank forces. Fortunately the German Army was equally exhausted. Once again both prepared for new summer offensives. This time Stalin elected to wait for the Germans to strike first.

The German plan was codenamed Operation Citadel and was intended to cut off and destroy the troops in the Kursk salient. However, delays in the launching of Citadel, which didn't begin until 5 July, 1943, allowed the Soviet forces to rebuild and fortify their positions. Kursk was to be the rock against which the steel fist of the Nazi forces was to shatter itself.

Thunderstorms at Kursk

As summer thunderstorms rolled overhead, *3-y Mechanizirovanniy Korpus* once again rolled into battle against its old enemy—the *Grossdeutschland Division*. Attacking south from Kursk, the Corps aimed to stop the German 48th Panzer Corps' thrust towards Oboyan. T-34 tanks of *3-y Mechanizirovanniy Korpus* repeatedly clashed with enemy armour. On 8 July the brave tankists engaged the fearsome Tiger heavy tanks of *Grossdeutschland* outside the town of Syrtsevo. The following day the German thrust was turned aside at heavy cost to the enemy. The ill-fated German offensive would now meet its doom upon the reckoning ground of Prokhorovka in one of the largest tank battles in history.

On 12 July, the same day as the mighty tank clash at Prokhorovka, the Red Army launched a major offensive against the Germans around Orel immediately to the north of the Kursk salient. Over a month of hard fighting followed, as the Soviet attack inflicted heavy losses upon the enemy forces and gradually drove them back. After this the Red Army would never be defeated again.

Guards Mechanised Corps

3-y Mechanizirovanniy Korpus was given little time to rest following its victory at Kursk, and was in the thick of the fray in the Soviet offensives that followed. Belgorod was recaptured, as too was Kharkov for the final time.

As a reward for its brave fighting at Kursk and after, *3-y Mechanizirovanniy Korpus* was renamed *8-y Gvardeyskiy Mechanizirovanniy Korpus* (8th Guards Mechanised Corps) on 23 October 1943. On that same day the Red Army captured Melitopol north of the Crimean peninsular.

The Red Tide Flows

How far the Red Army had come from the dismal days of a year before is shown in their new cavalry-mechanised groups. Composed of a cavalry and a mechanised corps and fighting with new-found operational skill, these groups advanced ahead of the main force, keeping the defenders off-balance. With these mobile groups in the vanguard, the red tide swept westwards. The Dnepr River became the finish line in a race between the German Army Group Centre rushing to reach the western bank and fortify it, and the advancing Soviets attempting to cut them off. The German Army won, narrowly, but a few Soviet bridgeheads across the Dnepr would ultimately prove their undoing.

Triumphant March

1944 saw the Red Army finally liberating the rest of the Soviet Union in Operation Bagration (launched on the third anniversary of Hitler's invasion) and the Lvov-Sandomir operation in August that carried them to the Vistula River in central Poland.

In September, *8-y Gvardeyskiy Mechanizirovanniy Korpus* was withdrawn into reserve for a well-deserved rest and refit. It was back at the front by the beginning of 1945 driving relentlessly forward through the heavily fortified area from the Vistula to the Oder. The vengeful Red Army swept onwards and in May 1945, the battle-weary *8-y Gvardeyskiy Mechanizirovanniy Korpus* played it's final part in the bloody, but triumphant, storming of Berlin.

RZHEV

25 November 1942—Marshal Zhukov launches Operation Mars to eliminate the German Army Group Centre.

The Red Army breaks through the German frontlines in several places.

28 November 1942—Renewed Soviet attacks.

26 November 1942—Zhukov commits his reserve tanks to expand the bridgehead.

27 November 1942—German counterattacks cut off the armoured spearhead.

Further German counterattacks eliminate the spearhead.

5 July 1943—The German Army launches a massive offensive to crush the Soviet forces holding Kursk.

Incessant local counterattacks slow the German advance and wear down their forces.

16 July 1943—Hitler concedes defeat.

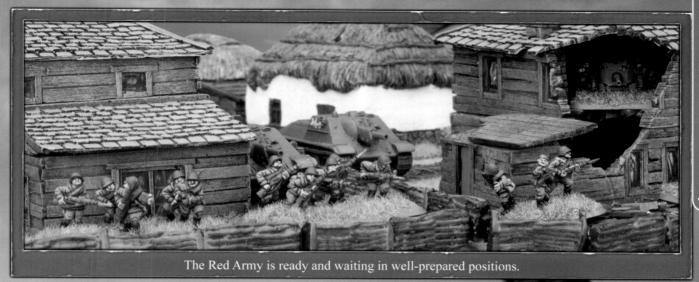

The Red Army is ready and waiting in well-prepared positions.

12 July 1943—Massed Soviet tank attacks halt the German spearhead.

18 July 1943—Germans withdraw to their start lines.

Order 227—Not One Step Back

The Supreme General Headquarters of the Red Army commands:

Military councils of armies and first of all army commanders should:

1. Unconditionally remove commanders and commissars who have accepted troop withdrawals from occupied positions without the order of the army command, take from them their orders and medals, and send them to the military councils for court martial.

2. Form within each army 3 to 5 well-armed blocking detachments, put them directly behind unstable divisions, and require them to shoot panic-mongers and cowards on the spot in the case of panic and scattered withdrawals and thus help the honest soldiers of the division execute their duty to the Motherland;

3. Form within each Front from one to three (depending on the situation) penal battalions where commanders and high commanders and appropriate commissars of all service arms who have been guilty of a breach of discipline due to cowardice or bewilderment will be sent.

Form within each Army up to ten (depending on the situation) penal companies where ordinary soldiers and low ranking commanders who have been guilty of a breach of discipline due to cowardice or bewilderment will be sent.

Put them at difficult sectors of the front to give them an opportunity to redeem by blood their crimes against the Motherland.

This order is to be read in all companies, cavalry squadrons, artillery batteries, commands and headquarters.

The National Commissar for Defence: I. Stalin

Characteristics

Boris Vasilevsky is a Warrior and a Command team. He is rated as **Fearless Conscript**.

Komissar Vasilevsky is always accompanied by his Blocking Detachment of a deputy Komissar team and three Maxim HMG teams. The Blocking Detachment counts as a platoon for all purposes and Vasilevsky is its Command team.

Komissar Vasilevsky and his Blocking Detachment can join a Strelkovy Batalon for 135 points, a Gvardeyskiy Strelkovy Batalon for 105 points, or an Batalon Opolcheniya for 165 points.

Special Rules

For Stalin: Vasilevsky and his Blocking Detachment always pass Motivation tests on a roll of 2+.

Not One Step Back: If Vasilevsky is adjacent to the Battalion Command team when it takes a Company Morale Check, the Command team rolls again if it failed its Motivation test. The result of the second roll is final.

Blocking Detachment: If any part of a Soviet company is In Command and within 24"/60cm and line of sight of a Maksim HMG team of the Blocking Detachment that is also In Command, fails a Motivation test it must re-roll the test as if the Battalion's Company Command team was within 6"/15cm of its Command team.

If the company fails the Motivation test (after re-rolling for the blocking detachment and the company's Komissar), then roll a die. The result is the number of hits scored by the Maksim HMG teams on the company in an effort to motivate them. Apply the hits to teams visible to the Maksim HMG teams, starting with those closest to the Blocking Detachment. Roll the normal save for any teams hit. The company is automatically Pinned Down if it wasn't before.

Born into a peasant family in the Crimea, Mariya was one of ten children. In 1925 she married a young army officer and in tribute to the October Revolution she and her husband changed their surname to Oktyabrskaya.

Her husband was killed in the fighting around Kiev in August 1941 but the news took a year to reach her. Her desire for revenge led her to sell all of her possessions to raise funds to purchase a tank for the Red Army. Mariya placed one condition on this donation: she must be allowed to drive it! Realising the publicity opportunities, High Command approved her request and, at the age of thirty-eight,

she commenced training.

In September 1943, she was assigned to *26ya Gvardeyskaya Tankovaya Brigada* (26th Guards Tank Brigade) as a mechanic/driver. When Mariya arrived at her unit in a T-34 tank emblazoned with the turret slogan *'Boyevaya Podruga'* or 'Fighting Girlfriend', the tankists viewed her with scepticism and considered the assignment a publicity stunt.

This attitude changed to one of respect following Mariya's participation in battle. In combat during October and November 1943, Mariya distinguished herself as a skilled and fearless driver, manoeuvring her tank like a veteran and accounting for many enemy

troops and guns in close assaults during her rampage of revenge. In several engagements enemy shells damaging the tracks halted her T-34. Mariya, often disregarding orders not to, would jump out of the tank while under fire, effect repairs to get back into action as fast as possible.

In January 1944 she was hit in the head by shrapnel while repairing a broken track and killed. In August she was posthumously decorated becoming the first female tankist to be awarded the Hero of the Soviet Union—the Red Army's highest award for military valour.

Characteristics

Mariya Oktyabrskaya is a Warrior and has the same characteristics as the platoon she is part of.

Mariya may be assigned as the driver of your battalion's Company Command tank or any Tank team in a Tankovy Company for a cost of +25 points.

Special Rules

Vengeance: Any tank driven by Mariya passes all Motivation tests on a roll of 2+.

For the Motherland: Any tank driven by Mariya passes all Skill Tests on a roll of 2+

Fighting Girlfriend: Mariya's ability to anticipate her commander/gunner's shooting allows her to halt at the right moments to give him the best shots. As a result, any tank driven by Mariya does not reduce the ROF of its main gun if firing while moving. However, a tank driven by Mariya still obeys the Hen and Chicks special rule.

БОЕВАЯ
ПОДРУГА

Known as 'Vasha' to his friends, V G Zaytsev was taught marksmanship in the taiga (Siberian forest) by his grandfather. When twenty-four years old, and a payroll clerk with the Soviet Navy's Pacific Fleet, *Glavstarshiny* (Chief Petty Officer) Zaytsev insisted on volunteering for frontline service in one of the new Siberian divisions.

Zaytsev crossed the Volga with the 284th Siberian Rifle Division at the end of September 1942. Soon after landing at Stalingrad, Zaytsev shot a German machine-gunner several hundred meters away. Impressed by Zaytsev's accuracy, his commander, Colonel Nikolai Batyuk, immediately ordered Zaytsev be issued with a rifle with telescopic sights.

Before long his sniping was widely known to the embattled defenders of Stalingrad—and to the Germans, who became increasingly fearful of Soviet snipers. His tally of Germans at Stalingrad was 242. It is said that he spent 243 bullets to make that score.

Batyuk recognised the importance of sniping, and a school was set up just behind the front-line to train new snipers under Zaytsev's expert instruction. Amongst Zaytsev's students were sniper aces such as Anatoli Chekov, Viktor Medvedev (who would go on to Berlin and kill even more Germans than Zaytsev), and Tania Chernova (who became his lover). Zaytsev was the star amongst many other snipers whose exploits became staple fare for Soviet propaganda.

Soviet sources claimed that a German super-sniper, Major Koenig, was sent to Stalingrad to kill Zaytsev, but after a three-day duel Zaytsev managed to kill Koenig (or Colonel Thorvald as some sources call him).

In January 1943, Zaytsev was wounded in the eyes, but once recovered he was promoted to *Mladshi Leytenant* (Junior Lieutenant) and continued to elect and train snipers. He was awarded the Soviet Union's highest decoration—Hero of the Soviet Union in February 1943.

After the war he became a professor of engineering at the University of Kiev and died in 1992.

"...await the right moment for one, and only one well-aimed shot"

Characteristics

Zaytsev is a Sniper and a Warrior. He is rated as **Fearless Veteran**.

Zaytsev can join any Strelkovy Batalon for +100 points.

Special Rules

Crack Shot: Zaytsev is a crack shot. Re-roll any failed rolls to hit when he shoots.

Little Hares: Zaytsev trains his students well. Any Sniper team in the same Strelkovy Batalon as Zaytsev may re-roll any failed roll to hit when shooting.

One Well-aimed Shot: Zaytsev learned his trade hunting deer in Siberia. He never wastes a bullet. Any team hit by Zaytsev must re-roll successful saves.

62-YA ARMIYA—Soviet Army, Stalingrad, November 1942
General V I Chuikov

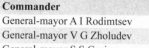

Divisions	Regiments	Commander
13-ya Gvardeyskaya Strelkovaya Diviziya	34, 39, & 42	General-mayor A I Rodimtsev
37-ya Gvardeyskaya Strelkovaya Diviziya	109, 114, & 118	General-mayor V G Zholudev
39-ya Gvardeyskaya Strelkovaya Diviziya	112, 117, & 120	General-mayor S S Guriev
45-ya Strelkovaya Diviziya	10, 61, & 253	Podpolkovnik V P Sokolov
95-ya Strelkovaya Diviziya	90, 161, & 241	General-mayor V A Gorishny
112-ya Strelkovaya Diviziya	385, 416, & 524	Unknown
138-ya Strelkovaya Diviziya	344, 650, & 768	General-mayor I I Lyudnikov
193-ya Strelkovaya Diviziya	604, 683, & 685	General-mayor F N Smekhotvorov
196-ya Strelkovaya Diviziya	863, 884, & 893	Polkovnik S P Ivanov
244-ya Strelkovaya Diviziya	907, 911, & 913	Polkovnik G A Afanasiev
284-ya Strelkovaya Diviziya	1043, 1045, & 1047	Polkovnik N F Batyuk
308-ya Strelkovaya Diviziya	339, 347, & 351	Polkovnik L N Gurtiev
10-ya Strelkovaya Diviziya NKVD	269, 270, 271, 272, 282	Diviziya Komissar Rogatin
92-ya Brigada Morskoi Pekhoty		Polkovnik Tarasov
42-ya Brigada Opolcheniya		Polkovnik M S Batrakov
115-ya Brigada Opolcheniya		Polkovnik K M Andryusenko
124-ya Brigada Opolcheniya		Polkovnik S F Gorokov
149-ya Brigada Opolcheniya		Mayor I D Durnev
160-ya Brigada Opolcheniya		Unknown
84-ya Tankovy Brigada	200 & 202 Tk bns, 84 MR bn	Polkovnik D N Bely
189-ya Tankovy Brigada	135 & 178 Tk bns, 189 MR bn	Podpolkovnik K S Udovichenko

Armiya = Army, Gvardeyskaya Strelkovaya Diviziya = Guards Rifle Division, Strelkovaya Diviziya = Rifle Division, Strelkovaya Diviziya NKVD = NKVD Rifle Division, Brigada Morskoi Pekhoty = Naval Infantry Brigade, Brigada Opolcheniya = Militia Brigade, Tankovy Brigada = Tank Brigade, 62-ya = 62nd.

The RKKA, the Workers and Peasants Red Army, expanded from 177 rifle divisions at the start of the war to some 407 by 1943. In the meanwhile it had lost 191 rifle divisions in the encirclement battles of 1941 and 1942. As a result it is almost impossible to list every rifle division, let alone their histories. Instead, here is a list of the divisions fighting in Stalingrad in November 1942 with Chuikov's 62-ya Armiya. The dire lack of experienced senior officers after the early disasters led to the Red Army dissolving its rifle corps and putting the troops directly under the army commanders.

6. ARMEE—German Army, Stalingrad, November 1942
General der Panzertruppen Friedrich Paulus

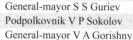

Division	Regiments	Commander
XI Armeekorps		**General der Infanterie Karl Strecker**
384. Infanteriedivision	534, 535, & 5362	Generalleutnant Freiherr Eccard von Gablenz
44. Infanteriedivision	131, 132, & 134	Generalmajor Heinrich Deboi
376. Infanteriedivision	672, 673, & 767	Generalmajor Edler von Daniels
VIII Armeekorps		**General der Artillerie Walter Heitz**
113. Infanteriedivision	260, 261, & 268	Generalleutnant Hans-Heinrich Sixt von Armin
76. Infanteriedivision	178, 203, & 230	Generalmajor Carl Rodenburg
XIV Panzerkorps		**General der Panzertruppen Hans Hube**
16. Panzerdivision	2 Pz, 64, & 79	Generalmajor Günther Angern
3. Infanteriedivision (mot)	8 & 29	Generalmajor Helmuth Schlömer
60. Infanteriedivision (mot)	92 & 120	Oberst i.G. Hans-Adolf von Arenstorff-Oyle
94. Infanteriedivision	267, 274, & 276	Generalleutnant Georg Pfeiffer
LI Armeekorps		**General der Artillerie Walther von Seydlitz-Kurzbach**
71. Infanteriedivision	191, 194, & 211	Generalleutnant Alexander von Hartmann
79. Infanteriedivision	208, 212, & 226	Generalmajor Richard von Schwerin
295. Infanteriedivision	516, 517, & 518	Oberst Otto Korfes
305. Infanteriedivision	576, 577, & 578	Oberst Bernard Steinmetz
389. Infanteriedivision	544, 545, & 546	Generalmajor Erich Magnus
24. Panzerdivision	24 Pz, 21, & 26	Generalmajor Arno von Lenski
100. Jägerdivision	54 & 227	Generalleutnant Werner Sanne
	369. Croatian	Oberst Viktor Pavicic
Armeetruppen		
9. Flakdivision (mot)		Generalmajor Wolfgang Pickert
14. Panzerdivision	36 Pz, 103, & 108	Generalmajor Johannes Baessler
1. Romanian Cavalry Division		Generalmajor Constantin Bratescu

Armee = Army, Armeekorps = Corps, Infanteriedivision = Infantry Division, Panzerdivision = Armoured Division,

Jägerdivision= Light Infantry Division, Armeetruppen = Army Troops, Flakdivision = Anti-aircraft Division, mot = motorised.

While 6. Armee was certainly the largest German Army with four corps and twenty divisions, it was still only a small cog in the German war machine. For the invasion of the Soviet Union the German Army fielded 80 infantry divisions in six armies. Two years later there were 139 infantry divisions spread across four army groups along the 1200 mile (2000 km) Eastern Front.

The Russians use the Cyrillic alphabet. The table below shows the approximate pronunciation of each letter.

А	а	a	father	К	к	k	kiss	Х	х	kh	loch
Б	б	b	bank	Л	л	l	fill	Ц	ц	ts	sits
В	в	v	victor	М	м	m	mother	Ч	ч	ch	church
Г	г	g	good	Н	н	n	north	Ш	ш	sh	short
Д	д	d	dog	О	о	o	port	Щ	щ	shch	fresh cheese
Е	е	ye	yes	П	п	p	penguin	Ъ	ъ		hard sign
Ё	ё	yo	yogurt	Р	р	r	red	Ы	ы	y	ill
Ж	ж	zh	massage	С	с	s	soon	Ь	ь		soft sign
З	з	z	zebra	Т	т	t	tea	Э	э	e	let
И	и	i	see	У	у	u	fool	Ю	ю	yu	youth
Й	й	y	goodbye	Ф	ф	f	fun	Я	я	ya	yacht

Англичанин (an-gli-cha-nin): Englishman. Nickname for Marks II & III British lend-lease tanks.

БА, Бронеавтомобиль (BA, bro-nye-av-to-mo-bil): Armoured car.

Бей Фашистов (bye-y fa-shist-ov): Slogan 'Crush the Fascists'.

Боевая Подруга (bo-ye-va-ya po-dru-ga): Slogan 'Fighting Girlfriend'.

Братская могила на шестерых (brats-ka-ya mo-gi-la na shye-stye-rykh): 'Grave for six brothers'. Nickname of lend-lease M3s medium tank.

Бронетранспортер (bro-nye-trans-por-tyer): Armoured transporter.

Валентайн (va-lyen-tayn): Valentine. Lend-lease Mark III tank.

ВВС, Военно Воздушный Силы (VVS, vo-yen-no voz-dush-ny-y si-ly): Military Air Force.

Великая Отечественная Война (vyel-i-ka-ya ot-ye-chyest-vyen-na-ya voy-na): Great Patriotic War. The Second World War.

Вперед На Зарад (vpye-ryed na za-rad): Slogan 'Forward to the West'.

Голожопий Фэрдинант (go-lo-zho-pi-y fer-di-nant): Bare-ass Ferdinand, derogatory nickname for SU-76M assault gun.

Ефрейтор (ye-frye-y-tor): Corporal.

За Сталина (za sta-li-na): Slogan 'For Stalin'.

За Родину (za ro-di-nu): Slogan 'For the Motherland'.

Зверобой (zvye-ro-bo-y): 'Animal Killer'. Nickname given the SU-152 assault gun for killing the German Tigers and Panthers.

Казак (ka-zak): Cossack.

Казачья Сотня (ka-zach-ya sot-nya): Cossack hundred, squadron.

Капитан (ka-pi-tan): Captain. Company officer.

Катюша (ka-tyu-sha): Little Katy. BM-13 rocket launcher.

КВ, Климент Ворошилов (KV, kli-ment vo-ro-shi-lov): Commissar of Defence. KV tank named after him.

КВ-1э (KV-1e): 'Ekranirovannyy' or uparmoured KV-1 tank.

КВ-1с (KV-1s): 'Skorostnoy' or fast KV-1 tank.

Коломбина (ko-lom-bi-na): Columbine. Nickname for SU-76M.

Комиссар (ko-mis-sar): Senior political officer.

Красноармец (kras-no-ar-myets): Red Armyman. Private soldier..

Легкий (leg-ki-y): Light.

Лейтенант (lye-y-tye-nant): Lieutenant. Junior officer.

Ли (li): Lee. Lend-lease M3 medium tank.

М3л (M3l): M3 'legkiy' or light tank.

М3с (M3s): M3 'sredniy' or medium tank.

Матильда (ma-til-da): Matilda. Lend-lease Mark II tank.

Механизированная Бригада (me-kha-ni-zi-ro-van-na-ya bri-ga-da): Mechanised brigade.

Механизированный Корпус (me-kha-ni-zi-ro-van-ny-y kor-pus): Mechanised corps.

Мотострелковый Батальон (mo-to-stryel-ko-vy-y ba-ta-lon): Motor-rifle battalion.

обр, Образца (obr, o-braz-tsa): Model.

Победа (po-bye-da): Slogan 'Victory'.

Полковник (pol-kov-nik): Colonel. Regimental officer.

Подполковник (pod-pol-kov-nik): Sub-colonel. Lt. Colonel.

Пуп (pup): Pup. Nickname for lend-lease Mark III tank.

Разведчики (raz-ved-chi-ki): Scouts.

РККА, Рабоче-Крестьянская Красная Армия (RKKA, ra-bo-che kryest-yan-ska-ya kras-na-ya ar-mi-ya): Workers and Peasants Red Army.

Родина Мать (ro-di-na mat): Motherland.

Сержант (ser-zhant) : Sergeant.

Скоростной (sko-rost-noy): Fast.

Славянин (slav-ya-nin): Slav. Nickname for Soviet soldier.

Средний (sryed-ni-y): Medium.

СССР, Союз Советских Социалистических Республик (SSSR, so-yuz, so-vyetsk-ikh so-tsi-al-ist-its-yesk-ikh rves-pub-lik): Union of Soviet Socialist Republics.

Сталин (sta-lin): Iosif Stalin, Soviet leader.

СУ, Самоходная Установка (SU, sa-mo-khod-na-ya u-sta-nov-ka): Self-propelled mounting. Assault gun.

Сука (su-ka): Bitch. Nickname for SU-76M assault gun.

Танк (tank): Tank.

Танковый Батальон (tan-ko-vy-y ba-ta-lon): Tank battalion.

Танковая Бригада (tan-ko-va-ya bri-ga-da): Tank brigade.

Танковый Корпус (tan-ko-vy-y kor-pus): Tank corps.

Танкодесантник (tan-ko-dye-sant-nik): Tank-rider.

Тачанка (ta-chan-ka): Horse-drawn machine-gun cart.

Товарищ (to-va-rishch): Comrade.

Тяжелый (tya-zhye-ly-y): Heavy.

Тридцатьчевёрка (trid-stat-chyet-vyor-ka): Thirty-four. Nickname for T-34 tank.

USA, Убейат Сукинсйна Адолфа (u-bye-yat su-kin-sy-na a-dolf-a): USA, 'Kill that son-of-a-bitch Adolf'. Pre-painted slogan on American lend-lease vehicles.

Фриц (frits): Fritz. Nickname for German soldier.

Фронтовник (front-ov-nik): Front-line soldier.

Черчилль (chyer-chill): Churchill. Lend-lease mark IV tank.

Шваб (shvab): Schwabian Nickname for Germans.

Шерман (shyer-man): Sherman. Lend-lease M4 tank.

экранированный (ek-ra-ni-ro-van-ny-y): Shielded.

Эмча, Эм Четыре (em-cha, em che-tyr-ye): M4. Nickname for lend-lease M4 tank.

TANKOVY BATALON

(TANK COMPANY)

A force based around a Tankovy Batalon must contain:

- a Company HQ, and
- two or three Light and Medium Tankovy Companies.

Weapons Companies available to a Tankovy Batalon are:

- a Heavy Anti-tank Company,
- a Tank Rider Company, and
- a Motorised Mortar Company.

Support Companies for a Tankovy Batalon can be:

- an Armoured Car Company,
- Heavy Mortar Companies
- Motostrelkovy Companies,

- Light Armoured Car Platoons,
- Armoured Transporter Platoons,
- a Kazachya Sotnya, and
- Corps Support Companies.

You may have up to **one** Support Company attached to your company for each Tankovy Company you field.

Motivation and Skill

Many Soviet tank crews gain their first experience of battle after only the briefest training. Those that survive learn, but many perish first. A Tankovy Batalon is rated as **Fearless Conscript**.

HEADQUARTERS

1 Battalion HQ

Headquarters
Light Tanks

T-60 obr 1942	**25 points**
T-70 obr 1942	**35 points**
T-70 obr 1943	**40 points**
Mark III (Valentine II)	**45 points**
M3l (M3A1 Stuart)	**40 points**

- Arm M3l tank with AA MG for +5 points.

Medium Tanks

T-34 obr 1941 or 1942	**90 points**

- Upgrade T-34 obr 1942 tank with a Cupola for +5 points.

Mark II (Matilda II)	**65 points**
Mark II 76mm (Matilda II CS)	**65 points**
M3s (M3 Lee)	**85 points**

- Arm M3s tank with a long M3 75mm tank gun in place of the short M2 75mm tank gun for +10 points.

M4 (M4A2 Sherman)	**100 points**

- Arm M4 tank with .50 cal AA MG for +5 points.

Options

- Mount a Tankodesantniki SMG team on T-34, Mark II, M3s, or M4 tank for +15 points.
- Add Anti-aircraft Platoon for +45 points.

A Tankovy Batalon must contain at least one Tankovy Company equipped with the same type of tank as the Battalion HQ.

PODPOLKOVNIK

PODPOLKOVNIK

Company Command tank

BATTALION HQ

KAPITAN
MEDIUM TANKOVY COMPANY

KAPITAN
TANKOVY COMPANY

KAPITAN
TANKOVY COMPANY

KAPITAN
TANK RIDER COMPANY

KAPITAN
HEAVY ANTI-TANK COMPANY

LEYTENANT

DShK AA MG on truck

DShK AA MG on truck

DShK AA MG on truck

ANTI-AIRCRAFT PLATOON

KAPITAN
MORTAR COMPANY

TANKOVY BATALON

The devastating losses suffered by the Soviet tank forces at the hands of the Nazi invaders have now been made good. Thanks to the dedication of the factory workers and the steady supply of lend-lease vehicles from our allies, the tankists are now ready to smash the arrogant fascists with their puny Panzers upon the battlefields of Mother Russia.

COMBAT PLATOONS

A Tankovy Batalon must have two or three Tankovy Companies. At least one of the companies must be a Medium Tankovy Company and at least one of the companies must be equipped with the same type of tank as the Battalion HQ Platoon.

1 or 2 Medium Tankovy Companies

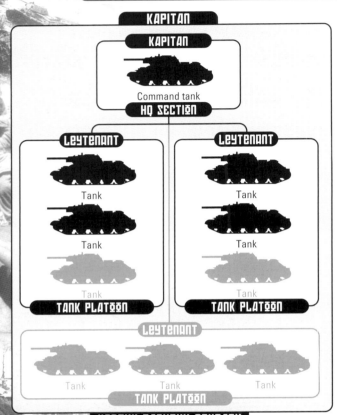

KAPITAN

KAPITAN

Command tank

HQ SECTION

LEYTENANT

Tank

Tank

Tank

TANK PLATOON

LEYTENANT

Tank

Tank

Tank

TANK PLATOON

LEYTENANT

Tank

Tank

Tank

TANK PLATOON

MEDIUM TANKOVY COMPANY

Tanks are extremely vulnerable to infantry tank-hunter teams at close quarters. The *tankodesantniki* (pronounced tank-o-dye-sant-nik-i), or tank riders, protect the tanks. Tankodesantniki never go far from their tank.

Company

	10	9	8	7	6	5	
T-34 obr 1941 or 1942	715	665	615	555	490	425	points

- Replace up to three T-34 obr 1942 tanks with T-34/57 tanks for +15 points per tank.
- Upgrade any or all T-34 obr 1942 or T-34/57 tanks with Cupolas for +5 points per tank.

	10	9	8	7	6	5	
Mark II (Matilda II)	530	485	440	395	350	300	points

- Replace any or all Mark II (Matilda II) tanks with Mark II 76mm (Matilda II CS) tanks at no cost.

	10	9	8	7	6	5	
M3s (M3 Lee)	635	590	545	490	435	375	points

- Arm any or all M3s tanks with long M3 75mm tank guns in place of their short M2 75mm tank guns for +10 points per tank.

	10	9	8	7	6	5	
M4 (M4A2 Sherman)	815	755	695	630	560	485	points

- Arm any or all M4 tanks with .50 cal AA MG for +5 points per tank.

Option

- Mount Tankodesantniki SMG teams on all T-34, Mark II, M3s, or M4 tanks for +15 points per team.

0 to 2 Light Tankovy Companies

Better armed and armoured than their German counterparts, our light tanks are the steel wolves circling and snapping at the fascist beasts and dragging them down into smoking ruin.

While most of our tanks come from the factories of Leningrad, Stalingrad and Tankograd in the Urals, our British and American allies have sent numbers of their own tanks through the lend-lease program as well. These 'Valentines' and 'General Stuarts' are reliable, but undergunned. Still, every little bit helps.

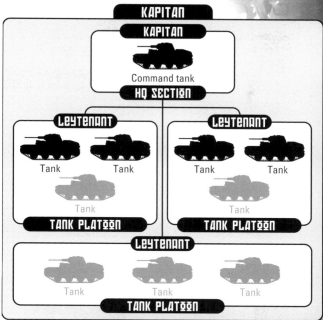

Company

	10	9	8	7	6	5	
T-60 obr 1942	195	185	165	150	135	115	points
T-70 obr 1942	275	255	230	210	190	160	points
T-70 obr 1943				220	195	165	points
Mark III (Valentine II)	355	330	305	275	245	210	points

- Replace any or all Mark III (Valentine II) tanks with Mark III (Valentine VIII) tanks for +15 points per tank.

	10	9	8	7	6	5	
M3l (M3A1 Stuart)	300	280	255	230	205	175	points

- Arm any or all M3l tanks with AA MG for +5 points per tank.

 WEAPONS PLATOONS

0 to 1 Heavy Anti-tank Company

Company
HQ Section with:

2 Anti-tank Platoons	**150 points**
1 Anti-tank Platoon	**80 points**

Option
- Add Komissar team for +5 points.

The soldiers of the heavy anti-tank company play a key role in the work of the Tankovy Batalon. While the brave tank commanders drive hard towards the enemy, the anti-tank guns fire round after round at the fascist panzers. Once the tanks overcome the enemy, the artillerists quickly hitch their guns to the trucks and follow in the pursuit of the enemy.

The 76mm ZIS-3 guns of a Heavy Anti-tank Company can not fire Artillery Bombardments.

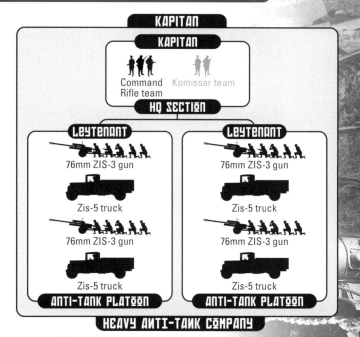

TANKOVY BATALON

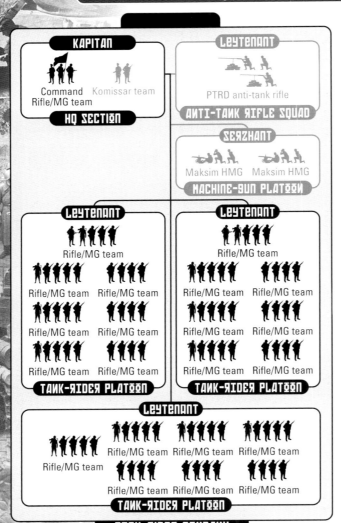

0 to 1 Tank-rider Company

Company
HQ Section with:

3 Tank-rider Platoons	**320 points**
2 Tank-rider Platoons	220 points
1 Tank-rider Platoon	120 points

Options
- Replace all Rifle/MG teams with SMG teams in one Tank-rider Platoon at no cost.
- Add Komissar team for +5 points.
- Add Maksim HMG teams for +20 points per team.
- Add PTRD anti-tank rifle team for +20 points.

Like Alexander Nevski and the warrior knights of old, the bold tank-riders mount their steel-clad chargers to lead the attack. Fighting closely with the tanks, they will drive out the Nazi invaders as Nevski drove out their Teutonic ancestors.

While the tanks are the undoubted masters of the Steppe, the tank-riders are vital for clearing the villages and woods in their path. Together they are unstoppable.

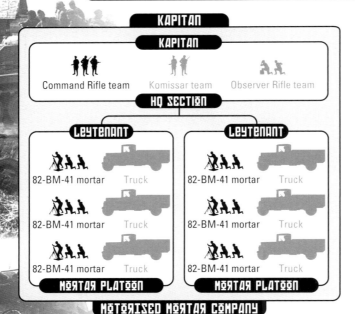

0 to 1 Motorised Mortar Company

Company
HQ Section with:

2 Mortar Platoons	**135 points**
1 Mortar Platoon	75 points

Options
- Add Trucks to the platoon at no cost.
- Add Komissar team for +5 points.
- Add Observer Rifle team for +30 points.

When attacking infantry the *tankovy batalon* is vulnerable to tank-hunters and anti-tank guns. The massed fire of the mortar company batters the enemy, keeping their heads down. Their task may not be the heroic work of the tank crews, but many a tankist has been thankful for the storm of mortar rounds pounding the enemy.

SUPPORT PLATOONS

0 to 1 Armoured Car Company

Company	
10 BA-10M	400 points
9 BA-10M	375 points
8 BA-10M	345 points
7 BA-10M	310 points
6 BA-10M	275 points
5 BA-10M	240 points
4 BA-10M	195 points
3 BA-10M	150 points

The armoured car battalions that survived to fight with the tank corps were pre-war units stationed in the East away from the fighting. They had plenty of time to train before going into battle and are well trained.

Armoured Car Companies are Reconnaissance Platoons

Armoured Car Companies are rated as **_Fearless Trained_**

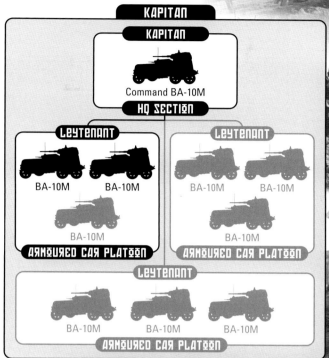

0 to 1 Heavy Mortar Company

Company	
HQ Section with:	
3 Heavy Mortar Platoons	195 points
2 Heavy Mortar Platoons	135 points
1 Heavy Mortar Platoon	75 points

Options
- Add Trucks to the platoon at no cost.
- Add Komissar team for +5 points.
- Add Observer Rifle team for +30 points.

Heavy mortar companies provide the Red Army with mobile artillery, applying pressure to the capitalist lines through unrelenting bombardment. They keep the fascist cowards hiding in their holes and divert their attention from the brave socialist soldiers sent to purge them from the Soviet Union.

Unlike the lighter battalion mortars, the big 120-PM-38 heavy mortar has the explosive power in its shells to destroy the fascists in their defences rather than merely neutralising them.

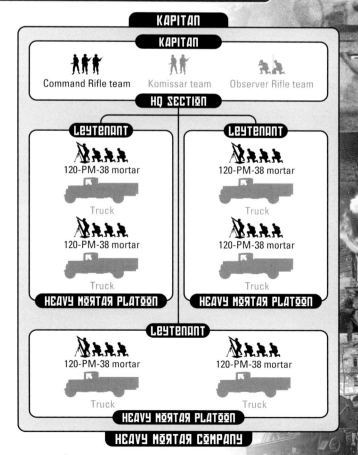

MIXED TANKOVY BATALON

(TANK COMPANY)

A Mixed Tankovy Batalon is organised the same as a Tankovy Batalon, except that it may only have one Tankovy Company of each type, but can also have one Heavy Tankovy Company as well. If the battalion has only two Tankovy Companies, they may be any two of the three types.

HEADQUARTERS PLATOON

1 Battalion HQ

The Battalion HQ of a Mixed Tankovy Batalon does not have any tanks. In battle the battalion commander rode in one of the tanks in a combat company. Before deployment, you may remove one tank from any Tankovy Company and make it into the Battalion Command Tank.

COMBAT PLATOONS

0 to 1 Light Tankovy Company

This is organised and equipped like the Light Tankovy Company shown on page 141, except that it may not have more than eight tanks and may not have T-70 obr 1943 or Mark III (Valentine VIII) tanks.

0 to 1 Medium Tankovy Company

This is organised and equipped like the Medium Tankovy Company shown on page 140, except that it may not have T-34 obr 1942, T-34/57, or M4 (M4A2 Sherman) tanks and M3s (M3 Lee) tanks may not be armed with Long 75mm guns.

- You may equip all of your T-34 obr 1941 tanks with extra armour for +10 points per tank.

0 to 1 Heavy Tankovy Company

This is organised like the Medium Tankovy Company shown on page 140, except that it may have as few as three tanks and not have more than seven tanks. All of these tanks must be KV-1e, KV-1s, or KV-2 tanks for the following points.

Company

	7	6	5	4	3	
KV-1e	755	670	580	480	360	points

- Replace any or all KV-1e tanks with KV-2 tanks at no cost.

	7	6	5	4	3	
KV-1s	755	670	580	480	360	points

Option

- Mount Tankodesantniki SMG teams on all KV tanks for +15 points per team.

T-26 Tankovy Company

The first versions of the T-26 entered service in 1933, and for its day it was an outstanding tank. It was manufactured in greater quantities than any other tank of its time and by the start of the war the Red Army had 11,000 of them in service. Most of these were lost in the months following the German invasion in June 1941. However, some survived in areas distant from the fighting and in the desperate days at the start of 1942 they were sent into battle despite their obsolescence.

Any Light, Medium, or Heavy Tankovy Companies in a Mixed Tankovy Batalon may be replaced with T-26 Tankovy Companies for the following points cost.

Company

	10	9	8	7	6	5	
T-26s obr 1939	245	230	215	195	170	145	points

MOTOSTRELKOVY BATALON

(INFANTRY COMPANY)

A force based around a Motostrelkovy Batalon must contain:

- a Company HQ, and
- two or three Motostrelkovy Companies.

Weapons Companies available to a Motostrelkovy Batalon are:

- a Machine-gun Company,
- a Motorised Anti-tank Rifle Company,
- two Motorised Mortar Companies,
- a Motorised Anti-tank Company,
- a Submachine-gun Company,
- a Motorised Artillery Battalion,
- a Truck Section,
- a Light or Medium Tankovy Company.
- a Light Armoured Car Platoon, and

- an Armoured Transporter Platoon.

Support Companies for a Motostrelkovy Batalon can be:

- Tankovy Companies,
- an Armoured Car Company,
- Heavy Mortar Companies,
- a Kazachya Sotnya, and
- Corps Support Companies.

You may have up to **one** Support Company attached to your company for each Motostrelkovy Company you field.

Motivation and Skill

The desperate need for fresh units to replace casualties means that few Soviet troops receive much training before being committed to battle. A Motostrelkovy Batalon is rated as **Fearless Conscript**.

HEADQUARTERS

1 Battalion HQ

Headquarters

Battalion HQ	25 points

Option

- Add Anti-aircraft Platoon for +45 points.

The combined effort required to cast off the yoke of the despised Nazi invaders is epitomized in the composition of the versatile Motostrelkovy Company. Our troops of the brave *motostrelkovy* fight arm-in-arm with their comrades from the artillery, reconnaissance and tank forces. The commander of a Motostrelkovy Company has a devastating array of support arms at his disposal. Anti-tank weapons, artillery, machine-guns, all are at his beck and call. This versatility combined with the mobility of motorised infantry will prove too much for the over-stretched Fritzes.

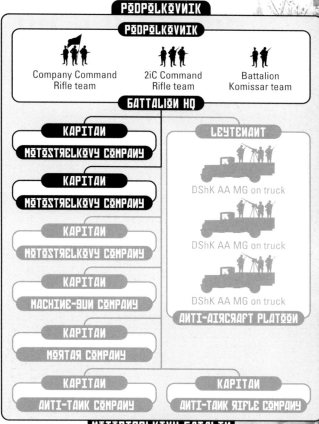

COMBAT COMPANIES

2 or 3 Motostrelkovy Companies

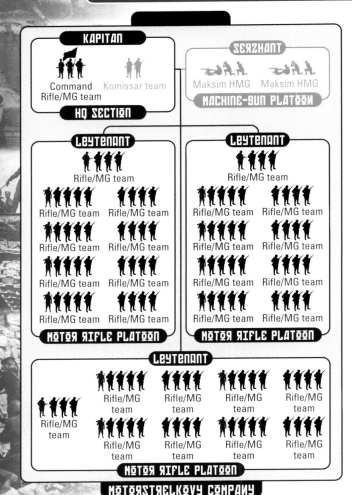

KAPITAN

Command Rifle/MG team — Komissar team

HQ SECTION

SERZHANT

Maksim HMG — Maksim HMG

MACHINE-GUN PLATOON

LEYTENANT

Rifle/MG team

Rifle/MG team — Rifle/MG team
Rifle/MG team — Rifle/MG team
Rifle/MG team — Rifle/MG team

MOTOR RIFLE PLATOON

LEYTENANT

Rifle/MG team

Rifle/MG team — Rifle/MG team
Rifle/MG team — Rifle/MG team
Rifle/MG team — Rifle/MG team

MOTOR RIFLE PLATOON

LEYTENANT

Rifle/MG team

Rifle/MG team — Rifle/MG team — Rifle/MG team — Rifle/MG team
Rifle/MG team — Rifle/MG team — Rifle/MG team — Rifle/MG team

MOTOR RIFLE PLATOON

MOTORSTRELKOVY COMPANY

Company

HQ Section with:

3 Motor Rifle Platoons	**420 points**
2 Motor Rifle Platoons	**285 points**
1 Motor Rifle Platoon	**150 points**

Options

- Replace all Rifle/MG teams with SMG teams in one Motor Rifle Platoon at no cost.
- Add Komissar team for +5 points.
- Add Maksim HMG teams for +20 points per team.

The motostrelkovy companies are the pick of the Red Army's infantry. While tanks alone can only attack, the motor-riflemen are more versatile. The brave *motostrelkovy* keep pace with the rapidly advancing tanks in the attack. As fast as the enemy flees before the might of the vengeful Red Army the *motostrelkovy* pursue. Yet when the enemy turns at bay and launches a desperate counterattack, the *motostrelkovy* dig in and hold on until a new attack can be launched.

WEAPONS COMPANIES

0 to 1 Machine-gun Company

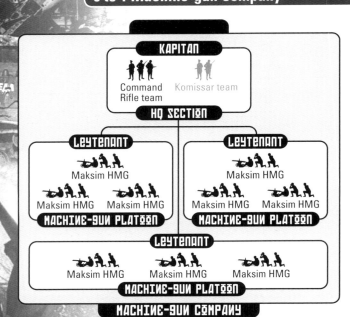

KAPITAN

Command Rifle team — Komissar team

HQ SECTION

LEYTENANT

Maksim HMG

Maksim HMG — Maksim HMG

MACHINE-GUN PLATOON

LEYTENANT

Maksim HMG

Maksim HMG — Maksim HMG

MACHINE-GUN PLATOON

LEYTENANT

Maksim HMG — Maksim HMG — Maksim HMG

MACHINE-GUN PLATOON

MACHINE-GUN COMPANY

Company

HQ Section with:

3 Machine-gun Platoons	**200 points**
2 Machine-gun Platoons	**140 points**
1 Machine-gun Platoon	**80 points**

Option

- Add Komissar team for +5 points.

The machine-gun is still the best defence against the counterattacks of the desperate Hitlerite infantry. The deadly fire of the *Maksim* scythes down the fascists like the first wheat of summer.

0 to 1 Motorised Anti-tank Rifle Company

Company

HQ Section with:

3 Anti-tank Rifle Platoons	125 points
2 Anti-tank Rifle Platoons	90 points
1 Anti-tank Rifle Platoon	50 points

Option

• Add Komissar team for +5 points.

The anti-tank rifle company is responsible for protecting the entire battalion. To do this it is often broken up into detachments.

A Motorised Anti-tank Rifle Company may make Combat Attachments to Combat Platoons.

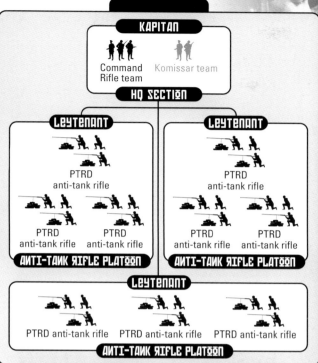

The half-tracks and armoured cars of the invaders are the favourite prey of our anti-tank riflemen. Dug in amongst the riflemen, they leave any of Fritz's tanks foolish enough to attack burning upon the battlefield.

0 to 2 Motorised Mortar Companies

The Mortar Companies of a Motostrelkovy Batalon are organised like those on page 142. You may convert one Mortar Company in your force to a Heavy Mortar Company by replacing each 82-BM-41 mortar with a 120-PM-38 mortar for +30 points per Mortar Platoon.

0 to 1 Motorised Anti-tank Company

Company

HQ Section with:

2 Anti-tank Platoons	100 points
1 Anti-tank Platoon	55 points

Option

• Replace all 45mm obr 1937 guns with 45mm obr 1942 guns for +5 points per platoon.

• Add Komissar team for +5 points.

The ingenuity of the Soviet weapons designers has taken the German 3.7cm Pak36 gun, improved upon it, and turned it back upon the fascists. With their 45mm gun, effective against both tanks and infantry, the anti-tank company is a useful and versatile part of the Red Army.

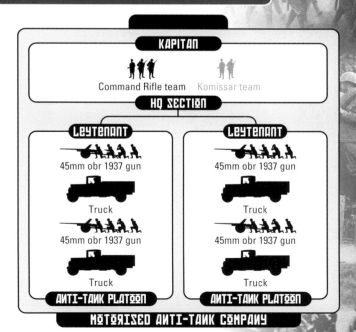

147

0 to 1 Submachine-gun Company

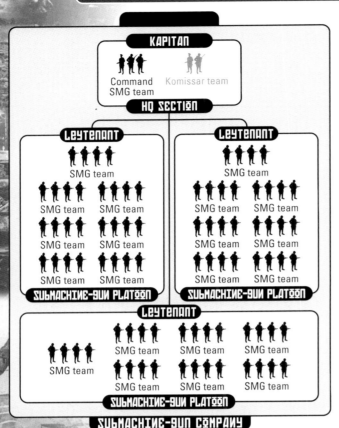

Company
HQ Section with:

3 Submachine-gun Platoons	320 points
2 Submachine-gun Platoons	220 points
1 Submachine-gun Platoon	120 points

Option
• Add Komissar team for +5 points.

The role of the submachine-gun company is simple: to lead the assault against the enemy and destroy them. Wherever the fighting is thickest, the need most desperate, and the enemy the toughest is where the *avtomatchiki*, the submachine-gunners, are. They lead the way, storming enemy positions with speed and ferocity.

0 to 1 Transport Platoon

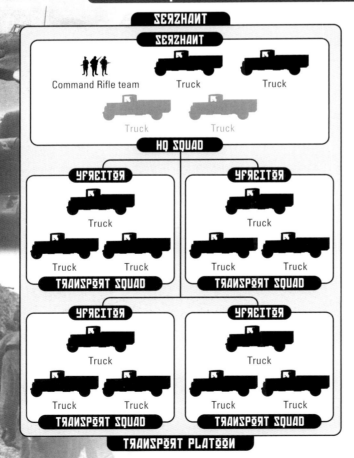

Platoon
HQ Squad with:

4 Truck Squads	75 points
3 Truck Squads	60 points
2 Truck Squads	45 points
1 Truck Squad	30 points

Option
• Add trucks to HQ Squad for +5 points per truck.

A Transport Platoon is a Transport Platoon.

The scarcity of transport in the Red Army means that trucks are highly prized. Without them the *motostrelkovy* could not keep pace with the Red tide sweeping the fascists from the Motherland.

Trucks
The most common trucks in the Red Army at the start of the war were the four-wheeled ZIS-5 truck, a Soviet copy of the American Autocar truck, and the ZIS-6, a six-wheeled version. The need for more tanks curtailed truck production, so US-supplied Dodge and 'Studebekker' trucks became the backbone of the Red Army from 1943.

MOTOSTRELKOVY BATALON

SOVIET

0 to 1 Motorised Artillery Battalion

Company

HQ Section with:

6 Gun Platoons	355 points
4 Gun Platoons	285 points
2 Gun Platoons	170 points
1 Gun Platoon	100 points

Options

- Add Komissar team for +5 points.
- Add Observer team for +30 points.
- Add trucks at no cost.

The motorised artillery battalion is armed with the versatile 76.2mm ZIS-3 gun. This fine weapon can deliver devastating barrages, but is often at its best rolling forward and pounding the fascists with hard-hitting direct fire. A massed battery firing over open sights is the surest way to guarantee a successful assault.

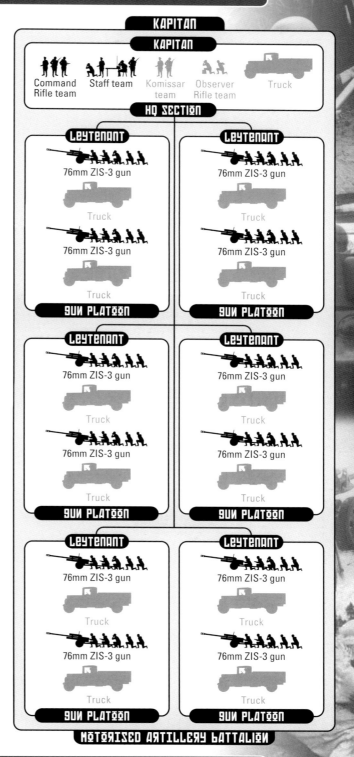

0 to 1 Light or Medium Tankovy Company

The Soviet economy was not particularly mechanised before the war, and the losses of 1941 made trucks even more scarce. With few trucks and no armoured personnel carriers, the Red Army turned to the one thing it did have in numbers to motorise its infantry—tanks! Every mechanised brigade included a tank regiment specifically to transport the infantry into battle.

A Motostrelkovy Batalon may have one Medium Tankovy Company from page 140 or one Light Tankovy Company from page 141 as a Weapons Platoon.

MOTOSTRELKOVY BATALON

0 to 1 Light Armoured Car Platoon

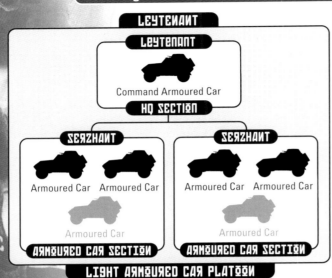

A Light Armoured Car Platoon is a Reconnaissance Platoon.

Platoon

HQ Section with:

7 BA-64	195 points
6 BA-64	175 points
5 BA-64	150 points
4 BA-64	125 points
3 BA-64	95 points

- Replace the AA MG on up to two armoured cars with a hull-mounted PTRD-41 anti-tank rifle at no cost.

5 BA-10M	240 points
4 BA-10M	195 points
3 BA-10M	150 points

*The reconnaissance troops are picked from the most resourceful and experienced troops. Light Armoured Car Platoons and Armoured Transporter Platoons are rated as **Fearless Trained** and operate independently from the rest of their company. They are not subject to the Centralised Control special rule.*

0 to 1 Light Armoured Transporter Platoon

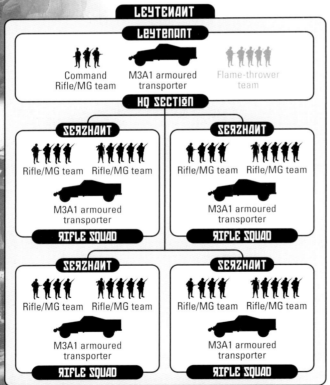

Equipped with armoured transporters and the best weapons, the *razvedchiki*, the scouts, move swiftly to strike the enemy with deadly force. Operating with the most forward elements of the Red Army these soldiers stand out even amongst the many heroes of the Great Patriotic War.

Platoon

HQ Section with:

4 Rifle Squads	295 points
3 Rifle Squads	230 points
2 Rifle Squads	165 points

Options

- Replace all Rifle/MG teams with SMG teams at no cost.
- Add Flame-thrower team for +50 points.
- Replace AA MG on any or all M3A1 armoured transporters with 0.5" AA MG's for +5 points per vehicle.
- Replace all M3A1 armoured transporters with BA-10M or captured Sd Kfz 251 armoured transporters at no cost.
- Replace all M3A1 armoured transporters with one Universal Carrier armoured transporter per Rifle/MG team for +10 points per Rifle Squad. .
- If HQ Section has a Universal Carrier armoured transporter, add another for the Flame-thrower team for +15 points.
- Replace all M3A1 armoured transporters with one Motorcycle team per Rifle/MG team for -10 points per Rifle Squad and -10 points for the HQ Section
- If HQ Section has a Motorcycle team, add another for the Flame-thrower team for +5 points.

ROTA RAZVEDKI

(RECONNAISSANCE MECHANISED COMPANY)

The reconnaissance force of the mechanised troops is their rota razvedki *or reconnaissance company. It has the only truly mechanised infantry in the entire Red Army. The* razvedchiki *ride into battle in armoured transporters. These are a mix of lend-lease scout cars and carriers, converted armoured cars, and captured half-tracks.*

A force based around an Rota Razvedki must contain:
- a Company HQ, and
- one or two Armoured Transporter Platoons.

Weapons Platoons available to a Rota Razvedki are:
- a Light Armoured Car Platoon,
- a Mortar Company, and
- a Heavy Anti-tank Company.

Support Companies for a Rota Razvedki can be:
- Tankovy Companies,
- an Armoured Car Company,
- Heavy Mortar Companies,
- Motostrelkovy Companies,
- a Kazachya Sotnya, and
- Corps Support Companies.

You may have up to **one** Support Company attached to your company for each Armoured Transporter Platoon you field.

Motivation and Skill

A Rota Razvedki is rated as **Fearless Trained**.

HEADQUARTERS

1 Company HQ

Headquarters

Company HQ	50 points

Options
- Add Komissar team and Motorcycle team for +10 points.
- Add Anti-aircraft Platoon for +60 points.

COMBAT PLATOONS

1 or 2 Armoured Transporter Platoons

The Armoured Transporter Platoons are organised as shown on the previous page.

WEAPONS PLATOONS

0 to 1 Light Armoured Car Platoon

The Light Armoured Car Platoon is organised as shown on the previous page.

0 to 1 Mortar Company

The Mortar Company is organised as shown on page 142. Their higher Skill rating increases the points cost by +20 points per Mortar Platoon and +10 points for the Observer team.

0 to 1 Heavy Anti-tank Company

The Heavy Anti-tank Company is organised as shown on page 141. Their higher Skill rating increases the points cost by +35 points per Anti-tank Platoon.

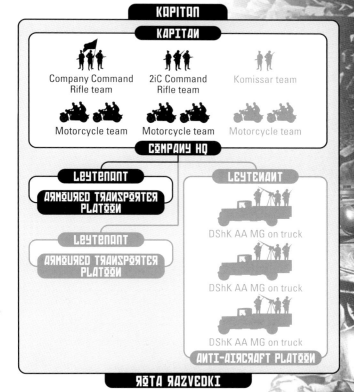

GVARDEYSKIY TANKOVY BATALON

(GUARDS TANK BATTALION)

Stavka, the Soviet high command, distinguished successful units with the 'Guards' designation. These were always units that had succeeded in capturing their objectives in heavy fighting. A *Gvardeyskiy Tankovy Batalon*, a Guards Tank Battalion, is such a unit. The reward was the best equipment available—and the most difficult assignments!

You may upgrade your Tankovy Batalon or Mixed Tankovy Batalon to Guards status making the Training rating of the entire battalion and its supporting troops **Trained** rather than **Conscript**. If you do this the number of points you have available to spend on your force *decreases* as follows:

Normal Force	Guards Force
1000 points	775 points
1500 points	1165 points
2000 points	1550 points

A Gvardeyskiy Tankovy Batalon has the following differences from a normal Tankovy Batalon.

- It may not field T-26 tanks.

- Light Armoured Car Platoons, Armoured Transporter Platoons, and Armoured Car Companies remain Trained, but decrease in cost by -15 points for every full 50 points that you spend on them.

- A supporting Kazachya Sotnya remains Trained, but decreases in cost by -15 points for every full 50 points that you spend on them.

- Guards Heavy Tank Companies and Guards Rocket Mortar Batteries remain Trained, but decrease in cost by -15 points for every full 50 points that you spend on them.

GVARDEYSKIY MOTOSTRELKOVY BATALON

(Guards Motor Rifle Battalion)

Like the Tank Corps, the Mechanised Corps were also rewarded with Guards status for successful combat actions. By the end of 1943 almost half of the Mechanised Corps had won the Guards honour.

You may field a *Gvardeyskiy Motostrelkovy Batalon*, a Guards Motor Rifle Battalion, using the changes above, but applying them to the Motostrelkovy Batalon instead of the Tankovy Batalon.

GVARDEYSKIY ROTA RAZVEDKI

(Guards Reconnaissance Company)

A Mechanised Brigade's *rota razvedki* or reconnaissance company was always in the lead, and always took the brunt of the inevitable German counterattack. As a result casualties were high and few lived long enough to acquire much experience.

If you field a *Gvardeyskiy Rota Razvedki*,

a Guards Reconnaissance Company, your HQ Platoon, Combat Platoons and Weapons Platoons remain Trained. However all of your Support choices must be upgraded to a Skill rating of Trained for +15 points for each 50 points or part thereof that you spend on them, unless they are already rated as Trained.

...Mariya Oktyabrskaya, Dnepr 1943...

Yefimovich grasps his mug of acorn coffee tightly and slumps tiredly down onto an ammunition crate beside his comrades. "Yefimovich, tell Gregori about what happened today with Tovaritsch Mariya" urges Volskova.

"Da, very well" he begins, taking a long gulp of his coffee.

"It was mid-afternoon and we had just broken through the German lines, or so we thought. It had seemed too quiet, too subdued. That fool Tolistov had blundered ahead yet again and we had become separated when the whole world seemed to erupt around our very ears! It was obvious that Tolistov had led us all into an ambush, blast his eyes. The first shot, bang! Hit us on the flank. The boy Pavel was hysterical, screaming for his mother. But Mariya refused to panic. We were reversing when, bang, another hit! This one was louder, closer, the impact sending us back, skidding until we came to a halt. Then we waited, that cold silence, not knowing whether we'd start burning. Fjedor shouted down from the turret 'Left track - out!' We weren't going anywhere. Mariya picked up the tool kit from the floor. 'Where the hell do you think you're going?' demanded Fjedor. 'A still tank is a dead tank' shouted Mariya. She turned to the rest of us. 'Who's with me?' Pavel was sobbing still; Fjedor for all his protests muttered something about his back. She looked at me, what could I do? Next thing I know, we are clambering out from the tank. In one, two, three movements we hit the hard ground."

"Outside was chaos, smashed tanks, bodies, fire-terrible! Clank, clank, clank, Mariya hammered at the buckled links. The damage wasn't as bad as we feared but still bad enough to leave us exposed. Soon enough they had our range and bullets were zipping all around us."

"You know what she did?" asks Yefimovich with a smile. "She threw her hammer up at the turret to where Fjedor was skulking. 'Fjedor! One hundred yards, ten o'clock, continuous fire, keep their heads down, now!' There was enemy fire coming from ahead of us, I wasn't sure exactly where but somehow she knew where to aim Fjedor at. My heart was pounding, my mouth dry with fear. We shouldn't be out here! I thought."

"We heard Fjedor grumbling but soon he was firing. By the gods, it was loud! Still Mariya kept hammering at the buckled track, her hands bruised and cut. Soon enough we had beaten the last link into place and the track was good once more. The fire was getting heavier; Mariya had her heel clipped by a stray shot but she just pushed me head first back into the tank and dropped back into her seat. 'Let's go and find Tolistov'".

154

KAZACHYA SOTNYA

(MECHANISED COMPANY)

A force based around an Kazachya Sotnya must contain:

- a Company HQ, and
- two to four Kazachya Platoons.

Weapons Platoons available to an Kazachya Sotnya are:

- a Tachanka Platoon,
- a Cossack Anti-tank Rifle Platoon,
- a Cossack Mortar Company, and
- a Cossack Regimental Gun Company.

Support Companies for an Kazachya Sotnya can be:

- a Horse Artillery Battery,
- Motostrelkovy Companies,
- Armoured Transporter Platoons,
- an Armoured Car Company,

- Heavy Mortar Companies,
- Tankovy Companies, and
- Corps Support Companies.

You may have up to **one** Support Company attached to your company for each Kazachya Platoon you field.

Motivation and Skill

Cossacks learn to ride when they learn to walk. Combine this with a long military tradition and you get some of the finest soldiers in the Red Army.

A Kazachya Sotnya is rated as **Fearless Trained**.

The platoons of an Kazachya Sotnya are an exception to the Centralised Control special rule. They operate as normal platoons.

HEADQUARTERS

1 Company HQ

Headquarters

Company HQ	45 points

Options

- Add Komissar team for +10 points.
- Add up to 3 DShK AA MG on trucks for +20 points each.

Before the game begins you may amalgamate two Kazachya Platoons with the Company HQ to form one large platoon under the 2iC Command team. The Company Command team, Komissar team, and Anti-aircraft Platoon are not fielded in this case. The platoons' Command teams become normal Rifle/MG teams.

The Kazachya Sotnya In Support

When taking a Kazachya Sotnya as a Support Platoon you can either take a single Kazachya Platoon, or you may take the Company HQ and two Kazachya Platoons amalgamated as described above as a single support choice.

In either case you may take a Tachanka Platoon as part of the same Support Platoon.

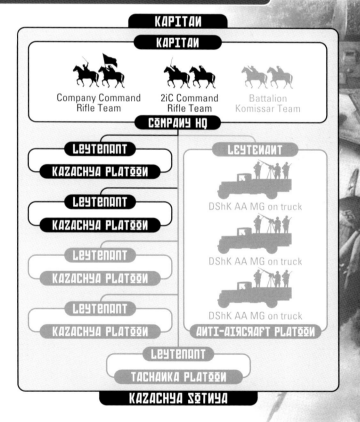

2 to 4 Kazachya Platoons

LEYTENANT

LEYTENANT

Command Rifle/MG Team

HQ SECTION

SERZHANT

Rifle/MG Team

Rifle/MG Team

KAZACHYA SQUAD

SERZHANT

Rifle/MG Team

Rifle/MG Team

KAZACHYA SQUAD

KAZACHYA PLATOON

Platoon

HQ Section with:

2 Kazachya Squads	**130 points**

The fearsome Cossacks are horse-warriors of old. In this age of mechanised warfare they fight on, their ferocity and skill undiminished. They penetrate deep into the enemy lines taking advantage of their mobility in rough terrain, not to mention the option of delivering an old-style charge if the opportunity arises.

WEAPONS PLATOONS

0 to 1 Tachanka Platoon

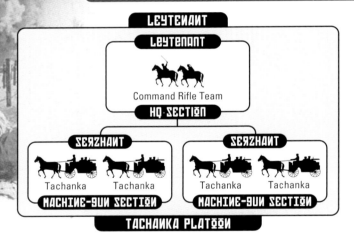

LEYTENANT

LEYTENANT

Command Rifle Team

HQ SECTION

SERZHANT

Tachanka   Tachanka

MACHINE-GUN SECTION

SERZHANT

Tachanka   Tachanka

MACHINE-GUN SECTION

TACHANKA PLATOON

Platoon

HQ Section with:

2 Machine-gun Sections	**115 points**
1 Machine-gun Section	**70 points**

Option

- Allow Maxim HMG to fire as a Self-defence Anti-aircraft weapon for +5 points per Tachanka.

The Tachanka

The *tachanka* machine-gun cart was invented by the Ukrainian Anarchist forces during the Russian Civil War of 1918 to 1922 and quickly adopted by their Red Army opponents. The concept was simple and uniquely suited to the circumstances—a marriage of the deadly Maksim heavy machine-gun with the fast *tachanka* cart common in the area.

This combination used four horses abreast, chariot-style, to give the *tachanka* the speed to keep up with the light cavalry that formed the strike forces of both sides and provide them with the fire support they desperately needed.

With Russian battlefields lacking the impenetrable barbed wire entanglements of the Western Front, cavalry were a powerful force limited only by the enemy machine-guns' ability to stop them. With the *tachanka* carts racing into position, wheeling around and firing their own machine-guns back, the cavalry could pin down the enemy machine-guns, then charge and rout their infantry.

With the Civil War long over and a new enemy threatening, the Soviet Cossacks find their *tachanka* carts as useful as ever. While they dismount to assault well-prepared positions, the combination of speed and *firepower* their partnership produces allows them to overrun less prepared foes with ease. As long as fast tanks remain in short supply, the *tachanka* will have its place in the Red Army.

0 to 1 Cossack Anti-tank Rifle Platoon

Platoon

HQ Section with:

3 AT Rifle Squads	**85 points**
2 AT Rifle Squads	**60 points**

Option

- Mount all teams as Cavalry teams for +5 points per team.

The anti-tank rifle platoon provides anti-tank support close to the forward positions occupied by the Cossack squadrons. The anti-tank rifle finds its mark in the soft flanks and bellies of the steel beasts of Hitler's army.

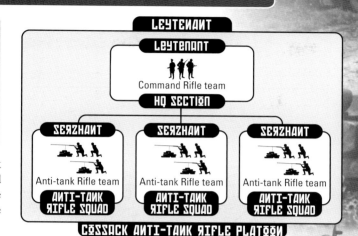

0 to 1 Cossack Mortar Company

Company

HQ Section with:

2 Mortar Platoons	**170 points**
1 Mortar Platoon	**90 points**

Options

- Add Komissar team for +5 points.
- Add Observer Rifle team for +40 points.
- Add one-horse carts at no cost.

In the age of modern warfare, the Cossacks rely upon the mortar company for close artillery support. Their weapon is the standard 82mm mortar, light enough to keep pace with the fast moving cavalry squadrons.

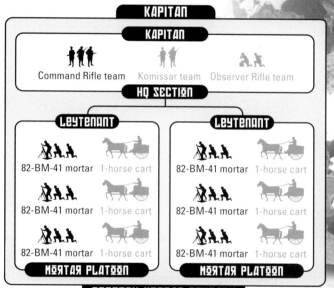

0 to 1 Cossack Regimental Gun Company

Company

HQ Section with:

2 Regimental Gun Platoons	**120 points**
1 Regimental Gun Platoon	**65 points**

Options

- Replace all 76mm obr 1927 guns with 45mm obr 1937 guns for +25 points per platoon or with 45mm obr 1942 guns for +40 points per platoon.
- Add Komissar team for +5 points.
- Mount Command Rifle team and Komissar team as Cavalry teams at no cost.
- Add Cavalry limbers at no cost

The Cossacks need artillery support that is as fast-moving as they are. The horse drawn guns provide a mobile, and powerful, solution.

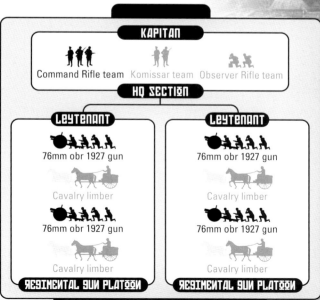

SUPPORT PLATOON

0 to 1 Horse Artillery Battery

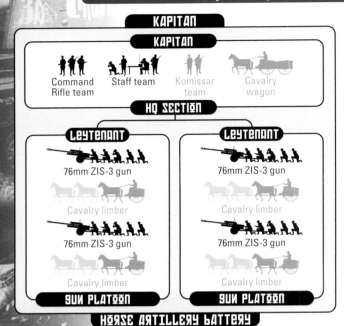

KAPITAN

KAPITAN

Command Rifle team | Staff team | Komissar team | Cavalry wagon

HQ SECTION

LEYTENANT | LEYTENANT

76mm ZIS-3 gun — Cavalry limber
76mm ZIS-3 gun — Cavalry limber

76mm ZIS-3 gun — Cavalry limber
76mm ZIS-3 gun — Cavalry limber

GUN PLATOON | GUN PLATOON

HORSE ARTILLERY BATTERY

Company

HQ Section with:

2 Gun Platoons	**285 points**
1 Gun Platoon	**160 points**

Options

- Add Komissar team for +5 points.
- Mount Command Rifle team and Komissar team as Cavalry teams at no cost.
- Add cavalry wagon to carry the Staff team at no cost.
- Add cavalry limbers at no cost.

Representing the triumphant combination of tradition with Soviet technical excellence, the horse artillery battery is armed with the fine, new 76mm ZIS-3 field gun. Its light yet strong construction is ideal for mobile artillery support.

Crash Action

The Cossack artillery has a long tradition of close support for their countrymen. They endlessly practice getting their guns into action as fast as possible to protect their brothers with their fire.

A Cossack Regimental Gun Company or Horse Artillery Battery may use the Horse Artillery Special Rule.

GVARDEYSKIY KAZACHYA SOTNYA

(GUARDS COSSACK SQUADRON)

The time the Cossacks spent training together before entering battle made them far superior to the run-of-the-mill infantry and most were already Guards by the start of the summer of 1942. However their casualties were high and time for integrating replacements short, so they were unable to improve much further.

If you field a Gvardeyskaya Kazachya Sotnya, a Guards Cossack Squadron, your HQ Platoon, Combat Platoons and Weapons Platoons remain Trained. However all of your Support Choices must be upgraded to a skill rating of Trained for +15 points for each 50 points or part thereof that you spend on them, unless they are already Trained. Note that their own horse artillery battery is already rated as Trained.

STRELKOVY BATALON

(INFANTRY COMPANY)

A force based around a Strelkovy Batalon must contain:

- a Battalion HQ, and
- two or three Strelkovy Companies.

Weapons Companies available to a Strelkovy Batalon are:

- a Scout Platoon,
- two Machine-gun Companies,
- a Submachine-gun Company,
- an Anti-tank Rifle Company,
- an Anti-tank Company,
- a Mortar Company,
- a Heavy Mortar Company,
- a Regimental Gun Company, and
- a Storm Group.

Support Companies for a Strelkovy Batalon can be

- a Tankovy Company,
- a Flame-thrower Platoon,
- a Flame-tank Platoon,
- an Artillery Battalion, and
- Divisional Support Companies.

You may have up to **one** Support Company attached to your battalion for each Strelkovy Company you are fielding.

Motivation and Skill

Soviet troops are poorly trained, but determined. A Strelkovy Batalon is **Fearless Conscript**.

 HEADQUARTERS

1 Battalion HQ

Headquarters

Battalion HQ	25 points

Options

- Add Anti-tank Rifle Platoon for +50 points.
- Add Anti-tank Platoon for +40 points.
- Replace both 45mm obr 1937 guns with 45mm obr 1942 guns for +5 points.
- Add Anti-aircraft Platoon for +45 points.
- Add Sapper Platoon of five Pioneer Rifle teams for +75 points.
- Add four additional Pioneer Rifle teams for +60 points.
- Equip Sapper Platoon with a Pioneer Supply wagon for +20 points.

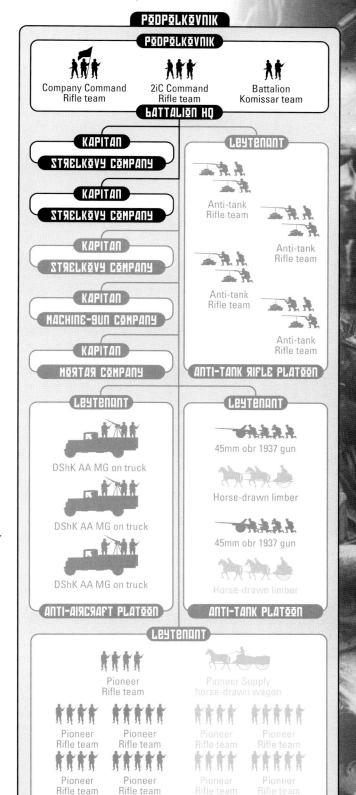

STRELKOVY BATALON

'The soldiers of the Workers and Peasants Red Army are heroes defending the people against the fascist vipers. The riflemen of the Strelkovy Batalon fight with socialist vigour, destroying the Hitlerite invaders and freeing our beloved Mother Russia from their tyranny.'

-Kapitan P. Kalishnikov

COMBAT COMPANIES

2 or 3 Strelkovy Companies

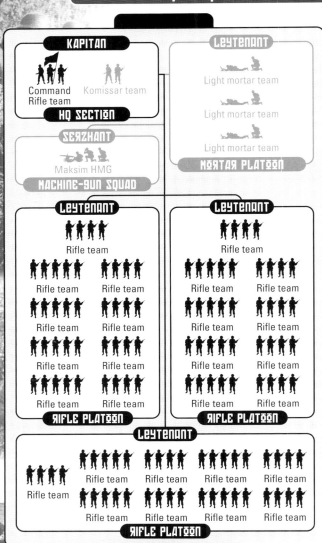

Company

HQ Section with:

3 Rifle Platoons	**285 points**
2 Rifle Platoons	**195 points**
1 Rifle Platoon	**105 points**

Options

- Replace all Rifle teams with Rifle/MG teams for +45 points per platoon.
- Replace all Rifle/MG teams with SMG teams in one Rifle Platoon at no cost.
- Add Komissar team for +5 points.
- Add Maksim HMG team for +20 points.
- Add up to three Light mortar teams for +10 points per team.

The Red Army soldier knows how highly victory is prized in the Red Army, and that nothing can be allowed to interfere with this exalted goal. Neither the futile resistance of the fascist enemy or any selfish thoughts of personal survival can be allowed to hinder the socialist victory. The individual is meaningless when compared to the survival of International Communism.

There are many Hitlerites infesting our state, and many workers have died heroic deaths eradicating them, but Russia is a vast country, and one thing it is not short of is people that are willing to fight to the last breath in defence of the Motherland.

SHTRAF COMPANY

Stalin's infamous Order 227—Not One Step Back formed *Shtrafniye Roti* or Penal Companies in each Army. These were used as assault troops and for risky tasks like mine-clearing under fire where they could redeem themselves with their blood.

You may take a Shtraf Company as a Support Platoon. It is organised like a normal Strelkovy Company, but it may not have any options other than adding a Komissar team, which it must have. Your Shtraf Company may not have more platoons than your smallest Strelkovy Company.

Because it is expected to die, the Shtraf Company does not add to the number of operational platoons when taking a Company Morale Check, nor does it count as destroyed if it suffers that fate. It is totally ignored for morale purposes.

For the same reason, its loss is of little military significance. Do not count it as a lost platoon when calculating Victory Points.

Since the soldiers of the Shtraf Company can only gain pardon for their crimes (such as spreading defeatist propaganda, failing to report defeatist talk, failing to shoot traitors attempting to desert or surrender, etc.) with their blood, they tend to be hard to stop.

A Shtraf Company always passes a Motivation Test on a roll of 2+.

HEAPON COMPANIES

0 to 1 Scout Platoon

Platoon
HQ Section with:

2 Scout Squads	**160 points**
1 Scout Squad	**100 points**

Option
- Add Komissar team for +5 points.

Your force may not contain more than one Scout Platoon, even it has more than one Strelkovy Batalon.

A Scout Platoon is rated as **Fearless Veteran**.

Scout Platoons are Reconnaissance Platoons

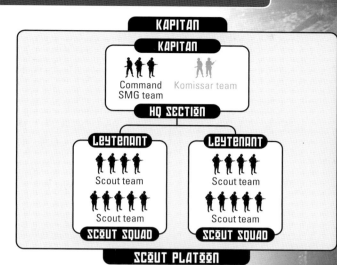

Red Army scouts probe enemy defences and prepare the way for the valiant Strelkovy Batalon to hound the fascist dogs all the way back to their kennel.

Scout Platoons are an exception to the Centralised Control special rule. They operate as a normal platoon.

0 to 2 Machine-gun Companies

The Machine-gun Companies of a Strelkovy Batalon are organised like those on page 148.

0 to 1 Submachine-gun Company

Company
HQ Section with:

3 Submachine-gun Platoons	**320 points**
2 Submachine-gun Platoons	**220 points**
1 Submachine-gun Platoon	**120 points**

Option
- Add Komissar team for +5 points.

The Red Army soldier knows no fear, bravely taking the battle to the cruel Hitlerite invaders. Armed with superior PPSh-41 *avtomat* guns, the Slavs of the *fusiler* Submachine-gun Companies throw Fritz back and cut him down as wheat before the Soviet sickle.

The submachine-gun company attacks the front line of the capitalist army. They take back the land and bread that has been stolen from us, liberating our socialist brothers and sisters from fascist tyranny.

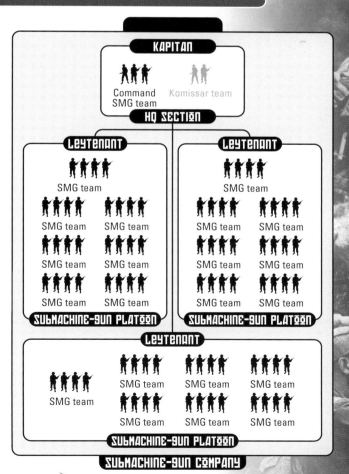

0 to 1 Anti-tank Rifle Company

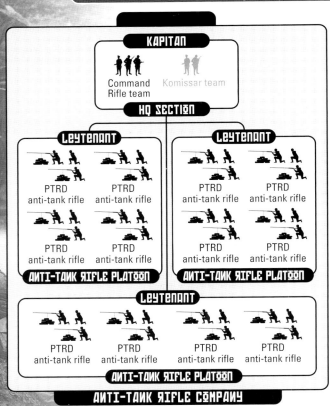

Company

HQ Section with:

3 Anti-tank Rifle Platoons	**165 points**
2 Anti-tank Rifle Platoons	**115 points**
1 Anti-tank Rifle Platoon	**65 points**

Option
- Add Komissar team for +5 points.

An Anti-tank Rifle Company may make Combat Attachments to Combat Platoons.

The Hitlerites underestimate out strength, they see no tanks and think we are defenceless. We are never defenceless.

While just one of our PTRD-41 anti-tank rifles may not be fearsome, a dozen or more wielded by brave socialist workers will tear apart light tanks and make heavier ones think twice. We shall lure them into our trap and destroy their tanks and they will fear us.

0 to 1 Anti-tank Company

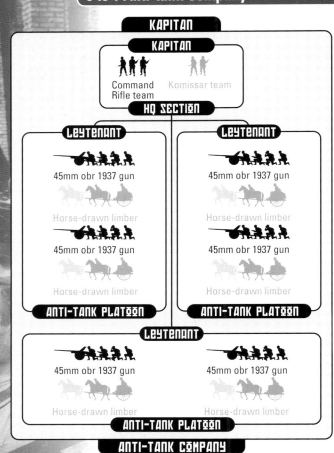

Company

HQ Section with:

3 Anti-tank Platoons	**140 points**
2 Anti-tank Platoons	**95 points**
1 Anti-tank Platoon	**50 points**

Options
- Replace all 45mm obr 1937 guns with 45mm obr 1942 guns for +5 points per platoon.
- Add Komissar team for +5 points.
- Add horse-drawn limbers at no cost.

Our brilliant engineers have defeated the Fascist monster again. With the opening of 1943, they have made our already formidable anti-tank guns even more effective.

Let the fascist army come. Let them bring their armoured tanks, we will be waiting with our guns and destroy them as easily as we have always done.

SOVIET

0 to 1 Mortar Company

Company

HQ Section with:

3 Mortar Platoons	**190 points**
2 Mortar Platoons	**130 points**
1 Mortar Platoon	**70 points**

Option

- Add Komissar team for +5 points.
- Add Observer Rifle team for +30 points.
- Add one-horse carts at no cost.

Every Red Army rifle battalion has a company of mortars. The battalion commander uses these to fire devastating bombardments at the fascist invaders neutralising the enemy before our attacks and wiping out their counterattacks.

A wise officer deploys his mortar company where it can see its target. Socialist workers do not instinctively know the complexities of firing artillery bombardments at targets out of sight, however, brave soviet soldiers can hit anything they can see. Of course more fortunate units have telephones, allowing them to neutralise a wider range of targets.

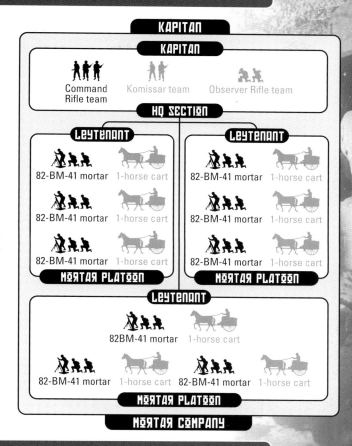

0 to 1 Heavy Mortar Company

The Heavy Mortar Company of a Strelkovy Batalon are organised like those on page 143.

0 to 1 Regimental Gun Company

Company

HQ Section with:

2 Regimental Gun Platoons	**95 points**
1 Regimental Gun Platoon	**50 points**

Options

- Add Komissar team for +5 points.
- Add Observer Rifle team for +30 points.
- Add horse-drawn limbers at no cost

The Hitlerites think we are cowards, hiding behind our big guns. We are not cowards, we do not hide behind hills throwing shells at them. They will then know who the cowards are when they see us run our guns forward. They will see us aiming at them down the barrel of our guns, before they run from our socialist fury.

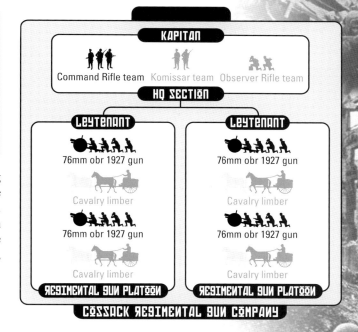

0 to 1 Storm Group

The Red Army has learned its trade quickly in the 'Street-fighting Academy of Stalingrad'. One of the lessons they have learned well is the use of *Shturmovye Gruppy* or Storm Groups to capture key buildings. Storm Groups are formed specifically for the task at hand. Although each one is unique, they have much in common.

The core of every Storm Group is the Assault Group, a small platoon armed with *Pepeshka* submachine-guns and *Fenyusha* hand grenades. The Assault Group makes the initial assault, taking and clearing the building.

The Reinforcement Group enters the building immediately after the Assault Group. Armed with machine-guns, anti-tank rifles, and mortars, and reinforced by sappers, their role is to protect the Assault Group and prevent the enemy from counterattacking the building.

The final part of the Storm Group is the Reserve Group. They can be detailed to form additional assault groups as needed or to strengthen the Reinforcement Group.

Only the best soldiers are picked for Storm Groups. As a result all storm groups are rated as **Fearless Trained**.

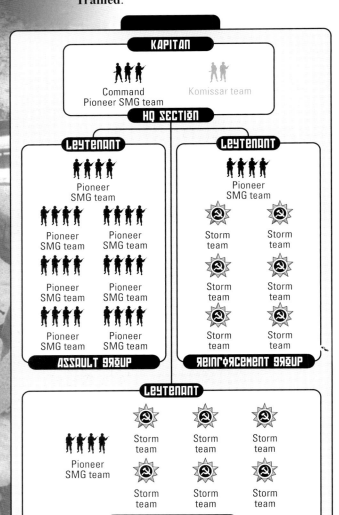

Company

HQ Section with:
    Assault Group and
    Reinforcement Group   **360 points**

Options

- Add Komissar team for +5 points.
- Add Reserve Group for +170 points.

A Storm Group is unusual in that the composition of the company can change from game to game. The Reinforcement and Reserve Groups are made up of Storm teams.

There is no actual team called a Storm team. Instead these can be any of the following types of teams:

- Pioneer SMG team,
- Pioneer Rifle/MG team,
- Light Mortar team,
- PTRD anti-tank rifle,
- Maksim HMG,
- 82-BM-41 mortar, or
- 76mm obr 1927 gun.

Your Storm Group cannot have more than four Storm teams of the same type.

You may replace three Storm teams with one Flame-thrower team or five Storm teams with two Flame-thrower teams at no extra cost.

You may replace two Storm teams with one 45mm obr 1937 gun or four Storm teams with two 45mm obr 1937 guns at no extra cost.

You must choose the composition of your Storm Group for each game before deployment begins.

The most experienced street fighters are chosen for special missions. Storm Groups are rated as **Fearless Trained**.

SUPPORT PLATOONS

0 to 1 Flame-thrower Platoon

Platoon

4 Flame-thrower Sections	320 points
3 Flame-thrower Sections	240 points
2 Flame-thrower Sections	160 points
1 Flame-thrower Section	80 points

The courageous flame-thrower operators bravely run forward to bathe the capitalist enemy in sheets of fire. They will burn the stench of the fascist invaders from the beloved Motherland with solid socialist vigour.

Flame-thrower Platoons must make Combat Attachments to Strelkovy Companies and SMG Companies with all of their sections.

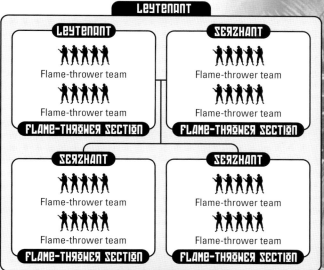

0 to 1 Flame-tank Company

Company

T-34 command tank with:

10 OT-34	625 points
9 OT-34	590 points
8 OT-34	550 points
7 OT-34	510 points
6 OT-34	465 points
5 OT-34	415 points

KV-8 command tank with:

4 KV-8	420 points
3 KV-8	350 points
2 KV-8	270 points

KV-8s command tank with:

4 KV-8s	450 points
3 KV-8s	375 points
2 KV-8s	290 points

Flame-throwing tanks are specialists at destroying the bunkers and trenches where the capitalist butchers cower. They are crewed by brave socialist soldiers who valiantly take their fire-spewing tanks toward the fascist lines, destroying the Hitlerites with their flames.

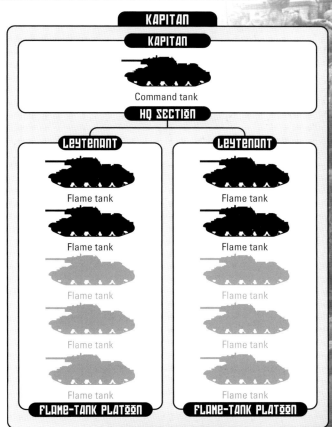

0 to 1 Tankovy Company

A Tankovy Company supporting a Strelkovy Batalon is organised like those on page 140. You may not field a Tankovy Company if your are fielding a Flame-tank Company.

0 to 1 Artillery Battalion

KAPITAN

KAPITAN

Command Rifle team | Komissar team | Observer Rifle team | Horse-drawn wagon | Staff team

HQ SECTION

LEYTENANT

76mm ZIS-3 gun
Horse-drawn limber

76mm ZIS-3 gun
Horse-drawn limber

GUN PLATOON

LEYTENANT

76mm ZIS-3 gun
Horse-drawn limber

76mm ZIS-3 gun
Horse-drawn limber

GUN PLATOON

LEYTENANT

76mm ZIS-3 gun
Horse-drawn limber

76mm ZIS-3 gun
Horse-drawn limber

GUN PLATOON

LEYTENANT

76mm ZIS-3 gun
Horse-drawn limber

76mm ZIS-3 gun
Horse-drawn limber

GUN PLATOON

LEYTENANT

122mm obr 1938 gun
Stalinets tractor

122mm obr 1938 gun
Stalinets tractor

PTRD anti-tank rifle

HOWITZER PLATOON

LEYTENANT

122mm obr 1938 gun
Stalinets tractor

122mm obr 1938 gun
Stalinets tractor

PTRD anti-tank rifle

HOWITZER PLATOON

ARTILLERY BATTALION

Company

HQ Section with:

4 Gun Platoons	**280 points**
2 Gun Platoons	**165 points**

- Add two Howitzer Platoons for +95 points for both platoons.

HQ Section with:

1 Gun Platoon	**95 points**
1 Howitzer Platoon	**95 points**

Options

- Add Komissar team for +5 points.
- Add Observer Rifle team for +30 points.
- Add PTRD anti-tank rifle teams to Howitzer Platoons for +20 points per team.
- Add horse-drawn wagon to carry the Staff team at no cost.
- Add horse-drawn limbers at no cost.
- Add Stalinets tractors at no cost

As the heroic army of the Soviet state advances, their artillery, the Red God Of War, neutralises the capitalist enemy ahead of them. The artillery arm opens holes for the spearhead of Socialism to reclaim despoiled land and lift the yoke of capitalist oppression.

Our guns are built light so the gunners can roll them forward, blasting the Hitlerites from their positions.

Socialist artillery disdains the imprecise, uneconomical bombardments of the enemy that saturate an area with shells. Instead, Soviet artillery prefers to fire over open sights, with well-placed shots, destroying the fascist enemy.

Our artillery battalions are exceptionally well equipped. The 76mm ZIS-3 divisional gun that equips four platoons out ranges most enemy artillery. These guns shell any target in view. The remaining two platoons are armed with 122mm obr 1938 divisional howitzers. These fire a heavy shell, adding destructive force to massed artillery bombardments.

 # БАТАЛОН ОПОЛЧЕНИЯ

(MILITIA BATTALION)

When Stalin issued his Not One Step Back order, it applied to civilians as well as soldiers. The workers of Stalingrad were not evacuated as the German Army approached. Instead, each part of a factory formed a *Batalon Opolcheniya* or Militia Battalion. These hastily raised formations held the line long enough for better troops to arrive, then held on through the bitter siege until the city was finally freed.

You may downgrade your Strelkovy Batalon to Militia reducing their Motivation rating and that of all supporting troops (except as noted below) to **Confident** rather than Fearless. If you do this the number of points you have available to spend on your force increases as follows:

Normal Force	Militia Force
1000 points	1200 points
1500 points	1800 points
2000 points	2400 points

As a result of their limited equipment, a Batalon Opolcheniya has the following restrictions.

- A Militia Battalion HQ may not have any Anti-tank Rifle, Anti-tank Gun, Anti-aircraft, or Sapper Platoons.

- A Militia Strelkovy Company may not have any upgrades aside from a Komissar.

- Your force cannot contain Scout Platoons, Submachine-gun Companies, Heavy Mortar Companies, Storm Groups, Assault Guns, or Tank Destruction Companies.

- A Militia force may not upgrade anti-tank guns. They are all 45mm obr 1937 models.

- A Militia force may only have one Machine-gun Company, but may have up to two Anti-aircraft Companies (often manned by women) from the city's defences.

Any Shtraf or Tankovy Companies, Guards Heavy Tank Companies, Guards Rocket Mortar Batteries, or Flame-tank Companies cost an additional +10 points for every 50 points or part thereof you spend on them. These troops remain Fearless when supporting a Batalon Opolcheniya.

GVARDEYSKIY STRELKOVY BATALON

(GUARDS RIFLE BATTALION)

With the horrendous losses of 1941 and early 1942, the Soviet high command, Stavka, needed to reward and distinguish those units that acquitted themselves well in combat. They introduced the title 'Guards' to mark these exceptional units. A *Gvardeyskiy Strelkovy Batalon* or Guards Rifle Battalion was issued the best equipment available, then rewarded with the most difficult assignments.

You may upgrade your Strelkovy Batalon to Guards status making the Training rating of the entire battalion and its supporting troops **Trained** rather than Conscript. If you do this the number of points you have available to spend on your force decreases as follows:

Normal Force	Guards Force
1000 points	775 points
1500 points	1165 points
2000 points	1550 points

A Gvardeyskiy Strelkovy Batalon has the following differences from a normal Strelkovy Batalon.

- A Guards Battalion HQ may have up to two Anti-tank Rifle Platoons.
- A Guards Strelkovy Company may have up to two Maksim HMG teams.

- A Guards Scout Platoon remains rated as Veteran but decreases in cost by -5 points for the HQ Section and -15 points for each Scout Squad in the platoon.
- A Guards Machine-gun Company has four rather than three Maksim HMG teams in each platoon at a cost of +20 points per platoon.
- A Guards force may have up to two Submachine-gun Companies as Weapons Platoon choices.
- A Guards Heavy Mortar Company may add a fourth platoon for +80 points.
- A Guards Storm Group remains rated as trained, but decreases in cost by -90 points for each Assault, Reinforced, and Reserve Group in the Storm Group.
- A Guards Heavy Tank Company or Guards Rocket Mortar Battery remains rated as Trained, but decreases in cost but -10 points for every 50 points or part thereof you spend on them.
- A Guards Shtraf Company remains rated as Conscript, but decreases in cost by -20 points for each Rifle Platoon in the Company.

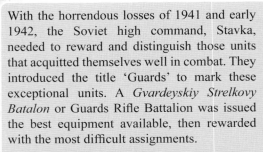

GVARDEYSKIY VOZDUSHNO-DESANTNIY BATALON

(GUARDS AIR-LANDING BATTALION)

Throughout the war the Red Army had the world's largest parachute force. Unfortunately they lacked the transport aircraft to use it and sent them into battle as elite infantry with the standard Guards Rifle Battalion organisation instead.

You may make your *Strelkovy Batalon* into a *Gvardeyskiy Vozdushno-Desantniy Batalon* or Guards Air-landing Battalion using the changes above in the same way you would make it a Guards Rifle Battalion.

CORPS SUPPORT

SOVIET

Corps Support Companies

Your force may have the following support companies:

- Anti-aircraft Company,
- Assault Gun Company,
- Guards Heavy Tankovy Company,
- Heavy Assault Gun Company,
- Guards Rocket Mortar Battery,
- Sapper Company,
- Tank Destruction Company.

Motivation and Skill

Like the soldiers they support, corps troops have little or no training but fight with Soviet passion to ensure a Socialist victory. All Corps Support companies are **Fearless Conscript** unless otherwise noted.

Air Support		
Aircraft	Limited Air Support	Sporadic Air support
I-153	120 points	90 points
Il-2 Shturmovik	200 points	145 points
P-39 Kobra	130 points	95 points

0 to 1 Anti-aircraft Company

Company	
HQ Section with:	
3 Anti-aircraft Platoons	135 points
2 Anti-aircraft Platoons	95 points
1 Anti-aircraft Platoon	55 points
Option	

- Add Komissar team for +5 points.

The gallant work of the comrades of the anti-aircraft company cannot be underestimated. The rapid-firing 37mm obr 1939 gun lights the skies of the Motherland with fire to protect the valiant Red Army. The shrieking harpies of the *Luftwaffe* beware!

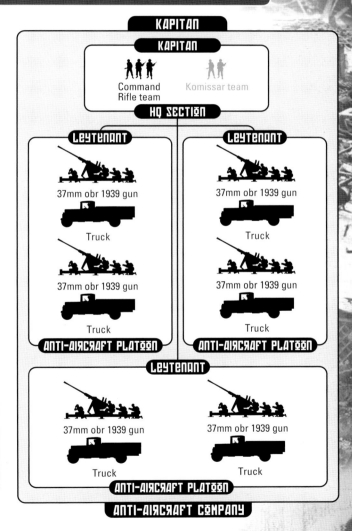

0 to 2 Assault Gun Companies

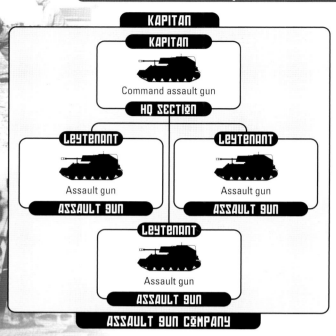

Company	
4 SU-76i	200 points
3 SU-76i	150 points
2 SU-76i	100 points
4 SU-76M	200 points
3 SU-76M	150 points
2 SU-76M	100 points
4 SU-122	245 points
3 SU-122	185 points
2 SU-122	125 points
4 SU-85	345 points
3 SU-85	260 points
2 SU-85	175 points

You may not field an Assault Gun Company with a Heavy Tank Company or a T-26 Tankovy Company.

You may not field SU-85 assault guns supporting a Strelkovy Battalion or its variants.

0 to 1 Guards Heavy Tank Company

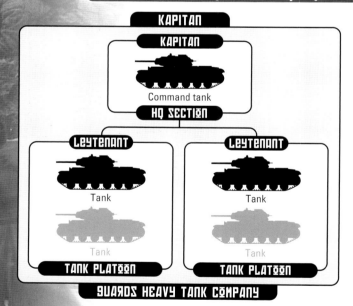

Company	
5 KV-1s	795 points
4 KV-1s	660 points
3 KV-1s	495 points
5 KV-85	1025 points
4 KV-85	845 points
3 KV-85	635 points

5 Mark IV (Churchill III or IV) 685 points

4 Mark IV (Churchill III or IV) 565 points

3 Mark IV (Churchill III or IV) 425 points

You may not field a Guards Heavy Tank Company with a Heavy Tank Company or a T-26 Tankovy Company.

You may not field both a Tankovy Company and a Guards Heavy Tank Company supporting a Strelkovy Battalion or its variants.

With such a high proportion of officers in the company, Guards Heavy Tank Companies use more sophisticated tactics than most Soviet troops. They are not affected by the Hen and Chicks special rule.

Heavy tanks are such a valuable resource that only the best are selected to crew them. Every tank has not one, but two officers in its crew when normally a platoon has just one in total!

As one would expect Guards Heavy Tank Companies are Guards troops. As such they are always rated **Fearless Trained**.

0 to 1 Heavy Assault Gun Company

Company

2 SU-152	245 points

You may not field a Heavy Assault Gun Company with a Heavy Tank Company or a T-26 Tank Company.

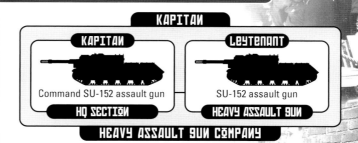

To kill a big cat you need a big gun. The SU-152 waits patiently for the enemy to appear and then the powerful shell from its gun will blast apart even a Tiger. Known as *zvyeroboy*, these animal-killers will skin many of the fascist cats.

0 to 1 Guards Rocket Mortar Battery

Company

HQ Section with:

2 Rocket Mortar Platoons	185 points
1 Rocket Mortar Platoon	105 points

Options

- Add Loading crews and trucks to all platoons for +60 points per platoon.
- Add Anti-aircraft Section for +30 points.
- Replace all DShK AA MG with towed 37mm obr 1939 guns for +20 points.

Loading Crews

It takes a lot of manpower to keep a Katyusha battery operational due to the vast amounts of ammunition that is fired with each salvo.

A BM-13 Katyusha rocket launcher with a Loading Crew adjacent to it counts as two weapons firing in a bombardment. A Loading Crew cannot fire as part of a bombardment in its own right.

Loading Crews are Gun teams, but have no weapons a-side from the rifles they use in self defence.

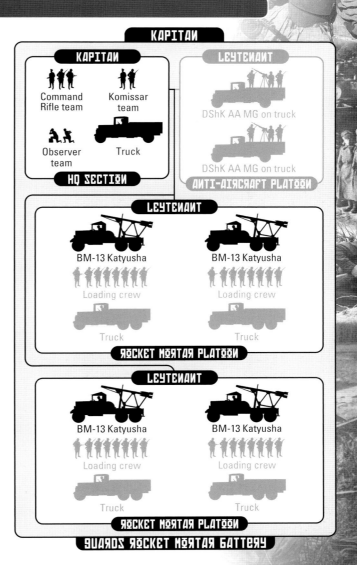

Like little Katy, the *Katyusha* of the popular song, our rockets wail as they scream their way to the enemy. While *Katyusha* longs for her beloved to return, our rocket launchers long for the destruction of the hated fascist invaders.

The Hitlerites call our rockets 'Stalin Organs' as their terrifying music demoralizes the fascist enemy with salvos of high explosive rockets.

0 to 1 Sapper Company

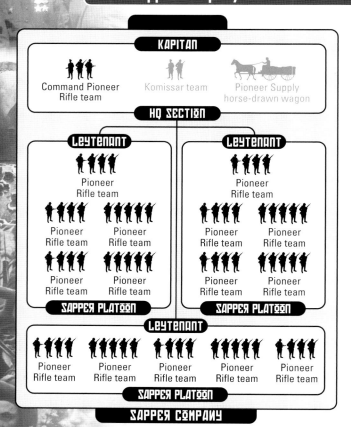

Company
HQ Section with:

3 Sapper Platoons	**235 points**
2 Sapper Platoons	**160 points**
1 Sapper Platoon	**85 points**

Options

- Add Komissar team for +5 points.
- Add Pioneer Supply horse-drawn wagon for +20 points.
- Replace Pioneer Supply horse-drawn wagon with Pioneer Supply truck for +5 points.
- Downgrade Pioneer Rifle teams to unarmed Pioneer teams for -10 points per platoon.

The Hitlerites have littered the soil of the Rodina with obstacles and mines in a desperate bid to delay the advance of the mighty Red Army. It is the job of the gallant sappers to detect and remove these obstacles, thus clearing the way to drive the reviled invaders from the Motherland.

Tank Destruction Company

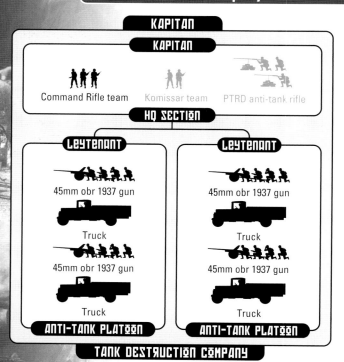

Company
HQ Section with:

2 Anti-tank Platoons	**100 points**
1 Anti-tank Platoon	**55 points**

Options

- Add Komissar team for +5 points.
- Add PTRD anti-tank rifle team for +20 points.
- Replace all 45mm obr 1937 guns with 45mm obr 1942 guns for +5 points per platoon, 57mm ZIS-2 guns for +65 points per platoon, or 76mm ZIS-3 guns for +25 points per platoon,.
- Replace all 45mm obr 1937 guns and trucks with 85mm obr 1939 guns and Stalinets tractors and equip HQ Section with a truck for +70 points per platoon.
- Model 85mm obr 1939 guns with eight or more crew and increase their ROF to 3 for +10 points per platoon.

You may not field more than one Tank Destruction Company armed with 57mm ZIS-2 or 85mm obr 1939 guns.

You may not field 85mm obr 1939 guns supporting a Strelkovy Battalion or its Variants.

The 76mm Zis-3 guns of a Tank Destruction can not fire Artillery Bombardments.

MODELLING GUIDE

By putting in a little extra effort in painting your models you can make them really stand out and impress your friends. Shown here are some easy painting techniques and tips that you can master with a little patience and a steady hand.

Preparing your miniatures

Step 1. To prepare your model for painting you will need some super-glue or epoxy glue, a modelling knife or scalpel, a cutting board, a modelling file and some newspaper to help catch the mess you make.

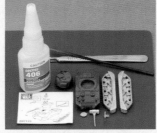

Step 2. Wash all your parts carefully in soapy water to remove any of the molding residues and dry. Use your knife or scalpel to remove any flash and file down any mould lines.

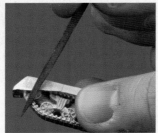

Step 3. Assemble your model using the assembly diagram. When the glue has dried, undercoat your model in black paint thinned with a little water and let it dry. Your model is now ready to paint!

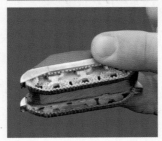

Adding Decals

Step 1. You will need a shallow container of warm water, a paint brush, paper towels, a pair of scissors or hobby knife, and a surface to cut on. First cut out the decals you need for your model and drop them into the water.

Step 2. After soaking for 30 seconds, use your brush to separate the decal from the paper. Then use the brush to pick up the decal from the water.

Step 3. Use the brush to float the decal onto the models surface. Once the decal is floating in a small pool of water, the brush can be slid from under it. While the decal is floating use the brush to adjust its position by sliding it around and when in the correct position use a dry brush to absorb the excess water.

Advanced Techniques

Ink Washing: After you have painted your model in the base colour use a very watered down black paint with a tiny drop of dish-washing detergent and apply liberally. The watered down paint will naturally pool into the recesses accentuating the detail.

Panel Painting: After you have undercoated your model in black, apply the base colour by painting each panel individually. Carefully painting up to the recessed panel lines and detail, leaving the black undercoat showing through in these areas.

Shadow painting: After you have base coated your model, use some thinned black paint to carefully paint in the recessed panel lines and around any detail you want to make stand out.

Basing

Step 1. Once you have glued your painted models to the base paint white glue on the top of the base and dip into a container of fine sand. Leave it to dry.

Step 2. Paint the base in a colour that suits your terrain.

Dry brush the base in a lighter shade of the colour made by mixing in a little white.

Your models are now based and ready for battle.

Step 3. If you want to add even more detail, glue on any extras.

This example has two different kinds of lichen, two small pebbles and the edge of the base has been painted brown. This extra detail can make every stand in your army unique.

Painting Infantry

1 After preparing your figures for painting, undercoat them with a black spray-can primer or thinned primer paint. Paint a base coat of **German Fieldgrey** on the uniforms and a basecoat of **German Grey** on the helmets.

2 Next highlight the uniforms. Mix **German Fieldgrey** with a little **White** paint (90:10) and dry brush this lighter colour onto the raised parts of the uniforms to add depth to the figures.

3 Finish the figures by painting the details with a fine brush. Paint faces and hands in **Flat Flesh**, rifles in **Beige Brown**, machine-guns in **Gunmetal Grey**, and boots **Black**. Now your troops are ready for battle. All you need to do now is to Mount them on their bases.

4 Once you have painted your army you may want to go back and add more details to your figures. Only do this if you wish to put a lot more time into your painting. You can paint the bread bag, water bottle, helmet straps and webbing, adding highlight for more depth .

German Colour List

Tanks, Trucks and Guns

Panzer Grey	German Grey (995)
Dark Yellow	Green Ochre (914)
Camouflage	
Winter white wash	White (951)
Chocolate Brown	German Camo Medium Brown (826)
Olive Green	Reflective Green (890)
Infantry	
Uniform	German Fieldgrey (830)
Helmet, gas mask	German Grey (995)
SMG ammo pouches and bread bag	German Camo Beige (821)
Greatcoat	German Fieldgrey (830)
Fallschirmjäger	
Jump smock	Green Grey (971)
Splinter jump smock	German Camo Beige (821)
Splinter green camo	Reflective Green (890)
Splinter brown camo	German Camo Medium Brown (826)
Pants	German Fieldgrey (830)
Common Colours	
Tracks, gun barrels	Gunmetal Grey (863)
Tool handles, rifle butt, belts,	
Water bottle, entrenching tool	Beige Brown (875)
Tyres, road wheels	Black (950)
Faces and hands	Flat Flesh (955)

Painting Tanks and Vehicles

1

Assemble your tanks using the diagram in the pack. Undercoat them with a black spray-can primer or thinned primer paint. Base coat your tanks in **German Grey** (for 1942), or **Green Ochre** (for 1943).

2

Mix a little **White** into the **German Grey** or **Green Ochre**. Dry brush this on the and highlight the top surfaces and raised details of the tank to highlight them. Scale miniatures benefit from accentuating detail in this way that would otherwise be lost to the eye.

3

Paint any camouflage at this stage. See below for some camouflage schemes. Highlight the camouflage with a dry brushed coat of lightened camouflaged colour. Finish off your tanks by painting your tracks **Gunmetal Grey**.

4

To take your Panzer to the expert level you can paint the tyres on the road wheels **Black**, the tool handles **Beige Brown** and their heads **Gunmetal Grey**. Paint the tracks with a **German Camo Medium Brown** and highlight with **Gunmetal Grey**. Adding Decals for the numbers and crosses and using some of the techniques shown on page 173 give your tank its final touches.

Tank Colours

Early Panzer Grey
German tanks fought in dark grey paint throughout 1942. This colour was designed to blend in with shadows when tanks were parked under trees and beside buildings .

Camouflaged Panzer Grey
In Russia the Panzers were painted with swatches of camouflage paint. In the summer of 1942, green and dark yellow were common, and brown less so.

Later Dark Yellow
From the summer of 1943 Panzer grey was replaced with a yellow brown called Dunkelgelb or dark yellow.

Camouflaged Dark Yellow
While dark yellow proved a better base colour then dark grey, camouflage still proved valuable. Many tanks were painted with swatches of colour to break up their outlines.

Three Colour Camouflage
Many units took advantage of the new camouflage paints to create elaborate three-colour camouflage schemes of green and brown on the basic dark yellow. These varied widely from blotches and spots to stripes of all sizes.

Follow the German Painting Infantry guide and refer to the colours for the Fallschirmjäger in the German Colour List on page 174. Painting complex camouflage can seem a daunting task, but breaking it down into easy steps will allow even a modest painter to achieve a good result.

Painting Splinter Camouflage

1 Paint your miniatures up to *Step 3* as shown on page 174. The miniature shown has had the pants painted in field grey (**German Fieldgrey**) and the jump smock and helmet cover painted in the splinter camo base colour of **German Camo Beige**.

2 Using **German Camo Medium Brown**, paint a series of small geometric shapes evenly spaced over the jump smock and helmet cover. Try and link two or three shapes together to make a line of shapes.

3 Using **Reflective Green**, paint a series of small geometric shapes evenly spaced over the jump smock and helmet cover. Paint a few of the **Reflective Green** shapes as a block of fine lines instead. Now paint the rest of the model following *Step 4* on page 174.

4 *Only attempt this step if you want to spend a lot more time on your miniatures. With practice and patience your miniatures will look stunning.*

Use a fine brush (*size: 00*) and some thinned **Black** paint to carefully add in the shadows in deep uniform folds and around any details. Paint the helmet band **Beige Brown**.

Finnish Tank and Gun Colours

Vehicles that were captured from the Soviet Army were quickly pressed into service in the original Soviet green colour with only the addition of Finnish Hakaristi (hooked cross) in prominent visible areas until an opportunity arose to paint them in Finnish colours.

Finnish tanks started adopting the distinct Finnish 3-colour camouflage in April 1943 after the winter white wash had been removed that was applied commonly during winter months of the war. Guns and some unarmoured vehicles had already been painted in the 3-colour camouflage which was introduced in September 1941. The camouflage scheme consisted of irregular shaped stripes with the lighter tan-grey being only 25-50% the width of the green and brown shapes.

Finnish Infantry And Crew

Use Painting Infantry on page 174 as a guide, but use the Finnish colours shown below instead of the German colours.

▼ BT-42 assault gun painted in Finnish 3-colour camouflage.

▲ Landsverk Anti-II self-propelled anti-aircraft tank painted in Finnish 3-colour camouflage.

▲ Captured T-26 left in the original Soviet green.

▼ 76 K/02 gun painted in Finnish 3-colour camouflage.

Paint Colours

Name	Vallejo Acrylic
Tanks and Guns	
Captured Soviet equipment	
Russian Green	Russian Green (924)
Finnish equipment	
Camo Tan-grey	Stone Grey (884)
Camo Brown	Beige Brown (875)
Camo Green	German Camo Bright Green (833)
Infantry	
Trousers, Winter Tunics and Side Caps	Grey Green (866)
Summer Tunics	Medium Sea Grey (870)
Helmet	Brown Violet (887)
Belts, Ammo Pouches	Chocolate Brown (872)
Bread Bag	German Camo Beige (821)
Boots	Black (950)

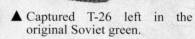

▼ Jalkaväki team.

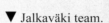

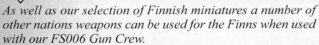

As well as our selection of Finnish miniatures a number of other nations weapons can be used for the Finns when used with our FS006 Gun Crew.

GE501 3.7cm PaK36 gun for the 37 PstK/37

SU500 45mm obr 1937 gun for the 45 PstK/37

GE510 5cm PaK38 gun for the 50 PstK/38

GE515 7.5cm PaK97/38 gun for the 75 PstK/97-38

GE520 7.5cm PaK40 gun for the 75 PstK/40

GE571 10.5cm leFH18 howitzer for the 105 H/33

GE542 2cm FlaK38 gun for the 20 ItK/38

US541 M1 Bofors gun for the 40 LtK/38

For vehicles not listed in the Finnish range use:

SU002 T-26s obr 1939 for the T-26

SU052 T-34 obr 1941 for the T-34

SU082 KV-1e for the KV-1

SU301 BA-10M for the BA-10M

SU422 ZIS-5 or GE431 Opel Blitz for the 3-ton trucks

Soviet figures (SS016 and SS017) can be used for tank crew.

Hungarian Tank and Gun Colours

Hungarian manufactured vehicles and guns are painted in a base colour of dark olive green with Czech-style camouflage consisting of ochre and brown blotches. Until 1942 this scheme was applied by brush with hard edges. In late 1942 some factories began to spray-paint the camouflage, though most of the vehicles at the front were still in the hard-edged version.

Vehicles and equipment obtained from Germany were left in Panzer Grey with the addition of Hungarian crosses.

Hungarian Infantry And Crew

Use Painting Infantry on page 174 as a guide, but use the Hungarian colours shown below instead of the German colours.

Hungarian Insignia and Markings

The Hungarians used a variation on Balkan Cross used by the Germans. The Hungarian version consisted of a red cross outlined in white with green triangles in the corners (though variations with the red and green transposed were often used).

The German supplied vehicles used the German numbering system on page 34, however the same system doesn't seem to have been applied to the Csaba, Toldi or Nimrod units.

▼ T-38G (Panzer 38(t)). Painted in the original German Grey.

▲ 40M Nimrod. Painted in Hungarian 3-colour camouflage.

▲ 38M Toldi I light tank.

▼ 39M Csába armoured car.

▼ Puskás team.

Paint Colours

Name	Vallejo Acrylic
Tanks and Guns	
Hungarian equipment	
Dark Olive Green	Reflective Green (890)
Camo Brown	German Camo Medium Brown (826)
Camo Ochre	Green Ochre (914)
German-supplied equipment	
Panzer Grey	German Grey (995)
Infantry	
Trousers, Tunics and Side Caps	English Uniform (921)
Helmet	Brown Violet (887)
Leather Boots, Belts, Ammo Pouches	Chocolate Brown (872)
Bread Bag	Khaki (988)

 **MINIATURES FOR YOUR HUNGARIAN FORCE**

As well as our selection of Hungarian Miniatures a number of other nations weapons can be used for the Hungarians when used with our HS005 Gun Crew.

GE501 3.7cm Pak36 gun for the 37mm 36M and 40mm 40M guns

GE510 5cm Pak38 gun for the 50mm 38M gun

GE515 7.5cm PaK97/38 gun for the 75mm 97/38M gun

GE520 7.5cm PaK40 gun for the 75mm 40M gun

IT570 75/27 gun for the 80mm 8/8M gun

IT580 100/17 howitzer for the 100mm 14M howtizer

GE571 10.5cm leFH18 howitzer for the 105mm 37M howtizer

BR540 Bofors 40mm gun for the 40mm 36M Bofors gun

For vehicles not listed in the Hungarian range use:

GE022 Panzer 38(t) for the T-38G

GE042 Panzer IV for the Panzer IV F$_1$ and F$_2$

GE400 BMW motorcycles & sidecars

GE412, GE413, GE425 and GE426 for field cars

GE430 and GE431 for Ford-Marmon trucks

GE272 for the Hansa-Lloyd half-track

German (GS017) or Italian (IS013) figures can be used for tank crew.

Italian Tank and Gun Colours

Italian vehicles and guns that went to the Eastern Front were left in the original colour of Italian Green. The L6/40 tanks however, arrived in Desert Yellow as they were originally destined for North Africa. The crews quickly camouflaged them with mud to make them blend in better!

Italian Infantry And Crew

Use Painting Infantry on page 174 as a guide, but use the Italian colours shown below instead of the German colours.

The Italian Eastern Front uniform is the same as the one worn in Sicily and Italy.

◀ L6/40 light tank in mud-camouflaged Desert Yellow.

▼ 47/32 anti-tank gun painted in Italian Green.

▼ 75/27 gun painted in Italian Green.

Paint Colours

Name	Vallejo Acrylic
Tanks	
Desert Yellow	Green Ochre (914)
Guns and Trucks	
Italian Green	German Fieldgrey (830)
Infantry	
Trousers, Tunics and Puttees	Olive Grey (888)
Helmet	German Fieldgrey (830)
Boots and Rifle butt	Beige Brown (875)
Webbing	Yellow Green (881)

▼ Fucilieri team.

Painting Romanian Forces

Romanian Tank And Gun Colours

Most Romanian equipment (including their R-2 tanks) was painted dark green without camouflage. German-supplied tanks remained in their original Panzer grey with the addition of Romanian markings. In the winter of 1942, some tanks received a hasty camouflage of white stripes over their basic colours.

Romanian Infantry And Crew

Use Painting Infantry on page 174 as a guide, but use the Romanian colours shown below instead of the German colours.

Romanian Insignia And Markings

The Cross of Michael and a red, yellow and blue roundel were used as national insignia on Romanian tanks. The cross was normally applied to the hull sides and the turret rear with a combined roundel and cross marking applied on the engine deck or top of the turret.

The Panzer III tanks were in the fourth company, while the Panzer IV tanks fought with the eight company.

Most tanks carried German style turret numbers (shown on page 34) to identify individual vehicles.

▲ T-4 (Panzer IV G) tank in German Grey.

▼ Romanian HQ team.

▲ R-2 (Panzer 35(t)) tank in Dark Olive Green.

▲ Model 1937 7.92mm ZB53 machine-gun team.

▼ Puscasi team.

Paint Colours

Name	Vallejo Acrylic
Tanks and Guns	
Romanian Equipment	
Dark Olive Green	Olive Grey (888)
German-supplied Equipment	
Grey	German Grey (995)
Infantry	
Trousers, Tunics and Side Caps	German Medium Camo Brown (826)
Helmet	Olive Grey (888)
Leather Boots, Belts, Ammo Pouches	Saddle Brown (940)
Bread Bag	Yellow Green (881)

MINIATURES FOR YOUR ROMANIAN FORCE

As well as our selection of Romanian miniatures a number of other nations weapons can be used for the Romanians when used with our RS004 Gun Crew:

GE501 3.7cm PaK36 gun for the TAC 37mm gun

IT560 47/32 gun for the TAC Bohler 47mm gun

GE510 5cm PaK38 gun for the TAC 938 50mm gun

GE515 7.5cm PaK97/38 gun for the TAC 938 75mm gun

FI570 76mm K/02 gun for the RF 75mm gun

IT580 100/17 Howitzer for the Skoda 100mm Howitzer

GE542 2cm FlaK36 gun for the Mitral 20mm gun

For vehicles not listed in the Romanian range use:

GE022 Panzer 38(t) for the T-38

GE034 Panzer III for the T-3

GE044 Panzer IV for the T-4

GE412, GE413, GE425, and GE426 for 1.5-ton trucks

GE430 and GE431 for 3-ton trucks

British (BS016 and BS017) figures can be used for tank crew.

PAINTING INFANTRY

1 After preparing your figures for painting, undercoat them with a black spray can primer or thinned primer paint. Paint a base coat of the main uniform colours. For Soviet infantry paint the uniform **Khaki Grey** and the helmets **Russian Green**.

2 Next highlight the uniform. Mix a little white paint with the original colour and dry brush this onto the raised parts of the uniform to add depth to the figure.

3 Finish the figure by painting the details with a fine brush. Paint the face and hands in a **Flat Flesh**, the machine-gun **Gunmetal Grey**, and the boots **Black**. Now your troops are ready for battle. All you need to do is put them on their bases (See page 173 for basing ideas).

4 Once you have painted your army you may want to go back and add more details to your figures.

Only do this if you wish to put a lot more time into your painting. You can paint the metalwork, helmet straps and webbing, adding highlight for more depth and much more if you want to.

SOVIET COLOURS

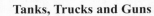

Tanks, Trucks and Guns	
Green	Russian Green (924)
Camouflage	
White	White (951)
Earth Brown	Flat Earth (983)
Sand Yellow	Yellow Ochre (913)
Tank Crews	
Overalls	Black (950)
Alternate uniform	Khaki Grey (880)
Helmet	Black (950)
Alternate colour	Beige Brown (875)
Infantry	
Uniform	Khaki Grey (880)
Helmet	Russian Green (894)
Ammo pouches and havesack	German Camo Beige (821)
Greatcoat	USA Tan Earth (874)
Cossacks	
Shirt	Khaki Grey (830)
Pants	Dark Blue (930)
Fur cap, belts	Black (950)
Common Colours	
Tracks, gun barrels, sabres	Gunmetal Grey (863)
Tool handles, rifle butt, belts	Beige Brown (875)
Boots, tyres, road wheels	Black (950)
Faces and hands	Flat Flesh (955)

PAINTING TANKS AND VEHICLES

1 Assemble your tanks using the diagram in the pack. Undercoat them with a black spray-can primer or thinned primer paint. Base coat your tanks with **Russian Green**.

2 Next highlight the tank. Mix **Russian Green** with a little **White** (90:10) and dry brush this onto the raised parts of the tank to add depth.

3 Finish off your tanks by painting your tracks **Gunmetal Grey** and the tyres on the road wheels **Black**.

The technique shown is also used to paint guns and trucks.

Your tanks are now ready to stalk their prey across the battlefield.

4 To take your tank to the expert level you can paint the tool handles **Beige Brown** and their heads **Gunmetal Grey**. Dry brush the tracks with **Flat Earth** and highlight with **Gunmetal Grey** to simulate mud and wear. Add decals for slogans or hand paint your own to give your tanks the final touches.

Once you have finished painting your tanks as shown above you can go a step further by adding tank camouflage. This will give your army a unique look and can be used to represent specific periods like white-wash camouflage for winter.

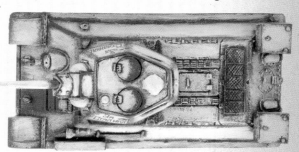

Whitewash. Whitewash is unusual as it is designed only to last through winter, after which it can be scrubbed off when the season changes revealing the original paint underneath. During operation this meant that areas of the whitewash were easily worn off by crew members clambering in and out of the tank as well as from snow and mud being thrown up from the tracks, washing away at the whitewash.

Once the tank is painted as shown above, roughly paint on **White**, leaving areas of the **Russian Green** showing through on the edges and anywhere where the crew or normal use would wear it off. Thinning the **White** paint with water and slowly building up layers of white paint will help simulate the look of a whitewashed tank.

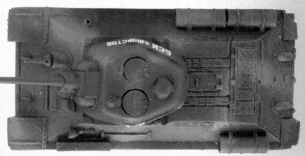

Earth Brown Camouflage. Once you have completed *Step 3* as shown opposite, add irregular patches of **Flat Earth** as camouflage, then add a small amount of **White** to the **Flat Earth** and dry brush the camouflage patches before moving on to *Step 4*.

Other variations of camouflage colour applied in this way are **Yellow Ochre** or **White**.

PAINTING COSSACKS AND HORSES

1

After preparing your figures for painting, undercoat them with a black spray-can primer or thinned primer paint. Paint a base coat of the main uniform colours. For Cossacks paint the shirt **Khaki Grey** and the pants and top patch of the hat **Dark Blue**. For the horse paint the entire body **Flat Earth**.

2

Next highlight the uniform and horse. Mix a little **White** paint with the original colours (90:10) and dry brush this onto the raised parts of the uniform and horse to add depth to the figure.

3

Finish the figure by painting the details with a fine brush. Paint the face and hands in **Flat Flesh**, the sabre, gun barrel, stirrups, and bit **Gunmetal Grey**, the horse's reins and saddle **Flat Earth**, and the gun butt **Beige Brown**, the battle flag **Red**, and the boots **Black**. Now your troops are ready for battle. Finally, put them on their bases.

4

Once you have painted your army you may want to go back and add more details to your figures.

Only do this if you wish to put a lot more time into your painting. You can paint the helmet straps and webbing on the soldiers and markings on the horse.

Visit *www.FlamesOfWar.com* for more detailed painting and reference guides.

ALTERNATIVE HORSE COLOURS

Mixing a variety of horse colours together in a unit will give you an overall more realistic and interesting force.

Grey: Mix **Black** and **White** together (50:50) on your painting palette for the base colour, add more **White** for the dry brush.

Dun: Mix **Khaki Grey** and **White** together (80:20) on your painting palette for the base colour, add more **White** for the dry brush.

Black: Mix **Black** and **German Camo Beige** together (90:10) on your painting palette for the base colour, add a little **White** for the dry brush.

183

MODELLING A RUINED BUILDING

There is nothing more inspirational than a battlefield covered in ruined buildings to make you want to test your army's street-fighting skills.

Start by making a one-storey building corner following the steps on these pages. Place two of these back-to-back to create a ruined building. Once you have your first building, make a bunch more, varying the design to create your own unique city.

Use the same techniques to build entire buildings in one piece. Simply cut a square base and four walls, leaving each floor separate to allow access to the troops inside.

Once you have got the hang of these simple buildings, have a go at making factories, apartment blocks and rail yards to add variety to your city.

The important thing is to give it a try, just follow this guide and you'll be fighting in the streets of Stalingrad in no time.

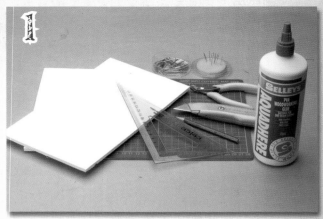

To make your buildings you will need a sharp knife, white glue, a ruler, dressmaker's pins, card or foam card, sand, paint and paint brush.

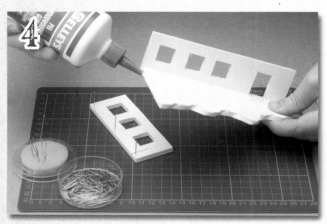

Once you have your walls, cut a 90 degree corner from card for your floor. Cut the other edge in a jagged line.

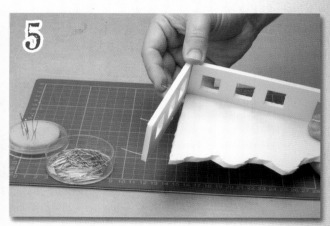

Cut two wall sections to fit your floor piece. Glue your wall sections onto the floor with white glue. Use dressmaker's pins to hold the walls in place while the glue dries.

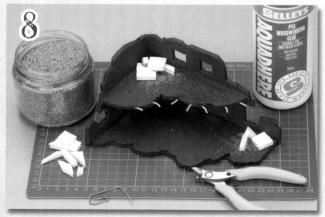

Now you have a ruin you could paint it and leave it as it is. Or you could go to town adding details such as rubble (all those offcuts) or re-enforcing steel rods (paperclips).

Make sure you leave room to put your infantry stands in the building.

The final touch is the paint work. Use a base layer of dark grey paint mixed with sand. Once this is dry, dry-brush with a lighter shade of grey. Finish with a dry-brush of black above the windows for a smoke effect. Dry-brush the edges of the building with a very light grey to finish.

Start by drawing up the walls on foam card. Mark out a strip 13/4"/45mm high for the wall. Draw in doors (5/8"/15mm wide by 1"/25mm high) and windows (5/8"/15mm square).

Start by drawing up the walls on foam card. Mark out a strip 13/4"/45mm high for the wall. Draw in doors (5/8"/15mm wide by 1"/25mm high) and windows (5/8"/15mm square).

Start by drawing up the walls on foam card. Mark out a strip 13/4"/45mm high for the wall. Draw in doors (5/8"/15mm wide by 1"/25mm high) and windows (5/8"/15mm square).

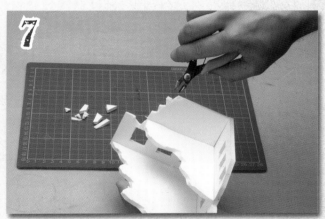

Once the glue dries, use a knife or wire cutters to create the ruined effect by cutting bits off to represent battle damage. Again, keep all the offcuts for rubble later.

Your building corner is ready. The city streets await your first battles.

For further ideas check out the **Flames Of War** website.

MODELLING A BRIDGE

1 Using a piece of 3mm hard board or similar, mark out a river and the area where you want a bridge (use a size and position suitable for your gaming table). Use a sharp craft knife to taper the edges of the board. Cut out the bridge from stiff card (leave an area of overhang over the river to mount the bridge sides on). Cut out two strips of card to act as the bridge support on the river bank.

Glue the bridge and supports in place, clamp down and let dry.

2 Use some ready-mixed filler to build up the river banks and add texture to the road surface of the bridge.

Hint: Use an unpainted tank track dipped in water (to stop the ready-mixed filler sticking to the track) and press it in to the road surface to represent vehicle tracks over the bridge.

A similar technique can also be used to make the foot prints of soldiers who have marched over the bridge.

3 Using kitty-litter or small pebbles and craft glue, build up the sides of the bridge, add strips of card to the top once the glue is dry.

You may also want to add some rocks in the river and on the banks.

Hint: Ensure the position and width of the river is constant on all of your river sections to allow you to mix and match them on your gaming table.

4 Paint the river, bank and bridge surface brown and paint the rocks and stone work grey. Dry-brush the painted areas with a lighter shade of the colours.

Once dry, paint on a thick coat of PVA glue into the river (PVA dries clear and gives the impression of water). Once the PVA is dry, add some static grass to the river banks.

Use these techniques to make additional river sections that can span your gaming table.

TIPS & TRICKS

- Plan out a whole river that can stretch across your gaming table, make it with straight and curved river sections so you can change the shape and position of the river.

- Build up two or three layers of PVA glue in the river, allowing the glue to dry clear between each layer, to add extra depth and realism to the river.

- Paint white streaks around stones and debris in the river to give the impression of water flow.

- Create reeds along the river bank by cutting off the bristles of cheap hard brushes and gluing clumps of the bristles to the river bank with PVA glue.

German Arsenal

Tank Teams

Name	Mobility	Front	Armour Side	Top	Equipment and Notes
Weapon	*Range*	*ROF*	*Anti-tank*	*Firepower*	

Tanks

Name	Mobility	Front	Side	Top	Equipment and Notes
Panzer II	Fully-tracked	3	1	1	Co-ax MG, Protected ammo.
2cm KwK38 gun	*16"/40cm*	*3*	*5*	*5+*	
Panzer 38(t)	Fully-tracked	3	1	1	Co-ax MG, Hull MG, Protected ammo.
3.7cm KwK38(t) gun	*24"/60cm*	*2*	*6*	*4+*	
Panzer III G, H, or J	Fully-tracked	5	3	1	Co-ax MG, Hull MG, Protected ammo.
5cm KwK38 gun	*24"/60cm*	*3*	*7*	*4+*	
Panzer III J (late)	Fully-tracked	5	3	1	Co-ax MG, Hull MG, Protected ammo.
5cm KwK39 gun	*24"/60cm*	*3*	*9*	*4+*	
Panzer III L or M	Fully-tracked	6	3	1	Co-ax MG, Hull MG, Protected ammo.
5cm KwK39 gun	*24"/60cm*	*3*	*9*	*4+*	
Panzer III N	Fully-tracked	6	3	1	Co-ax MG, Hull MG, Protected ammo.
7.5cm KwK37 gun	*24"/60cm*	*2*	*9*	*3+*	
Panzer IV E or F_1	Fully-tracked	5	3	1	Co-ax MG, Hull MG, Protected ammo.
7.5cm KwK37 gun	*24"/60cm*	*2*	*9*	*3+*	*Smoke.*
firing bombardments	*48"/120cm*	*-*	*2*	*6*	
Panzer IV F_2 or G	Fully-tracked	5	3	1	Co-ax MG, Hull MG, Protected ammo.
7.5cm KwK40 gun	*32"/80cm*	*2*	*11*	*3+*	
Panzer IV G (late) or H	Fully-tracked	6	3	1	Co-ax MG, Hull MG, Protected ammo.
7.5cm KwK40 gun	*32"/80cm*	*2*	*11*	*3+*	
Panther D (Kursk)	Fully-tracked	10	5	1	Co-ax MG, Hull MG, Wide tracks, Unreliable.
7.5cm KwK42 gun	*32"/80cm*	*2*	*14*	*3+*	
Tiger I E (early)	Fully-tracked	9	8	2	Co-ax MG, Hull MG, Protected ammo, Slow tank, Wide tracks, Unreliable.
8.8cm KwK36 gun	*40"/100cm*	*2*	*13*	*3+*	
T-70 obr 1942 (captured)	Fully-tracked	4	2	1	Co-ax MG, Limited vision, Unreliable.
4.5cm KwK(r)	*24"/60cm*	*2*	*7*	*4+*	
T-34 obr 1942 (captured)	Fully-tracked	6	5	1	Co-ax MG, Hull MG, Fast tank, Limited vision, Wide tracks, Unreliable.
7.62cm KwK(r)	*32"/80cm*	*2*	*9*	*3+*	
KV-1e (captured)	Fully-tracked	9	8	2	Co-ax MG, Hull MG, Turret-rear MG, Limited vision, Unreliable.
7.62cm KwK(r)	*32"/80cm*	*2*	*9*	*3+*	
Flammpanzer III	Fully-tracked	6	3	1	Co-ax MG, Fuel Tanks, Hull MG.
1.4cm Flammenwerfer	*4"/10cm*	*4*	*-*	*5+*	*Flame-thrower*

Assault Guns

Name	Mobility	Front	Side	Top	Equipment and Notes
StuG D or E	Fully-tracked	5	3	1	AA MG, Protected ammo.
7.5cm StuK36 gun	*24"/60cm*	*2*	*9*	*3+*	*Hull mounted.*
StuG F	Fully-tracked	5	3	1	AA MG, Protected ammo.
7.5cm StuK40 gun	*32"/80cm*	*2*	*11*	*3+*	*Hull mounted.*
StuG F/8 or G	Fully-tracked	7	3	1	Hull MG, Protected ammo.
7.5cm StuK40 gun	*32"/80cm*	*2*	*11*	*3+*	*Hull mounted.*
StuH42	Fully-tracked	7	3	1	Hull MG, Protected ammo.
10.5cm StuH42 gun	*24"/60cm*	*2*	*10*	*2+*	*Hull mounted.*
StuIG33B	Fully-tracked	7	4	1	Hull MG, Slow tank.
15cm sIG33 gun	*16"/40cm*	*1*	*13*	*1+*	*Bunker buster, Hull mounted.*
Brummbär	Fully-tracked	9	5	1	AA MG, Overloaded, Slow tank.
15cm StuH43 gun	*16"/40cm*	*1*	*13*	*1+*	*Bunker buster, Hull mounted.*

| Name | Mobility | Front | Armour Side | Top | Equipment and Notes |
Weapon	*Range*	*ROF*	*Anti-tank*	*Firepower*	

Infantry Guns (SP)

Name / Weapon	Mobility / Range	Front / ROF	Side / Anti-tank	Top / Firepower	Equipment and Notes
Sd Kfz 250/7 (8cm)	Half-tracked	1	0	0	Rear AA MG.
8cm GW34 mortar	*40"/100cm*	-	2	6	*Hull mounted, Portee, Smoke bombardment.*
Sd Kfz 250/8 (7.5cm)	Half-tracked	1	0	0	Rear AA MG.
7.5cm KwK37 gun	*24"/60cm*	2	9	3+	*Hull mounted.*
Sd Kfz 251/2C (8cm)	Half-tracked	1	0	0	Rear AA MG.
8cm GW34 mortar	*40"/100cm*	-	2	6	*Hull mounted, Portee, Smoke bombardment.*
Sd Kfz 251/9C (7.5cm)	Half-tracked	1	0	0	Rear AA MG.
7.5cm KwK37 gun	*24"/60cm*	2	9	3+	*Hull mounted.*
Grille (15cm sIG) H or K	Fully-tracked	2	1	0	Hull MG.
15cm sIG33 gun	*16"/40cm*	1	13	1+	*Bunker buster, Hull mounted.*
firing bombardments	*56"/140cm*	-	4	2+	
Sd Kfz 251/16C (Flamm)	Half-tracked	1	0	0	Fuel tanks, Hull MG.
Two 1.4cm Flammenwerfer	*4"/10cm*	3 (each)	-	6	*Side mounted, Flame-thrower.*

Tank-hunters

Name / Weapon	Mobility / Range	Front / ROF	Side / Anti-tank	Top / Firepower	Equipment and Notes
Panzerjäger I	Half-tracked	0	0	0	AA MG.
4.7cm PaK36(t) gun	*24"/60cm*	2	7	4+	*Hull mounted.*
Marder I	Fully-tracked	0	0	0	AA MG, Overloaded, Slow tank.
7.5cm PaK40 gun	*32"/80cm*	2	12	3+	*Hull mounted.*
Marder II	Fully-tracked	1	0	0	AA MG.
7.5cm PaK40 gun	*32"/80cm*	2	12	3+	*Hull mounted.*
Marder III (7.62cm)	Fully-tracked	1	0	0	Hull MG.
7.62cm PaK36(r) gun	*32"/80cm*	2	11	3+	*Hull mounted.*
Marder III H	Fully-tracked	1	0	0	Hull MG.
7.5cm PaK40 gun	*32"/80cm*	2	12	3+	*Hull mounted.*
Marder III M	Fully-tracked	0	0	0	AA MG.
7.5cm PaK40 gun	*32"/80cm*	2	12	3+	*Hull mounted.*
Hornisse	Fully-tracked	1	1	0	AA MG, Protected ammo.
8.8cm PaK43 gun	*40"/100cm*	2	16	3+	*Hull mounted.*
Ferdinand	Fully-tracked	15	8	2	AA MG, Overloaded, Slow tank, Unreliable.
8.8cm PaK43 gun	*40"/100cm*	2	16	3+	*Hull mounted.*

Artillery (SP)

Name / Weapon	Mobility / Range	Front / ROF	Side / Anti-tank	Top / Firepower	Equipment and Notes
Wespe	Fully-tracked	1	1	0	AA MG, Protected ammo.
10.5cm leFH18M howitzer	*24"/60cm*	1	10	2+	*Hull mounted, Smoke.*
firing bombardments	*72"/180cm*	-	4	4+	*Smoke bombardment.*
Hummel	Fully-tracked	1	1	0	AA MG, Protected ammo.
15cm sFH18 howitzer	*24"/60cm*	1	13	1+	*Bunker buster, Hull mounted, Smoke.*
firing bombardments	*80"/200cm*	-	5	2+	*Smoke bombardment.*
Panzerwerfer 42 (Maultier)	Half-tracked	0	0	0	AA MG, Armoured rocket launcher.
15cm PW42 rocket launcher	*64"/160cm*	-	3	4+	*Smoke bombardment.*
Panzer III OP	Fully-tracked	5	3	1	Hull MG.

Anti-aircraft (SP)

Name / Weapon	Mobility / Range	Front / ROF	Side / Anti-tank	Top / Firepower	Equipment and Notes
Sd Kfz 10/5 (2cm)	Half-tracked	-	-	-	
2cm FlaK38 gun	*16"/40cm*	4	5	5+	*Anti-aircraft.*
Sd Kfz 7/1 (Quad 2cm)	Half-tracked	-	-	-	
2cm FlaK38 (V) gun	*16"/40cm*	6	5	5+	*Anti-aircraft.*
Sd Kfz 7/2 (3.7cm)	Half-tracked	-	-	-	
3.7cm FlaK36 gun	*24"/60cm*	4	6	4+	*Anti-aircraft.*

Light Armoured Cars

Name / Weapon	Mobility / Range	Front / ROF	Side / Anti-tank	Top / Firepower	Equipment and Notes
Sd Kfz 221	Wheeled	0	0	0	AA MG.
Sd Kfz 221 (2.8cm)	Wheeled	0	0	0	
2.8cm sPzB41 anti-tank rifle	*16"/40cm*	2	7	5+	*Hull mounted, No HE.*
Sd Kfz 222 (2cm)	Wheeled	1	0	0	Co-ax MG.
2cm KwK38 gun	*16"/40cm*	3	5	5+	*Self-defence anti-aircraft.*
Sd Kfz 223 (early radio)	Wheeled	0	0	0	AA MG.
Sd Kfz 223 (radio)	Wheeled	1	0	0	AA MG.

Name	Mobility	Front	Armour Side	Top	Equipment and Notes
Weapon	*Range*	*ROF*	*Anti-tank*	*Firepower*	

Heavy Armoured Cars

Sd Kfz 231 (8-rad)	Jeep	2	0	0	Co-ax MG.
2cm KwK38 gun	*16"/40cm*	*3*	*5*	*5+*	
Sd Kfz 250/9 (2cm)	Half-tracked	1	0	0	Co-ax MG.
2cm KwK38 gun	*16"/40cm*	*3*	*5*	*5+*	*Self-defence anti-aircraft.*
Panzer II L Luchs	Fully-tracked	3	1	1	Co-ax MG, Light tank.
2cm KwK38 gun	*16"/40cm*	*3*	*5*	*5+*	
Panhard P-178(f)	Wheeled	1	1	0	Co-ax MG.
2.5cm KwK(f) gun	*16"/40cm*	*2*	*6*	*5+*	*No HE.*
Sd Kfz 233 (7.5cm)	Jeep	2	0	0	Hull MG.
7.5cm KwK37 gun	*24"/60cm*	*2*	*9*	*3+*	*Hull mounted.*
BA-10M	Wheeled	1	0	0	Co-ax MG, Hull MG, Limited vision.
4.5cm KwK(r) gun	*24"/60cm*	*2*	*7*	*4+*	

Gun Teams

Weapon	Mobility	Range	ROF	Anti-tank	Firepower	Notes
MG34 HMG	Man-packed	24"/60cm	6	2	6	ROF 2 when pinned down.
2.8cm sPzB41 anti-tank rifle	Man-packed	16"/40cm	3	7	5+	No HE.
7.5cm LG40 recoilless gun	Man-packed	16"/40cm	2	10	4+	Recoilless.
8.8cm RW43 (Püppchen) launcher	Man-packed	16"/40cm	1	11	5+	
8cm GW42 (Stummelwerfer) mortar	Man-packed	32"/80cm	-	2	6	Smoke bombardment.
8cm GW34 mortar	Man-packed	40"/100cm	-	2	6	Smoke bombardment.
10.5cm NbW35 mortar	Man-packed	40"/100cm	-	3	4+	Smoke bombardment.
12cm sGW43 mortar	Light	56"/140cm	-	3	3+	
7.5cm leIG18 gun	Light	16"/40cm	2	9	3+	Gun shield, Smoke.
firing bombardments		48"/120cm	-	3	6	
15cm sIG33 gun	Heavy	16"/40cm	1	13	1+	Bunker buster, Gun shield.
firing bombardments		56"/140cm	-	4	2+	
2cm FlaK38 gun	Light	16"/40cm	4	5	5+	Anti-aircraft, Gun shield, Turntable.
3.7cm PaK36 gun	Light	24"/60cm	3	6	4+	Gun shield.
firing Stielgranate		8"/20cm	1	12	5+	
4.2cm PJK41 gun	Light	24"/60cm	3	9	5+	Gun shield.
5cm PaK38 gun	Medium	24"/60cm	3	9	4+	Gun shield.
7.5cm PaK97/38 gun	Medium	32"/60cm	2	10	3+	Gun shield.
7.5cm PaK40 gun	Medium	32"/80cm	2	12	3+	Gun shield.
7.62cm PaK36(r) gun	Heavy	32"/80cm	2	11	3+	Gun shield.
8.8cm FlaK36 gun	Immobile	40"/100cm	2	13	3+	Gun shield, Heavy anti-aircraft, Turntable.
7.5cm GebG36 gun	Medium	16"/40cm	2	9	3+	Smoke.
firing bombardments		72"/180cm	-	3	6	Smoke bombardment.
10.5cm LG40 recoilless gun	Heavy	24"/60cm	1	12	3+	Gun shield, Recoilless, Smoke.
firing bombardments		64"/160cm	-	4	4+	Smoke bombardment.
10.5cm leFH18 howitzer	Immobile	24"/60cm	1	10	2+	Gun shield, Smoke.
firing bombardments		72"/180cm	-	4	4+	Smoke bombardment.
15cm NW41 rocket launcher	Light	64"/160cm	-	3	4+	Smoke bombardment.

Infantry Teams

Team	Range	ROF	Anti-tank	Firepower	Notes
Rifle team	16"/40cm	1	2	6	
Rifle/MG team	16"/40cm	2	2	6	
MG team	16"/40cm	3	2	6	
SMG team	4"/10cm	3	1	6	Full ROF when moving.
Light Mortar team	16"/40cm	1	1	5+	Can fire over friendly teams.
Anti-tank Rifle team	16"/40cm	2	4	6	
Flame-thrower team	4"/10cm	2	-	6	Flame-thrower.
Staff team	cannot shoot				Moves as a Gun team.

Additional Training and Equipment

Panzerknacker teams are rated as Tank Assault 5. Pioneer teams are rated as Tank Assault 4.

Transport Teams

Vehicle *Weapon*	Mobility *Range*	Front *ROF*	Armour Side *Anti-tank*	Top *Firepower*	Equipment and Notes
Trucks					
BMW & Sidecar or Kübelwagen jeep	Jeep	-	-	-	Optional Passenger-fired MG.
Schwimmwagen	Jeep	-	-	-	Amphibious, Passenger-fired MG.
Kettenkrad half-track or Horch Kfz 15 car	Jeep	-	-	-	
Horch, Krupp, or Steyr Kfz 70 truck	Wheeled	-	-	-	
Opel Blitz 3-ton truck	Wheeled	-	-	-	
Opel Maultier	Half-tracked	-	-	-	
Opel Kfz 68 radio truck	Wheeled	-	-	-	
RSO	Fully-tracked	-	-	-	Slow tank.
Horse-drawn wagon	Wagon	-	-	-	
Tractors					
Sd Kfz 10 (1t), Sd Kfz 11 (3t), or Sd Kfz 7 (8t) half-track	Half-tracked	-	-	-	
Horse-drawn limber	Wagon	-	-	-	
Armoured Personnel Carriers					
Sd Kfz 250 half-track	Half-tracked	1	0	0	Hull MG, Rear AA mount.
Sd Kfz 250/10 (3.7cm) *3.7cm PaK36*	Half-tracked *16"/40cm*	1 *2*	0 *6*	0 *4+*	Rear AA mount. *Hull mounted*
Sd Kfz 250/11 (2.8cm) half-track *2.8cm sPzB41*	Half-tracked *16"/40cm*	1 *2*	0 *7*	0 *5+*	Rear AA mount. *Hull mounted, No HE.*
Sd Kfz 251/1C half-track	Half-tracked	1	0	0	Hull MG, HMG Carrier, Rear AA mount.
Sd Kfz 251/10C (3.7cm) half-track *3.7cm PaK36*	Half-tracked *16"/40cm*	1 *2*	0 *6*	0 *4+*	Rear AA mount. *Hull mounted*
Sd Kfz 251/7C (Pioneer) half-track	Half-tracked	1	0	0	Hull MG, Rear AA mount, Assault bridge.
Sd Kfz 251/1C (Stuka) half-track *28cm sW40 rocket launcher*	Half-tracked *40"/100cm*	1 *-*	0 *3*	0 *1+*	Hull MG, Rear AA mount. *Hull mounted, Stuka zu Fuss.*
Sd Kfz 253 (StuG) or Sd Kfz 254 half-track	Half-tracked	1	0	1	AA MG.
Recovery Vehicles					
Sd Kfz 9 (18t) half-track	Half-tracked	-	-	-	Recovery vehicle.
Bergepanther recovery vehicle	Fully-tracked	10	5	0	AA MG, Wide tracks, Recovery vehicle.

Demolition Carriers

Name	Movement	Armour Front	Side	Top	Anti-tank	Firepower	Notes
Goliath	-	0	0	0	5/1	2+/4+*	Explodes easily.
Borgward BIV	Half-tracked	0	0	0	7/2	1+/2+*	Explodes easily.

*The first Anti-tank rating and Firepower ratings are used against targets adjacent to the demolition carrier when it explodes. The second rating is used against all other teams within 2"/5cm.

Aircraft

Aircraft	Weapon	To Hit	Anti-tank	Firepower	Notes
Ju 87D Stuka	Bombs	4+	5	1+	
Ju 87G Stuka	Cannon	3+	11	4+	
Hs 129B	Cannon	2+	9	4+	Flying Tank
Bf 109E or FW 190F	Cannon or Bombs	3+ 4+	7 5	5+ 2+	

Finnish Arsenal

Tank Teams

Name *Weapon*	Mobility *Range*	Front *ROF*	Side *Anti-tank*	Armour Top *Firepower*	Equipment and Notes *Notes*
Tanks					
T-26	Fully-tracked	1	1	1	Co-ax MG, Limited vision, Slow tank, Unreliable.
45mm obr 1934 gun	*24"/60cm*	*2*	*7*	*4+*	
T-28	Fully-tracked	4	3	2	Two Deck-turret MG, Turret-front MG, Turret-rear MG, Limited Vision, Slow tank, Unreliable.
76mm L-10 gun	*24"/60cm*	*2*	*7*	*3+*	
T-34	Fully-tracked	6	5	1	Co-ax MG, Fast tank, Hull MG, Limited vision, Wide-tracks.
76mm F-34 gun	*32"/80cm*	*2*	*9*	*3+*	
KV-1e	Fully-tracked	9	8	2	Co-ax MG, Hull MG, Turret-rear MG, Limited vision, Slow tank, Unreliable.
76mm F-34 gun	*32"/80cm*	*2*	*9*	*3+*	
Self-propelled Anti-aircraft					
Landsverk Anti-II	Fully-tracked	2	1	0	
40 ItK/38 gun	*24"/60cm*	*4*	*6*	*4+*	*Anti-aircraft.*
Armoured Cars					
BA-10	Wheeled	1	0	0	Co-ax MG, Hull MG, Limited vision.
45mm obr 1934 gun	*24"/60cm*	*2*	*7*	*4+*	
Assault Guns					
BT-42	Fully-tracked	1	1	1	Limited vision.
114 Psv.H/18 howitzer	*16"/40cm*	*1*	*7*	*2+*	
firing bombardments	*48"/120cm*	*-*	*4*	*4+*	

Gun Teams

Weapon	Mobility	Range	ROF	Anti-tank	Firepower	Notes
Maxim HMG	Man-packed	24"/60cm	6	2	6	ROF 2 when pinned down.
Lhati anti-tank rifle	Man-packed	16"/40cm	3	5	5+	
Tampella M/35 81mm mortar	Man-packed	40"/100cm	-	1	6	Smoke bombardment.
Tampella M/40 120mm mortar	Light	56"/140cm	-	3	3+	Smoke bombardment.
37 PstK/37 (3.7cm PaK36) gun	Light	24"/60cm	3	6	4+	Gun shield.
firing Stielgranate		8"/20cm	1	12	5+	
45 PstK/37 (45mm obr 1938) gun	Light	24"/60cm	3	7	4+	Gun shield.
50 PstK/38 (5cm PaK38) gun	Medium	24"/60cm	3	9	4+	Gun shield.
75 PstK/97-38 (7.5cm PaK97/38) gun	Medium	24"/60cm	2	10	3+	Gun shield.
75 PstK/40 (7.5cm PaK40) gun	Medium	32"/80cm	2	12	3+	Gun shield.
20 LtK/38 (2cm FlaK38) gun	Light	16"/40cm	4	5	5+	Anti-aircraft, Turntable.
40 LtK/38 (Bofors 40mm) gun	Immobile	24"/60cm	4	6	4+	Anti-aircraft, Turntable.
76 K/02 gun	Heavy	24"/60cm	2	8	3+	Gun shield, Smoke.
firing bombardments		60"/160cm	-	3	6	Smoke bombardment.
105 H/33 (10.5cm leFH18) howitzer	Immobile	24"/60cm	1	10	2+	Gun shield, Smoke.
firing bombardments		72"/180cm	-	4	4+	Smoke bombardment.

FINNISH

Infantry Teams

Team	Range	ROF	Anti-tank	Firepower	Notes
Rifle team	16"/40cm	1	2	6	
Rifle/MG team	16"/40cm	2	2	6	
SMG team	4"/10cm	3	1	6	Full ROF when moving.
Flame-thrower team	4"/10cm	2	-	6	Flame-thrower.
Staff team	cannot shoot				Moves as a Heavy Gun team.

Additional Training and Equipment

Close-defence and Pioneer teams are rated as Tank Assault 4.

Transport Teams

Name	Mobility	Front	Side	Top	Equipment and Notes
Trucks					
3-ton truck	Wheeled	-	-	-	
Horse-drawn wagon	Wagon	-	-	-	
Tractors					
Horse-drawn limber	Wagon	-	-	-	

(Armour: Front / Side / Top)

Aircraft

Team	Weapons	To Hit	Anti-tank	Firepower	Notes
Fokker CX	Machine-guns	3+	3	5+	
	or Bombs	4+	5	2+	

Hungarian Arsenal

Tank Teams

Name Weapon	Mobility Range	Front ROF	Armour Side Anti-tank	Top Firepower	Equipment and Notes
Tanks					
Toldi I	Fully-tracked	1	1	1	Co-ax MG.
36M anti-tank rifle	16"/40cm	3	5	5+	
T-38G	Fully-tracked	4	2	1	Co-ax MG, Hull MG, Protected ammo.
3.7cm KwK 38(t) gun	24"/60cm	2	6	4+	
Panzer IV F$_1$	Fully-tracked	5	3	1	Co-ax MG, Hull MG, Protected ammo.
7.5cm KwK 36 gun	24"/60cm	2	9	3+	
Panzer IV F$_2$	Fully-tracked	5	3	1	Co-ax MG, Hull MG, Protected ammo.
7.5cm KwK 40 gun	32"/80cm	2	11	3+	
Self-propelled Anti-aircraft					
Nimrod	Fully-tracked	2	1	0	
40mm 36M Bofors gun	24"/60cm	4	7	4+	*Anti-aircraft.*
Armored Cars					
Csaba 39M	Wheeled	1	0	0	Co-ax MG.
36M anti-tank rifle	16"/40cm	3	5	5+	

Gun Teams

Name	Mobility	Range	ROF	Anti-tank	Firepower	Weapons and Notes
7/31M HMG	Man-packed	24"/60cm	6	2	6	ROF 2 when pinned down.
36M anti-tank rifle	Man-packed	16"/40cm	3	5	5+	
81mm 36/39M mortar	Man-packed	40"/100cm	-	2	6	Smoke bombardment.
40mm 36M (Bofors 40mm) gun	Immobile	24"/60cm	4	7	4+	Anti-aircraft, Turntable.
37mm 36M (3.7cm PaK36) gun	Light	24"/60cm	3	6	4+	Gun shield.
40mm 40M gun	Light	24"/60cm	3	7	4+	Gun shield.
50mm 38M (5cm PaK38) gun	Medium	24"/60cm	3	9	4+	Gun shield.
75mm 38/97M (7.5cm PaK97/38) gun	Medium	24"/60cm	2	10	3+	Gun shield.
75mm 40M (7.5cm PaK40) gun	Medium	32"/80cm	2	12	3+	Gun shield.
80mm 5/8M (75/27) gun	Heavy	24"/60cm	2	8	3+	Gun shield, Smoke.
firing bombardments		64"/160cm	-	3	6+	Smoke bombardment.
100mm 14M (100/17) howitzer	Immobile	24"/60cm	1	9	2+	Gun shield.
firing bombardments		72"/180cm	-	4	4+	
105mm 37M (10.5cm leFH18) how	Immobile	24"/60cm	1	10	2+	Gun shield.
firing bombardments		80"/200cm	-	4	4+	

Infantry Teams

Team	Range	ROF	Anti-tank	Firepower	Weapons and Notes
Rifle team	16"/40cm	1	2	6	
Rifle/MG team	16"/40cm	2	2	6	
Light Mortar team	16"/40cm	1	1	4+	Can fire over friendly teams.
Staff team		cannot shoot			Moves as a Heavy Gun team.

Additional Training and Equipment

Páncélvadász and Pioneer teams are rated as Tank Assault 4

Transport Teams

Name	Mobility	Front	Armour Side	Top	Equipment and Notes
Trucks					
BMW motorcycle & sidecar	Jeep	-	-	-	
Horch or Steyr field car	Jeep	-	-	-	
Botond 38M 1.5-ton truck	Wheeled	-	-	-	
Ford-Marmon (Opel) 3-ton truck	Wheeled	-	-	-	
Horse-drawn wagon	Wagon	-	-	-	
Tractors					
Hansa-Lloyd (Sd Kfz 11) half-track	Half-tracked	-	-	-	
Horse-drawn limber	Wagon	-	-	-	

Aircraft

Team	Weapons	To Hit	Anti-tank	Firepower	Notes
Junkers Ju87D	Bombs	4+	5	1+	

Italian Arsenal

Tank Teams

Name *Weapon*	Mobility *Range*	Front *ROF*	Side *Anti-tank*	Armour Top *Firepower*	Equipment and Notes
Tanks					
L6/40	Half-tracked	2	1	1	Co-ax MG.
20/65 gun	*16"/40cm*	*2*	*5*	*5+*	
Self-propelled Guns					
Semovente 47/32	Half-tracked	3	1	0	
47/32 gun	*24"/60cm*	*2*	*7*	*4+*	
20/65 on 3-ton truck	Wheeled	-	-	-	
20/65 gun	*16"/40cm*	*4*	*5*	*5+*	*Anti-aircraft, Portee.*

Gun Teams

Name	Mobility	Range	ROF	Anti-tank	Firepower	Weapons and Notes
Mod37 HMG	Man-packed	24"/60cm	6	2	6	ROF 2 when pinned down.
81/14 mortar	Man-packed	48"/120cm	-	2	6	Smoke bombardment.
20/65 gun	Light	24"/60cm	4	5	5+	Anti-aircraft, Turntable.
65/17 gun	Light	16"/40cm	2	8	3+	
firing bombardments		64"/160cm	-	2	6	
75/27 gun	Heavy	24"/60cm	2	9	3+	Gun shield, Smoke.
firing bombardments		64"/160cm	-	3	6	Smoke bombardments.
75/39 (7.5cm PaK38/97) gun	Medium	24"/60cm	2	10	3+	Gun shield.
100/17 howitzer	Heavy	24"/60cm	1	10	2+	Gun shield, Immobile.
firing bombardments		72"/180cm	-	4	4+	

Infantry Teams

Team	Range	ROF	Anti-tank	Firepower	Weapons and Notes
Rifle team	16"/40cm	1	2	6	
Rifle/MG team	16"/40cm	2	2	6	
Flame-thrower	4"/10cm	2	-	6	Flame-thrower
Staff team		cannot shoot			Moves as Gun team.

Additional Training and Equipment

Passaglia bombs are Improvised Tank Assault 3. Pioneer teams are Tank Assault 4.

Transport Teams

Name	Mobility	Front	Armour Side	Top	Equipment and Notes
Trucks					
Motoguzzi motorcycle	Jeep	-	-	-	Remove when passengers dismount.
SPA TL-37 or SPA Dovunque 35 3-ton truck	Wheeled	-	-	-	
Lancia 3 RO 6-ton truck	Wheeled	-	-	-	Overloaded, Slow.

Aircraft

Name	Weapon	Range	Anti-tank	Firepower
Junkers Ju.87 Picchiatello	Bombs	4+	5	1+

...Don River, 1943...

Russian troops advanced on the frozen ground, some even venturing on the ice surface of the River Don as Italian mortar shells fell with steady, deadly precision among them. 'Bravo Francesco,' thought Sergente Beltrame, 'he measures his shells like he does his words.'

Beltrame looked at his men waiting in their snow holes and grimaced. The men looked as cold, tired, and hungry as they undoubtedly were. For weeks the alpini of Julia had endured the bitter Russian winter in thin clothes and summer boots. Food and ammunition were scarce. The German tanks, long promised, would never arrive. He was as sure of that as of the cold gun in his hand. They had been abandoned once again and it was a long and dangerous way home!

He shrugged and shifted his attention back to the assault. 'They keep coming,' Beltrame noted, impressed by the courage of the Russian soldiers. Italian machine gunners steadily pounded the open ground from the base of the ridge up to the river bank. The Russians scattered and slowed their advance, but a second wave was pouring out of their lines and a third one was gathering behind it. 'Like my alpini, they are tough as their weather,' he muttered to himself.

Bullets flew around him as the Russians came closer. The sergeant leveled his MAB sub-machine-gun and let off a short burst. The Russians were still out of range but it gave them something to think about. The alpini were firing all along the line now. Russians started to fall in greater numbers.

'Keep it up!' Beltrame yelled to his men. 'Keep firing, don't stop! Make every shot count!' A whistling sound drowned out his last words as the river ice erupted. The alpini cheered as another salvo landed amongst the Russians, breaking the momentum of the attack. 'L'artiglieria!', 'The artillery!', they shout, 'they finally remembered us!'

Romanian Arsenal

Tank Teams

| Name | Mobility | Front | Side | Armour Top | Equipment and Notes |
Weapon	Range	ROF	Anti-tank	Firepower	
Tanks					
R-2 (Panzer 35(t))	Fully-tracked	2	1	1	Co-ax MG, Hull MG, Unreliable, Protected ammo.
3.7cm KwK 35(t) gun	*24"/60cm*	2	6	4+	
T-38 (Panzer 38(t))	Fully-tracked	2	1	1	Co-ax MG, Hull MG, Unreliable, Protected ammo.
3.7cm KwK 35(t) gun	*24"/60cm*	2	6	4+	
T-3 (Panzer III N)	Fully-tracked	5	3	1	Co-ax MG, Hull MG, Protected ammo.
7.5cm KwK 36 gun	*24"/60cm*	2	9	3+	
T-4 (Panzer IV G)	Fully-tracked	5	3	1	Co-ax MG, Hull MG, Protected ammo.
7.5cm KwK 40 gun	*32"/80cm*	2	11	3+	
Armored Cars					
Sd Kfz 222	Wheeled	1	0	0	Co-ax MG.
2cm KwK 38 gun	*16"/40cm*	3	5	5+	*Self-defence Anti-aircraft.*
Sd Kfz 223	Wheeled	1	0	0	AA MG.

Gun Teams

Name	Mobility	Range	ROF	Anti-tank	Firepower	Weapons and Notes
ZB53 HMG	Man-packed	24"/60cm	6	2	6	ROF 2 while pinned down.
60mm Brandt mortar	Man-packed	24"/60cm	2	1	3+	Can fire over friendly troops.
firing bombardments		32"/80cm	-	1	6	
81.4mm Brandt mortar	Man-packed	40"/100cm	0	2	6	Smoke bombardment.
120-PM-38 mortar	Light	56"/140cm	-	3	3+	Smoke bombardment.
Mitral 20mm (2cm FlaK38) gun	Light	16"/40cm	4	5	5+	Anti-aircraft, Turntable.
TAC 37mm (3.7cm PaK36) gun	Light	24"/60cm	3	6	4+	Gun shield.
TAC Bohler 47mm (47/32) gun	Man-packed	24"/60cm	3	7	4+	
TAC 938 50mm (5cm PaK38) gun	Medium	24"/60cm	3	9	4+	Gun shield.
TAC 938 75mm (7.5cm PaK97/38) gun	Medium	24"/60cm	2	10	3+	Gun shield.
RF 75mm (76K/02) gun	Heavy	24"/60cm	2	8	3+	Gun shield, Smoke.
firing bombardments		64"/160cm	-	3	6	Smoke bombardment.
Skoda 100mm (100/17) howitzer	Immobile	24"/60cm	1	9	2+	Gun shield.
firing bombardments		72"/180cm	-	4	4+	

Infantry Teams

Team	Range	ROF	Anti-tank	Firepower	Weapons and Notes
Rifle team	16"/40cm	1	2	6	
Rifle/MG team	16"/40cm	2	2	6	
SMG team	4"/10cm	3	1	6	Full ROF when moving.
Flame-thrower	4"/10cm	2	-	6	Flame-thrower.
Staff team	cannot shoot				Moves as a Heavy Gun team.

Additional Training and Equipment

Vanator de Care and Pioneer teams are Tank Assault 4.

Transport Teams

Name	Mobility	Armour Front	Side	Top	Equipment and Notes
Trucks					
BMW motorcycle and sidecar	Jeep	-	-	-	
Steyr 1.5-ton truck	Wheeled	-	-	-	
Opel 3-ton trucks	Wheeled	-	-	-	
Tractors					
Horse-drawn limber	Wagon	-	-	-	
Horse-drawn wagon	Wagon	-	-	-	
Malaxa (Renault UE) tractor	Half-tracked	0	0	0	

Aircraft

Team	Weapons	To Hit	Anti-tank	Firepower	Notes
Junkers Ju87D	Bombs	4+	5	1+	

...Milo Mutanescu: 4th Infantry Division, South of Stalingrad 1942...

The bullets dance towards us, puckering up the soft forest floor, scattering leaves and bark. I duck low, huddling against the supply truck we have been emptying. Our retreat from Stalingrad has been costly in both men and supplies. Polev drops noiselessly. Baleav cries out as he falls dropping the three black loaves of bread he is carrying. This is madness! One year ago we had run Ivan from Odessa—it was a great victory—and now here we were, being chased down like stray curs, dying for a loaf of bread. Carefully I look around the shattered door of the truck. Sparks fly as more bullets slam into the vehicle.

'Trifon!' I call out 'Where is it coming from?' Trifon is hunkered down behind a rotten log, using a bandage from the truck to swathe Pedrag's chest. Pointless—we can all see that.

More bullets hit the truck shattering the last of the windows, the shards fly inwards, and the battered grille belches acrid smoke. Baleav's cries dissipate slowly until he is still. I remember him taking a machine-gun nest single-handed at Odessa—his chest swelled as he was decorated for that action. Now he lies dead in an unknown forest. Trifon's shouting brings me back to the present. 'Milo, Pedrag's dying, he needs help fast.' I know what to do now, my hands tremble as I slide the bayonet from the scabbard on my belt and, with a sharp click, mount it atop my rifle.

We had proved our worth at Odessa when we routed Ivan, I wasn't going to let the memory of the feats of my comrades die scrapping for food. Time seems to slow and stutter as I make my way from behind the burning truck. My pace quickens as my heart does, pounding hard within my chest. My rifle jolts as I loose off three shots from the hip, indiscriminately, hoping that I will hit something. Now my legs are moving faster, the ground thuds hard, reverberating against my boots. I run and run expecting not to hear the shot that will fell me here in this forest. Then ahead of me, three khaki-clad figures emerge noisily from the undergrowth. I don't stop, but fire twice more on the move, hitting the lead figure in the head and seeing him stumble back into the shrubs.

'Stoi! Stoi!' I hear one of them shout, as he fumbles with his rifle. I fire again and he falls like his comrade. My heart is beating furiously now as my legs carry me upon the third Russian. Our rifles clash violently, I grab his dirty webbing and we tumble over one another upon the forest floor. His weapon slips from his flailing grasp and I know what I have to do.

I bend down and pick up the three black loaves from the forest floor and put two into my belt. Trifon is supporting Pedrag who is now a deathly white pallor. 'This can't go on forever,' I think to myself. I have heard the whispers—change is in the air.

SOVIET ARSENAL

Tank Teams

Name *Weapon*	Mobility *Range*	Front *ROF*	Armour Side *Anti-tank*	Top *Firepower*	Equipment and Notes
Light Tanks					
T-26S obr 1939	Fully-tracked	1	1	1	Co-ax MG, Limited vision, Slow tank, Unreliable.
45mm obr 1934 gun	*24"/60cm*	*2*	*7*	*4+*	
T-60 obr 1942	Half-tracked	3	1	1	Co-ax MG, Limited vision.
20mm ShVAK gun	*16"/40cm*	*2*	*5*	*5+*	
T-70 obr 1942	Fully-tracked	4	2	1	Co-ax MG, Limited vision.
45mm obr 1938 gun	*24"/60cm*	*2*	*7*	*4+*	
T-70 obr 1942	Fully-tracked	4	2	1	Co-ax MG, Limited vision, Wide-tracks.
45mm obr 1938 gun	*24"/60cm*	*2*	*7*	*4+*	
Mark III (Valentine II)	Fully-tracked	6	5	1	Co-ax MG, Slow tank.
OQF 2 pdr gun	*24"/60cm*	*2*	*7*	*4+*	*No HE.*
Mark III (Valentine VIII)	Fully-tracked	6	4	1	Slow tank.
OQF 6 pdr gun	*24"/60cm*	*2*	*10*	*4+*	*No HE.*
M3l (M3A1 Stuart)	Fully-tracked	3	2	1	Co-ax MG, Hull MG, Light tank.
M5 37mm gun	*24"/60cm*	*2*	*7*	*4+*	
Medium Tanks					
T-34 obr 1941 or 1942	Fully-tracked	6	5	1	Co-ax MG, Hull MG, Fast tank, Limited vision, Wide-tracks.
76mm F-34 gun	*32"/80cm*	*2*	*9*	*3+*	
T-34 obr 1941 with extra armour	Fully-tracked	7	6	1	Co-ax MG, Hull MG, Limited vision.
76mm F-34 gun	*32"/80cm*	*2*	*9*	*3+.*	
T-34/57	Fully-tracked	6	5	1	Co-ax MG, Hull MG, Fast tank, Limited vision, Wide-tracks.
57mm ZIS-4 gun	*32"/80cm*	*2*	*11*	*4+*	
Mark II (Matilda II)	Fully-tracked	7	6	2	Co-ax MG, Slow tank.
OQF 2 pdr gun	*24"/60cm*	*3*	*7*	*4+*	*No HE.*
Mark II 76mm (Matilda II CS)	Fully-tracked	7	6	2	Co-ax MG, Slow tank.
OQF 3" gun	*24"/60cm*	*2*	*5*	*3+*	
M3s (M3 Lee)	Fully-tracked	5	3	1	Co-ax MG, Cupola MG.
M3 37mm gun	*24"/60cm*	*3*	*7*	*4+*	
M2 75mm gun	*32"/80cm*	*2*	*9*	*3+*	*Hull-mounted*
with long M3 75mm gun	*32"/80cm*	*2*	*10*	*3+*	*Hull-mounted*
M4 (M4A2 Sherman)	Fully-tracked	6	4	1	Co-ax MG, Hull MG.
M3 75mm gun	*32"/80cm*	*2*	*10*	*3+*	
Heavy Tanks					
KV-1e	Fully-tracked	9	8	2	Co-ax MG, Hull MG, Turret-rear MG, Limited vision, Slow tank, Unreliable.
76mm F-34 gun	*32"/80cm*	*2*	*9*	*3+*	
KV-2	Fully-tracked	8	7	2	Hull MG, Turret-rear MG, Limited vision, Slow tank, Unreliable.
152mm obr 1938/40 howitzer	*24"/60cm*	*1*	*10*	*1+*	*Bunker buster.*
KV-1s	Fully-tracked	8	6	2	Co-ax MG, Hull MG, Turret-rear MG, Wide-tracks.
76mm F-34 gun	*32"/80cm*	*2*	*9*	*3+*	
KV-85	Fully-tracked	9	7	2	Co-ax MG, Turret-rear MG, Slow tank.
85mm D-5T gun	*32"/80cm*	*2*	*12*	*3+*	
Mark IV (Churchill III or IV)	Fully-tracked	8	7	2	Co-ax MG, Hull MG, Slow tank, Wide tracks.
OQF 6 pdr gun	*24"/60cm*	*2*	*10*	*4+*	*No HE.*

SOVIET

Name *Weapon*	Mobility *Range*	Front *ROF*	Armour Side *Anti-tank*	Top *Firepower*	Equipment and Notes

Flame Tanks

Name *Weapon*	Mobility *Range*	Front *ROF*	Side *Anti-tank*	Top *Firepower*	Equipment and Notes
OT-34	Fully-tracked	6	5	1	Co-ax MG, Fast tank, Limited vision, Wide-tracks.
76mm F-34 gun	*32"/80cm*	*1*	*9*	*3+*	
ATO-42 flame-thrower	*4"/10cm*	*2*	*-*	*6*	*Flame-thrower, Hull-mounted.*
KV-8	Fully-tracked	9	8	2	Hull MG, Turret-rear MG, Limited vision, Slow tank, Unreliable.
ATO-41 flame-thrower	*4"/10cm*	*3*	*-*	*5+*	*Flame-thrower.*
45mm obr 1938 gun	*24"/60cm*	*2*	*7*	*4+*	
KV-8s	Fully-tracked	8	6	2	Hull MG, Turret-rear MG, Wide-tracks.
ATO-42 flame-thrower	*4"/10cm*	*3*	*-*	*5+*	*Flame-thrower.*
45mm obr 1938 gun	*24"/60cm*	*2*	*7*	*4+*	

Assault Guns

Name *Weapon*	Mobility *Range*	Front *ROF*	Side *Anti-tank*	Top *Firepower*	Equipment and Notes
SU-76i	Fully-tracked	3	2	1	
76mm ZIS-3 gun	*32"/80cm*	*2*	*9*	*3+*	*Hull mounted.*
SU-76M	Fully-tracked	3	1	0	Wide-tracked.
76mm ZIS-3 gun	*32"/80cm*	*2*	*9*	*3+*	*Hull mounted.*
SU-85	Fully-tracked	5	5	1	
85mm D-5 S-85 gun	*32"/80cm*	*2*	*12*	*3+*	*Hull mounted.*
SU-122	Fully-tracked	5	5	1	
122mm obr 1938 howitzer	*24"/60cm*	*2*	*10*	*2+*	*Hull mounted.*
SU-152	Fully-tracked	7	6	2	Slow tank.
152mm ML-20S gun	*32"/80cm*	*1*	*13*	*1+*	*Bunker buster.*

Armoured Cars

Name *Weapon*	Mobility *Range*	Front *ROF*	Side *Anti-tank*	Top *Firepower*	Equipment and Notes
BA-64	Jeep	0	0	0	AA MG.
with PTRD anti-tank rifle	*16"/40cm*	*2*	*5*	*5+*	
BA-10M	Wheeled	1	0	0	Co-ax MG, Hull MG, Limited vision.
45mm obr 1934	*24"/60cm*	*2*	*7*	*-4+*	

Rocket Launchers

Name *Weapon*	Mobility *Range*	Front *ROF*	Side *Anti-tank*	Top *Firepower*	Equipment and Notes
BM-13 Katyusha	Wheeled	-	-	-	
BM-13-16 rocket launcher	*64"/160cm*	*-*	*3*	*4+*	

Anti-aircraft Machine-guns

Name *Weapon*	Mobility *Range*	Front *ROF*	Side *Anti-tank*	Top *Firepower*	Equipment and Notes
DShK AA MG on truck	Wheeled	-	-	-	Awkward layout.
DShK AA MG	*16"/40cm*	*4*	*4*	*5+*	*Anti-aircraft, Portee.*

Cavalry Machine-guns

Name *Weapon*	Mobility *Range*	Front *ROF*	Side *Anti-tank*	Top *Firepower*	Equipment and Notes
Tachanka	Cavalry Wagon	-	-	-	
Maksim HMG	*24"/60cm*	*6*	*2*	*6*	*Portee, HMG Carrier.*

Gun Teams

Weapon	Mobility	Range	ROF	Anti-tank	Firepower	Notes
PTRD anti-tank rifle	Man-packed	16"/40cm	2	5	5+	Tank Assault 3.
Maksim HMG	Man-packed	24"/60cm	6	2	6	ROF 2 when pinned down.
82-BM-41 mortar	Man-packed	40"/100cm	-	2	6	
120-PM-38 mortar	Light	56"/140cm	-	3	3+	
76mm obr 1927 gun	Light	16"/40cm	2	5	3+	Gun shield.
firing bombardments		64"/160cm	-	3	6	
DShK AA MG	Man-packed	16"/40cm	4	4	5+	Anti-aircraft, Turntable.
37mm obr 1939 gun	Immobile	24"/60cm	4	6	4+	Anti-aircraft, Turntable.
85mm obr 1939 gun	Immobile	32"/80cm	2	12	3+	Heavy anti-aircraft, Turntable.
45mm obr 1938 gun	Light	24"/60cm	3	7	4+	Gun shield.
45mm obr 1942 gun	Light	24"/60cm	3	8	4+	Gun shield.
57mm ZIS-2 gun	Heavy	32"/80cm	3	11	4+	Gun shield.
76mm ZIS-3 gun	Heavy	32"/80cm	2	9	3+	Gun shield.
firing bombardments		80"/200cm	-	3	6	
122mm obr 1938 howitzer	Immobile	24"/60cm	1	7	2+	Gun shield.
firing bombardments		80"/200cm	-	4	3+	

Infantry Teams

Team	Range	ROF	Anti-tank	Firepower	Weapons and Notes
Rifle team	16"/40cm	1	2	6	
Rifle/MG team	16"/40cm	2	2	6	
SMG team	4"/10cm	3	1	6	Full ROF when moving.
Light Mortar team	16"/40cm	1	1	4+	Can fire over friendly teams
Flame-thrower team	4"/10cm	4	-	6	Flame-thrower.
Komissar team	4"/10cm	1	1	6	
Staff team		cannot shoot			Moves as a Heavy Gun team.

Additional Training and Equipment

Pioneer teams are Tank Assault 4.

Transport Teams

Vehicle	Mobility	Front	Armour Side	Top	Equipment and Notes
Trucks					
M-72 motorcycle and sidecar	Jeep	-	-	-	Passenger-fired MG.
ZIS-5 3-ton, ZIS-6 4-ton, Dodge 3/4-ton, or Studebekker 21/2-ton truck	Wheeled	-	-	-	
Horse-drawn wagon	Wagon	-	-	-	
Cavalry wagon	Cavalry Wagon	-	-	-	
Tractors					
Stalinets	Fully-tracked	-	-	-	Slow tank.
Horse-drawn limber	Wagon	-	-	-	
Cavalry limber	Cavalry Wagon	-	-	-	
Armoured Transporters					
M3A1 armoured transporter	Jeep	1	0	0	Passenger-fired AA MG.
BA-10M converted transporter	Jeep	1	0	0	Passenger-fired MG.
Captured Sd Kfz 251 half-track	Half-tracked	1	0	0	Passenger-fired MG.
Universal Carrier	Half-tracked	0	0	0	Passenger-fired MG.

Aircraft

Aircraft	Weapon	To Hit	Anti-tank	Firepower	Notes
I-153	MG	3+	3	6	
	or Rockets	4+	6	3+	
Il-2 Shturmovik	Cannon	3+	9	5+	
	or Bombs	4+	5	1+	
	or Rockets	3+	6	3+	
P-39 Kobra	MG	3+	6	5+	
	or Cannon	4+	9	4+	
	or Bombs	4+	5	2+	

THE GREAT BATTLE OF KURSK

Yesterday I interviewed General S M Krivoshein commanding *3-y Mechanizirovanniy Korpus* (3rd Mechanised Corps), the victors of the great battle of Kursk. This is his story.

The 5th of July opened to the thunder of the Red God of War and the song of the Katyushas as our artillery caught the Panzers in their marshalling areas and wreaked havoc upon them. Nevertheless, they regrouped and their offensive sprang towards us, led by 48th Panzer Corps heading for Oboyan. By 4 pm my men were in place behind *67-ya Gvardeyskaya Strelkovy Diviziya* (67th Guards Rifle Division), manning the impressive fortifications. We watched flight after flight of Vultures, German divebombers, dropping from the sky upon our comrades in the positions before us. Our brave fighter pilots were struggling to keep them away, but the *shvab* fighters were up in force as well. For every one of our brave pilots who fell from the sky I counted at least five of the Fascists fall, like burning stars. Every fallen comrade there was a *tuz*, an 'ace' as our allies call them!

The next morning marked the destruction of the tank brigades to our front. Their American-made tanks are very poor, but they helped stem the tide as 48th Panzer Corps surged forward into *67-ya Gvardeyskaya Strelkovy Diviziya*. The infantry took heavy losses, and but for the noble sacrifice of the tankists they could not have survived, but they struggled on. They fell back onto our positions and then my men became embroiled in it, fire and steel and the flash and crack of battle.

It was about now that I received a call from General Katukov. A gap had opened between the *67-ya* and *71-ya Gvardeyskaya Strelkovy Diviziya*. I issued a command and my men, with the comrades of the *90-ya Gvardeyskaya Strelkovy Diviziya*, deployed into the opening. We were only just in time. The elite German *Grossdeutschland* Division, our old foes from Operation Mars, crashed into us full force.

By midday the Fascists had reached the second defensive line, as our men struggled nobly against superior firepower. I myself witnessed the *1696-y Zenitno-artileriyskiy Polk*, the 1696th Anti-aircraft Regiment, give good service against both the half-tracks of the *Grossdeutschland* infantry and the Vultures that swarmed in the sky. The Germans kept on attacking, and although we gave a little, we did not break. I ordered a steady fire from our mortar battalions to cover a withdrawal. The men pulled back, fighting step-by-step, past Luchanino and Alexeievka to outside Dubrova. I spent all of that long day in my jeep, which became my mobile HQ.

Throughout the next day my tanks clashed with the *Grossdeutschland* Division outside Dubrova. The new Tigers and Panthers proved to be very tough for our guns to crack. Of the many reports of heroism I received that day one stands out above the rest. The third battery of *35-y Protivotankoviy Polk*, the 35th Anti-tank Regiment, held the line against an attack by 37 German tanks. They held their fire until their *shvab* faces could be seen clearly through the slits in their armour before opening a devastating fire which left five Tigers burning on the field.

Mid-morning I put in a request for air support and within an hour I heard the roar of our *shturmovik* assault aircraft over my tent. By the *rodina*, they gave Fritz's armour a good shake up! In spite of this, by early afternoon ceaseless enemy attacks had driven us back from the second defensive line. Soon thereafter *31-y Tankovy Korpus* (31st Tank Corps) joined our tanks in repulsing no fewer than three assaults by the 11th Panzer Division and *Grossdeutschland* along the Oboyan road. I stood atop a small rise to the east of the road and watched as our brave tankists threw themselves at the Germans. The sight of many burning Panzers gladdened my heart.

At dawn on the 8th of July, the weather

was warm and overcast. The grey clouds which rolled towards the German line must have filled the enemy with a sense of foreboding. They only filled me with confidence. The very *rodina* herself was preparing to throw off the fascist invaders! Taking advantage of our excellent air support we went over to the offensive. Our attack, in conjunction with the *200-ya Tankovaya Brigada* (200th Tank Brigade) and the *51-ya* and *67-ya Gvardeyskaya Strelkovy Diviziya*, threw back the German spearheads. Losses were acceptable, but sufficient to discourage further exploitation of our excellent tactical situation. I chose to make our own position secure rather than follow the foolish German example and push on against increasing enemy capability.

The Germans attacked in turn, pushing on towards Verechopenie with *Grossdeutschland* in the lead once more. I pulled *1-ya Gvardeyskaya Tankovaya Brigada* (1st Guards Tank Brigade) and *1-ya* and *3-ya Mechanizirovannaya Brigada* (1st and 3rd Mechanised Brigades) up to counter this thrust. A fierce engagement ensued in which our brave tankists fought their '34's against the monstrous German machines at point blank range, blunting Fritz's onrush.

The following day, as the weather worsened, the Germans resumed their offensive. At midday *Grossdeutsch-land* attacked Verechopenie along with heavy support from their air force. Aided by the poor conditions we fought them step for step. By day's end they had advanced a mere 10 kilometres, in some places no more than six. The brave sacrifice of my noble soldiers had stopped the Fascists in their tracks.

The next two days saw repeated, increasingly desperate attempts by the German forces to break through our positions. Throughout the Pena valley pockets of our noble comrades held out to the last round and the final 'Urrah!' despite being surrounded. Their sacrifice gutted the Germans. The main *shvab* thrust had been broken, and I received word from General Katukov that we were finally going onto the offensive again.

The 12th of July was the turning point of the whole battle. Two whole tank armies went on the offensive on a fifty kilometre front with some 800 tanks! *5-ya Gvardeyskaya Tankovaya Armiya*, 5th Guards Tank Army, attacked around Prokhorovka into the teeth of the German SS Panzer Corps, halting them in their tracks and then pushing them back. At the same time our *1-ya Tankovaya Armiya*, 1st Tank Army, attacked south down the Oboyan road. Attacking with *31-y Tankovy Korpus* again we reduced the German forward positions inflicting heavy casualties and drawing them into costly counterattacks.

I received a report of one such action taking place outside the village of Yakovlevo where 70 tanks of *Grossdeutschland* counterattacked *1-ya Gvardeyskaya Tankovaya Brigada*. An attempted outflanking manoeuvre by the enemy had been repulsed by Lt. Shalandin and the men of his command. Between them, they destroyed 26 tanks, including 2 Tigers. For this feat I have recommended Lieutenant Shalandin be awarded the title 'Hero of the Soviet Union'.

This young officer's heroism is symbolic of the bravery of all of the men of *3-y Mechanizirovanniy Korpus* throughout this battle. I am proud of each and every one of the comrades who have fought under my command during the struggle. In my eyes they are all Heroes of our glorious Soviet Republic fighting for Stalin and the *Rodina*.

These final attacks marked the high tide of the German advance. We are now pushing them back at all points along the line and are preparing for our own strategic offensive that will push Fritz back to the very borders of the Soviet Union. With their armour shattered against the strength of our positions it is only a matter of time now before we cleanse our Motherland of the stain of Fascist occupation.

GE884 Oberfeldwebel Schmidt's Assault Platoon

GE122 StuG F/8

GE411 Schwimmwagen (x4)

GE104 Marder III (7.62cm)

GE550 8.8cm FlaK36 gun

IT010 L6/40 (x2)

GE762 Fallschirmjäger or Pioneer Platoon

HU702 Puskás Platoon

FI702 Jalkavä Platoon

FI010 BT-42

GE060 Panther D (Kursk)

HU010 Toldi Light Tank

Germany

GEAB03	German Grenadier 1500pt Army	
GBX01	Armoured Panzergrenadier Platoon	
GBX03	Panzer IV F$_1$/F$_2$ Platoon	
GBX06	Grenadierkompanie	
GBX07	10.5cm leFH18 Artillery Battery	
GE010	Panzer II C	
GE011	Panzer II F	
GE020	Panzer 35(t)	
GE022	Panzer 38(t) B, C	
GE031	Panzer III G	
GE032	Panzer III H	
GE033	Panzer III J	
GE034	Panzer III L, N	
GE035	Panzer III M	
GE036	Panzer III L, N (Schürzen)	
GE037	Flammpanzer III	
GE042	Panzer IV F$_1$, F$_2$	
GE044	Panzer IV G	
GE045	Panzer IV G (late)	
GE046	Panzer IV H	
GE060	Panther D (Kursk)	
GE061	Panther A	
GE071	Tiger I E (Zimmerit)	
GE072	Tiger I E (Kursk)	
GE102	Marder I	
GE103	Marder II	
GE104	Marder III (7.62cm)	
GE105	Marder III H	
GE106	Marder III M	
GE107	Hornisse	
GE121	StuG D	
GE122	StuG F/8	
GE123	StuG G	
GE125	StuH42	
GE129	Brummbär	
GE131	Ferdinand	
GE133	StuIG 33B	
GE141	Wespe	
GE143	Grille H (15cm sIG)	
GE145	Hummel	
GE147	15cm Panzerwerfer 42	
GE160	Sd Kfz 10/5 (2cm)	
GE166	SdKfz 7/1 (Quad 2cm)	
GE167	SdKfz 7/2 (3.7cm)	
GE168	SdKfz 7/1 (Armoured Quad 2cm)	
GE169	SdKfz 7/2 (Armoured 3.7cm)	
GE200	Sd Kfz 250/1, /10 (3.7cm) (early)	
GE205	Sd Kfz 250/7 (early, 8cm)	
GE207	Sd Kfz 250/8 (early, 7.5cm)	
GE209	Sd Kfz 250/9 (early, 2cm)	
GE216	Sd Kfz 253 (StuG)	
GE240	Sd Kfz 251/1C, /10C (3.7cm)	
GE241	Sd Kfz 251/1D, /10D (3.7cm)	
GE242	Sd Kfz 251/1C (Stuka)	
GE244	Sd Kfz 251/2C (8cm)	
GE249	Sd Kfz 251/7D (Pioneer)	
GE252	Sd Kfz 251/9C (7.5cm)	
GE256	Sd Kfz 251/16C (Flamm)	
GE258	Sd Kfz 251/17C (2cm)	
GE271	Sd Kfz 7 (8t) tractor (x2 resin)	
GE272	Sd Kfz 11 (3t) tractor (x2 resin)	
GE273	SD Kfz 10 (1t) tractor (x2 resin)	
GE274	Opel Maultier half-track (x2)	
GE276	RSO tractor (x2 resin)	
GE300	Sd Kfz 221 (MG/Pz bush)	
GE301	Sd Kfz 222 (2cm)	
GE302	Sd Kfz 223 (command)	
GE340	Sd Kfz 231 (8-Rad)	

GE341	Sd Kfz 233 (7.5cm)	
GE342	Sd Kfz 263 (radio)	
GE400	BMW & sidecar (x4)	
GE402	Kettenkrad (x4)	
GE409	Kübelwagen (x3 resin)	
GE411	Schwimmwagen (x4)	
GE413	Horch Kfz 15 car (x2 resin)	
GE420	Krupp Kfz 70 truck (x2)	
GE425	Steyr Kfz 70 truck (x2)	
GE426	Steyr Kfz 70 truck (x2 resin)	
GE431	Opel Blitz 3-ton truck (x2 resin)	
GE490	Opel Blitz radio truck	
GE501	3.7cm PaK36 gun (x2)	
GE510	5cm PaK38 gun (x2)	
GE515	7.5 PaK38/97 (x2)	
GE520	7.5cm PaK40 gun (x2)	
GE525	7.62cn PaK 36(r) gun (x2)	
GE542	2cm FlaK38 gun (x2)	
GE550	8.8cm FlaK36 gun	
GE560	7.5cm leIG18 gun (x2)	
GE565	15cm sIG33 gun (x2)	
GE571	10.5cm leFH18 how (x2)	
GE590	15cm Nebelwerfer 41 (x3)	
GE610	Borgward B IV (remote control) (x4)	
GE670	German Stowage	
GE701	Company HQ	
GE702	Grenadier Platoon	
GE703	Panzergrenadier Platoon	
GE704	Machine-gun Platoon	
GE705	Mortar Platoon	
GE709	German Artillery HQ	
GE720	Grenadier Platoon (Winter)	
GE721	Company HQ (late)	
GE722	Grenadier Platoon (late)	
GE724	Machine-gun Platoon (late)	

GE725	Mortar Platoon (late)	
GE726	Pioneer Platoon	
GE737	Assault Rifle Platoon	
GE881	Generalmajor Otto-Ernst Remer	
GE883	Major Bruno Koenig's Snipers	
GE884	Oberfeldwebel Schmidt's Assault Platoon	
GE940	German Stalingrad decals	
GE941	German tank decals	
DD003	German Dice	
AT523	German Token Set	
GBX08	Fallschirmjägerkompanie	
GE502	3.7cm PaK36 or 4.2cm PJK41 (FJ)	
GE543	2cm FlaK38 gun (FJ)	
GE563	7.5cm GebG36 or 10.5cm LG40 (FJ)	
GE561	7.5cm LG40 (FJ)	
GE762	Fallschirmjäger or Pioneer Platoon	
GE763	Fallschirmjäger Platoon (Battle worn)	
GE764	Machine-gun Platoon (FJ)	
GE765	Mortar Platoon FJ	

Italian

WD109	Avanti Savoia	
ITAB01	Italian 1500pt Army Box	
IPS01	Italian Paint Set	
ITBX01	Compagnia Bersaglieri	
IBX02	M14/41 Platoon	
IBX03	Raggruppamento Artiglieria	
IT010	L6/40 (x2)	
IT040	M14/41	
IT060	R.35	
IT101	Semovente 47/32 (x2)	
IT110	Carro Comando M41	
IT111	Semovente 75/18	